Estate Planning
SMARTS

"*Estate Planning Smarts* is absolutely fantastic!
It captures many complicated aspects of federal
estate tax law and makes them readable for the lay
person. This book is an incredible resource for both
financial advisers and their clients."

> — **Jeffrey H. Thomasson, CFP**
> CEO and Managing Director
> Oxford Financial Group, Ltd.

"A comprehensive and accurate guide to estate
planning that tackles all the issues in clear,
easy-to-read style. This book will save you time
and your family money."

> — **Natalie B. Choate**
> Estate planning lawyer and author,
> *Life and Death Planning for Retirement Benefits*

Planning Smarts

" Deborah L. Jacobs has one of the clearest voices in America today on estate planning. Her book is thorough, precise and makes complicated issues understandable. **"**

> — **Rorie Michelle Sherman**
> Editor in Chief
> *Trusts & Estates*

" I have watched clients avoid estate planning because of the complexities and mysteries surrounding the topic. *Estate Planning Smarts* explains the subject matter in concise and readable fashion and is sprinkled with many fascinating and relevant items about people in the news. I particularly liked the "To-Do List" at the end of each chapter, which gives readers a road map to a successful estate plan. I will encourage my clients to read this book because an informed client makes better decisions."

> — **Dennis I. Belcher, President,**
> American College of Trusts and Estates Counsel;
> Past Chairman of the American Bar Association's
> Real Property Trust and Estates Section

DEBORAH L. JACOBS

Estate Planning
SMARTS

A Practical, User-Friendly, Action-Oriented Guide

A Note to the Reader

This book is intended for educational purposes, to provide useful ideas in the area of estate planning. Every effort has been made to ensure that the information contained in the book is complete and accurate at the time of publication. However, neither the author nor the publisher is engaged in rendering professional advice or services to the individual reader. The book is sold with that understanding. Neither the author nor the publisher can be held responsible for any loss incurred as a result of tax, estate planning or investment decisions the reader makes. To prepare your estate plan, you should rely on a lawyer licensed to practice in the state where you live. This notice is also meant to comply with IRS Circular 230.

This book is available at special discounts when purchased in bulk for premiums and sales promotions, as well as for fund-raising or educational use. Special editions or book excerpts can be created by the author to specification. For details, visit *www.estateplanningsmarts.com* or contact deborah@estateplanningsmarts.com.

First printing December 2009 by DJWorking Unlimited Inc.

Publisher's Cataloging-in-Publication
(Provided by Quality Books, Inc.)

    Jacobs, Deborah L., 1956-
        Estate planning smarts : a practical, user-friendly,
    action-oriented guide / by Deborah L. Jacobs.
        p. cm.
        Includes bibliographical references and index.
        LCCN 2009905123
        ISBN-13: 9780615297545
        ISBN-10: 0615297544

        1. Estate planning—United States—Popular works.
        2. Trusts and trustees—United States—Popular works.
        3. Tax planning—United States—Popular works.   I. Title.

    KF750.Z9J33 2009   346.7305'2
                           QBI09-200049

Edited by Joshua Mills
Designed by Laura Zavetz

To Ken and Jack

❧

Acknowledgements

Writing a book is labor-intensive and sometimes lonely work. I am deeply indebted to the many people who provided me with information, guidance and good humor along the way.

I am extremely grateful to Lawrence P. Katzenstein, Lloyd Leva Plaine, Gideon Rothschild and Howard M. Zaritsky, estate planning lawyers who spent an enormous amount of time commenting on drafts of various chapters and the Glossary.

Special thanks to these experts, who gave generously of their time and reviewed draft chapters: Susan T. Bart, Lawrence Brody, Natalie B. Choate, Michael N. Delgass, Keith Bradoc Gallant, Wendy S. Goffe, Jonathan E. Gopman, Steven B. Gorin, David A. Handler, Richard Harris, Stephanie E. Heilborn, Bernard A. Krooks, Carlyn S. McCaffrey, Michael D. Mulligan, Barry C. Picker and Pam H. Schneider.

I would probably would not have written much about estate planning were it not for Robert W. Casey. He is the editor who started me on that beat for Bloomberg, answering my initial objections by challenging me to "learn something new."

To bring this book to life, I had the privilege of working with a master editor: Josh Mills. His attention to detail, editorial judgment and wordsmithing were an asset at every turn. *Estate Planning Smarts* looks unlike any other personal finance book, and I have Laura and Craig Zavetz to thank for that. Laura designed a book that graphically conveys a life well lived, even as the text deals with the subject of mortality. Craig deftly implemented her highly creative vision and also designed the book's Web site, *www.estateplanningsmarts.com.*

In producing this book and the materials to go with it, I relied on Wayne Kirn, an expert production manager.

And where would I be without my husband Ken Stern, who has always been my biggest booster. His marketing know-how gave me the confidence to undertake this project, and the stability that he brings to our home life has enabled me to take greater risks in my professional one. Following his example, our son Jack never complained that I was distracted during the many months of writing this book, and found his own way of being supportive – by quietly doing his sixth-grade homework on the floor of my office.

Table of Contents

Shape the Future With Your Estate Plan

If the thought of doing an estate plan gives you goosebumps, you are not alone. But if you do not address this subject, the government will handle it for you, and things may not turn out the way you would have wanted.

Consider, for example, what happens without a will. State law determines how your belongings are distributed. If your children are minors and you were a single or surviving parent, a court will appoint a guardian for them. And your family members may wind up paying more tax than necessary on their inheritance.

Like many people, I didn't used to think much about any of this. Longevity ran in my family; it seemed like hardly anyone ever died. When my grandmother tried to talk about her will, I would brush her aside with a dismissive, "Stick around." To me, people who took an interest in other people's wills were moneygrubbers. Those who wrote wills themselves were flirting with the grim reaper. In short, I found the whole subject extremely unpleasant.

Then, in the space of three months, I became a parent, I lost a parent, and I found myself in charge of a trust that my grandmother had set up for my aunt, which my father had overseen until his death. Soon after, I was asked to write about estate planning on a continuing basis for two magazines, and I agreed.

Today, after being immersed in this field for 12 years, I have learned that estate planning is, above all, a way to take care of yourself and the people you love. It can minimize the hardships of your old age and ensure that less of what you leave behind goes to taxes – and more to family, friends and the causes important to you, whether it's your alma mater, the local symphony or a homeless shelter. If you are married or in any other committed relationship, estate planning is about leaving a financial cushion for your spouse or partner. It also includes providing funds for a child's or a grandchild's education and subsidizing less fortunate family members. For parents of young children, estate planning is a way to make sure someone will care for them if you suddenly perish.

The 21st Century started with stark reminders of our mortality. Whether a cruel terrorist incident or a natural disaster like Hurricane Katrina, the lesson is that life is precious and sometimes fleeting. With an estate plan in place, we can find a measure of comfort in the hope that things will go on as well as possible after we're gone.

Regardless of your net worth, a good estate plan should accomplish these essential goals:

Caring for yourself by authorizing people to handle your affairs if you no longer can because of illness or disability

Specifying who gets what after you pass away

Providing for children who are minors or who have special needs.

In many estate plans, trusts play a crucial role. Although they are commonly associated with saving taxes and financing lavish lifestyles, they serve other key purposes. Trusts can be used to hold money for minors, forestall spendthrift family members, protect assets from former spouses or creditors, or even make provisions to care for a pet that survives you.

If you already have an estate plan, you should determine if it needs revisions, to reflect changes in the law and other developments. In several respects, the estate planning landscape has been radically altered by events of recent years. The amount of an estate that is exempt from taxes soared, from $675,000 in 2001 to $3.5 million ($7 million for married couples) in 2009. As a result, plans done 10 years ago, or even 5, may be hopelessly out of date, because they relied on tax-saving strategies that are no longer necessary for many people because their estates are not large enough to be subject to federal tax. Nor are older plans likely to take account of estate taxes that many states have added.

Your estate planning may well have been disrupted by the economic meltdown that began in 2008. As I was writing this book, the stock market lost half its value, entire industries were devastated and many wealthy people were scammed by the largest fraud in Wall Street history. Although the long-term effect of the financial crisis remains unclear, it's possible that many of us, especially the baby boomers and their parents, will need to be more careful about money for the rest of our lives. And now, more than ever, the planning process is not just about money but also about love, family and legacy.

To-Do List

Make Sure You Have The Essential Documents

Regardless of your personal balance sheet, your estate plan should include the following key documents:

❧ *Will:* the cornerstone of many estate plans, it should transfer assets, appoint a guardian for minor children and name an executor or personal representative – the individual or institution that takes charge of your estate after you die and distributes property as you have specified.

❧ *Living trust or revocable trust:* safeguards your assets and provides for your care if you can no longer handle your affairs, then determines who will receive the property when you die.

❧ *Personal property memorandum:* provides guidance or direction (depending on state law) to your executor about whom you want to receive jewelry, art and other personal property not described in the will.

❧ *Durable power of attorney:* appoints a trusted family member, friend or adviser as an agent to act on your behalf in a variety of financial and legal matters.

❧ *Health care proxy:* also called a health care agent or health care power of attorney, authorizes someone to make medical decisions on your behalf.

❧ *HIPAA release:* gives doctors and hospitals permission to share medical records with people in addition to your health care agent.

❧ *Living will:* also called an advance directive, expresses preferences about certain aspects of end-of-life care, rather than simply leaving them up to the person named in your health care proxy.

Chapter 1

Nothing Lasts Forever

*Read this chapter even if you
are hearty and clear-headed.*

The first step in any estate plan is to provide for your own needs, anticipating that at some point you might become physically or mentally unable to manage your finances or make medical choices. Typically this is a function of old age, but it can also happen to much younger people who are injured or become ill unexpectedly. That risk of incapacity, meaning that you don't know what assets you have, what you want to do with them and who your family members are, lurks for us all.

Advancements in medical science and care may enable us to live fuller, longer lives. But that also means more of us are likely to suffer, eventually, from incapacity, which can strike suddenly and mercilessly.

Once you become incapacitated, it is generally too late legally to make changes in your estate planning documents. And unless you have made other, binding arrangements, your family may need to ask a court to appoint a conservator (also called a guardian) to oversee your finances. This can be an expensive and an embarrassing ordeal, and for many families involves unpleasant, even acrimonious, exchanges.

So it is much better to address these issues while you are active. You can set things up to preserve your independence for as long as possible, knowing that certain systems that you have designed will take effect should you decline. The key element of a plan for incapacity is that it must be in place before you need it.

In This Chapter...

- ⚓ *Who Will Take Over Your Finances?*
- ⚓ *Who Decides When You Are Incapacitated?*
- ⚓ *Who Will Make Health Care Decisions?*
- ⚓ *What Are Your Final Wishes?*

Who Will Take Over Your Finances?

If you become incapacitated, someone needs to be able to take over your finances – from paying bills to authorizing stock trades, and everything in between. Whomever you choose, you should have two separate documents: a durable power of attorney and a living trust or revocable trust.

A durable power of attorney authorizes a trusted family member, friend or adviser to act as your agent in a variety of financial and legal matters. The power of attorney may be effective from the moment you sign it or may specify that it is activated by a specific event, such as when you become incapacitated. Many people mistrust these documents, which give unbridled power to your agent. So some people sign them to appease their lawyers but never give them to the person designated to handle their affairs. If you're nervous about giving the signed document to your designated agent, leave it with your lawyer with instructions on when to turn it over. In that case, remember to tell your agent whom to contact.

Either way, make sure you name a second person who can become the agent if, for any reason, the first person cannot do the job. Some lawyers use pre-printed forms for the power of attorney and will include it as part of the estate-planning package at no additional cost.

Many financial institutions require that you fill out their own power of attorney form. If so, do the paperwork but also sign a power of attorney that your lawyer drafts to cover your other assets. A broadly worded power of attorney could give your agent the authority to implement a variety of estate planning strategies, such as making gifts (Chapter 15), adding assets to a trust (Chapter 6), prepaying charitable bequests (Chapter 17) and amending retirement plan beneficiary designation forms (Chapter 7).

A living trust or revocable trust holds assets for your benefit while you are alive and names the people who will receive them when you die. This is especially important in planning for incapacity and works in conjunction with the durable power of attorney – you need both.

You'll find a basic primer on trusts in Chapter 6. Basically, here's how this one works. You set up a trust, designed for your own benefit, with the idea that a person or financial institution that you designate (the trustee) will ultimately manage the funds and distribute the money for your care. Until then, you can be a co-trustee or the sole trustee.

The trust can describe in detail how the assets are managed, how principal and income are distributed and who receives the property when you die. It can also spell out exactly how to identify incapacity and who should determine it. When you are acting as trustee, it should include a procedure to bring in a successor trustee should you become incapacitated.

Depending on your circumstances, these trusts can be unfunded, partially funded or fully funded at the time they are set up. For example, you can keep some cash to manage yourself and transfer other assets into the trust. Or, you can leave the trust unfunded until someone certifies that you have become incapacitated. At that point, the designated agent could fund the trust for you. (See Chapter 2 for other purposes these trusts can serve.)

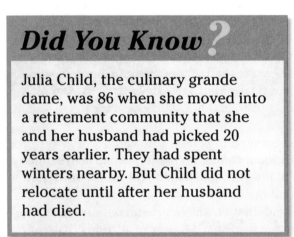

Did You Know?

Julia Child, the culinary grande dame, was 86 when she moved into a retirement community that she and her husband had picked 20 years earlier. They had spent winters nearby. But Child did not relocate until after her husband had died.

The elderly or other people who find financial matters overwhelming might prefer to put everything in the trust except for life insurance, retirement assets and a checking account that holds the grocery money. This bank account is needed, if for nothing else, to deposit Social Security checks (preferably by direct deposit), since they cannot be made payable to a trust.

It would be a mistake to rely exclusively on a revocable trust and not sign a power of attorney. For example, if you do not initially put all the assets in the trust, it is important that the agent with power of attorney be authorized to add assets to the trust at some later point. And while the trust works well for assets under its umbrella, it does not cover quasi-personal functions, like filing tax returns, applying for Social Security benefits, signing a nursing home contract and even picking up mail.

Keep Financial Data Accessible

The person with your durable power of attorney will need access to your financial records, which can be kept in your home in a file cabinet or safe that is fireproof and reasonably secure. If you pay bills and manage investments online, compile user names, passwords and the answers to secret questions needed to gain access. Even if you print out this information, also save a copy on a flash drive or burn it onto a CD, and keep it with copies of any other important records. They include:

- A list of all the financial institutions where you have accounts (don't forget bank CDs), including the account numbers and the type of account (for example, checking, savings or retirement)
- A beneficiary designation form for each retirement account
- Account numbers of credit cards
- Insurance policies
- A copy of documents creating any family limited partnership or limited liability company in which you have an interest (see Chapter 16)
- A list of monthly and quarterly bills that you pay. Include recurring bills that are automatically debited from your bank account
- Paperwork for all debts
- The title to your car and deed to a cemetery plot if you have bought one
- If you have a family business, a copy of the succession plan and buy-sell agreement for that company (see Chapter 12)
- Tax returns
- Records of accounts for which you are the custodian of investments for minor children (for example, savings bonds, brokerage accounts and college accounts)
- Copies of all trusts that involve you: those you have created, those of which you are a beneficiary, and those in which you serve as an individual trustee (see Chapter 6)
- Photocopies of original documents that you have put in a safe deposit box

Avoiding an Astor Disaster

Unless something goes wrong, courts generally do not supervise either powers of attorney or revocable trusts, because they are considered private arrangements. And while abuses are rare, they can be dramatic.

A notable example involved Brooke Astor, the New York philanthropist, who lived to be 105. Astor had a strained relationship with her son, Anthony D. Marshall, yet she gave him her power of attorney and entrusted him with supervising her care in old age. As Astor became incapacitated with Alzheimer's, friends complained that Marshall and his wife were diverting Astor's money for their own uses. One of Marshall's sons, Philip, filed a lawsuit in July 2006, basically accusing his father, who was 82, of elder abuse.

After several months of legal wrangling, the parties called a truce. The court appointed Annette de la Renta, a close friend of Astor's, as her guardian and put JPMorgan Chase in charge of her money. Astor died in August 2007 with an estimated net worth of $131 million.

At the end of a six-month criminal trial in New York, in October 2009 a jury convicted Marshall of stealing tens of millions of dollars from his mother. Some of the most serious charges involved abusing the power of attorney. In the same trial, Francis X. Morrissey, Jr., one of Marshall's lawyers and co-executor of Astor's will, was convicted of conspiring with Marshall to take advantage of Astor's diminished capacity and forging an amendment to the will. As this book went to press, a will contest was expected in surrogate's court asserting that Astor had been coerced to change her will to Anthony Marshall's benefit after she was already incapacitated.

What can we learn from this sad tale? Whether you are choosing a trustee for your living trust or an agent to hand your power of attorney, select someone you trust absolutely. And create a system of checks and balances that can guard against an Astor-style disaster. Naming joint agents for a power of attorney or co-trustees of a living trust is one possibility. Another is to appoint a protector, such as an attorney, an accountant or a family friend, to supervise the arrangement (see Chapter 6).

Who Decides When You Are Incapacitated?

Depending on how you set things up, the power of attorney and the revocable trust may remain inactive until you become incapacitated. Therefore, it is important to choose someone not involved in your financial affairs to decide when you have reached that state.

Traditionally, this has required a medical opinion. If that is your preference, you will need to provide the doctors of your choice the authorization to talk with your family members or advisers. Otherwise, the federal Health Insurance Portability and Accountability Act, or HIPAA, may prevent them from discussing your mental or physical condition. Without this kind of authorization, your family or advisers might need a court order to get the medical records necessary to implement a power of attorney or trigger a trustee provision.

The best approach is to indicate in the power of attorney or the living trust that the person in charge of finding out whether you lack capacity has the rights of a personal representative under HIPAA. According to the law, the personal representative has the same rights to medical information as the patient does. Back this up by signing a HIPAA release, authorizing doctors to disclose health information to the people you have listed, and store that with your other legal papers.

Another reasonable approach that leaves out the medical community is to name a committee of trusted family members, friends or advisers to come to a consensus about incapacity.

Who Will Make Health Care Decisions?

Separate from handling your finances, someone needs to be able to make medical decisions when you no longer can. To appoint this person, you will need a health care proxy – known in some states as a health care agent or health care power of attorney. Legally, the health care proxy also automatically gives the agent access to your medical records. (Some states have surrogate decision-making laws that give specific family members the right to make certain medical decisions for others.)

Other Reasons to Sign a HIPAA Release

Have you ever called a hospital to inquire about the condition of a friend or family member who is a patient there? If so, you may have been stymied by HIPAA. The federal Health Insurance Portability and Accountability Act, designed to protect medical privacy, prohibits doctors and hospitals from sharing medical information without the patient's permission (note, too, that this can apply to information about your own children once they reach age 18).

If you want concerned friends and relatives to be privy to the details, list them in a HIPAA release. You can also include lawyers, accountants and financial advisers who may need to stay current about your situation.

What Are Your Final Wishes?

If you have preferences about end-of-life care, you should create a living will (also called an advance directive) – a written statement that expresses your wishes. Although it is difficult to address every contingency, living wills typically cover pain relief and whether you would want treatments such as surgery, a ventilator, a feeding tube or resuscitation that might prolong your life but without necessarily ensuring your return to a functional state.

Likewise, funeral planning is a wrenching task for grief-stricken survivors and leaves them vulnerable to a predatory industry. You will ease the burden on loved ones if you let them know, orally or in a letter of instruction, how plain or fancy your funeral should be, and whether you have any special requests – about burial or cremation, for example. Keep in mind, too, that cash flow may be an issue. Expenses can be reimbursed from the estate, but someone must pay them upfront.

Left to their own devices, friends of Copeland Marks, who wrote cookbooks about exotic cuisines and died in 1999, organized a very meaningful, low-budget memorial. It consisted of a potluck dinner with each guest preparing one of Marks's recipes, and many sharing stories about their adventures with this fun-loving man.

To-Do List

Organize Important Records

Just as important as creating an estate plan is keeping all the documents and supporting records where your family can find them. That will greatly reduce the hassles for loved ones, both if you become incapacitated and after you are gone. While some records can be kept in a file cabinet at home (see "Keep Financial Data Accessible" on page 5), originals of documents that are difficult to replace belong in a safe deposit box. These include:

✤ Property deeds

✤ Birth certificate

✤ Social Security card

✤ Marriage certificate (this is more than a sentimental document – your spouse may need it to qualify for Social Security benefits)

✤ Savings bonds and other securities not held by a financial institution

Note that your will and the deed to your cemetery plot, if you have bought one, should *not* go in your safe deposit box. Why? Unless a family member has access to it (you must not only give that person a key, but also sign a form at the bank authorizing that designee to open it), the box could be sealed when you die, and it might take court action by your heirs to get it opened. Instead, keep one original copy of your will at home, along with any supporting documents your state requires (such as an affidavit of witnesses). Ask your lawyer or other trusted adviser to keep another copy. Be sure to leave contact information so family members know who the person is.

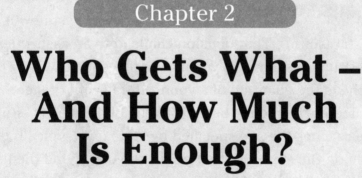

Chapter 2

Who Gets What – And How Much Is Enough?

Read this chapter if you want to provide for specific people, charities or pets in your estate plan.

T hinking about how to parcel out everything you leave behind might seem like a morbid chore, more so than any other aspect of estate planning. But consider what would happen if you did not make your wishes known.

Whatever is left after taxes would be distributed according to the law of intestacy. This law, which varies from state to state, establishes a ranking of inheritors of people who die without a will or living trust. Some newer laws say everything will go first to the spouse, then to children, parents and siblings. However, plenty of state laws still divide an estate between the surviving spouse and children in preset proportions (to check the law in your state, see www.mystatewill.com/specific_states.htm). That division can lead to an assortment of awkward situations, such as when a spouse ends up short of funds even as she is the guardian of a young child's inheritance. Whatever her needs, the money belongs to the child, who is entitled to it when she reaches the age specified by state law (typically 18 or 21, depending on the state). At that point, she can spend the funds as quickly or on whatever she wishes.

> ## In This Chapter...
>
> ⚜ *Dividing the Pie*
> ⚜ *Safeguarding an Inheritance*
> ⚜ *Basic Documents You Need*
> ⚜ *Who Implements Your Wishes*

With an estate plan, you have much more control over who gets what. Remember, though, that you send powerful messages in the way you distribute your assets – or fail to specify what you'd like. Deciding what you want means coming to grips with both emotional baggage and a sense of finality. But it's worth doing.

Dividing the Pie

Whether you are doing an estate plan for the first time or updating an existing one, the best way to start is by making a list of everything you own. This includes: your house and personal property (you can lump them together in a single estimate or identify the most valuable possessions separately); all your investments, whether in the form of bank or brokerage accounts, retirement plans, real estate or alternative investments, and any interests you hold in a family business or partnership. For each asset, note whether you are the sole owner or own it jointly with another person.

Think of these assets, which make up your estate, as a pie that may be divided into three parts. If the total is more than $3.5 million and you are not married, at least 45 cents of every dollar above that amount – except for what you leave to charity – could go to estate taxes. The rest can be divided among family and friends according to the details you provide in your estate plan.

How much goes to family? Many spouses start by leaving everything to each other. But whether you are married or single, you should consider all the contingencies. For each person whom you want to benefit from your estate plan – a spouse, a child, another relative or a friend – you must ask, and answer, this question: "If this person dies before me, what next?"

Thinking about these issues is especially important in second marriages when there are children from the first one. For example, you may want to arrange things, in case you die before your current spouse, so that your assets will at some point go to your own children, rather than ultimately passing to his (see Chapter 4).

Within a family, most people structure their estate plans to shift inheritances down a generation when one beneficiary dies, rather than distributing that person's share among the other members of the same generation. Let's say you have three grown children – Harry, Sam and Molly – whom you want to benefit equally in your will. If Harry dies before Molly and Sam, most people would give Harry's portion to his children, if he has any, rather than dividing it between Sam and Molly.

How family members are treated in an estate plan, and whether some feel they were dealt an unfair hand, is a common source of discord. To deter lawsuits, many estate plans include a no-contest or in terrorem clause, which provides that anyone who formally challenges the plan gets nothing – a practice permitted in most states.

Personal Possessions: A Lightning Rod for Conflict

Unlike financial assets, which can generally be divided easily among heirs, personal possessions – called tangible personal property – are unique.

If there are only one or two valuable possessions, your estate plan might direct the executor of the will or the trustee of a living trust to sell the diamond or the painting, for example, and divide the proceeds among the heirs. If one of them really wants a particular item (like Grandma's engagement ring) and has the funds, he or she could buy it from the estate for the fair market value. Another approach, if only one person asks for certain expensive pieces, is to honor those wishes and reduce the heir's share of other assets. To steer clear of conflicts, designate an independent third party to divide the assets or to referee.

If you want certain items to go to specific people, say so in your estate planning documents. For instance, in her will, Jacqueline Kennedy Onassis directed that most of her personal property go to her children, but she gave a handful of items to other people. She left her longtime companion, Maurice Tempelsman, a Greek alabaster head of a woman; her lawyer a copy of John F. Kennedy's inaugural address signed by Robert Frost and a close friend a couple of Indian miniatures.

The question is what to do about everything else. One possibility is to direct your heirs to divide belongings in substantially equal shares and if they sell anything, to use the cash to equalize things. Another is to map out a very specific rotation of choice – for instance, by birth order – so that everyone gets a turn at having first dibs on an item.

With or without such a clause, if a will is found to be invalid, assets are distributed according to the terms of a previous will or state law, depending on the circumstances. With a no-contest clause, those who lose a case to have the will thrown out, or bring one on lesser grounds, forfeit what they otherwise would have received.

The entertainer Michael Jackson, who died in 2009, reportedly included such a clause in his living trust, a private document that he used to dispose of most of his assets. After his death, questions arose about whether his mother, Katherine Jackson, would lose her 40 percent share of trust assets if she opposed the executors in his will. She asked the California Superior Court to rule on this issue, as state law permits, and the court found she could challenge the executors' authority without running afoul of the no-contest clause.

Tempting as it may be to tailor your plan to the personalities, abilities and needs of individual family members, remember that disparate treatment, particularly of children, can rekindle old rivalries or ignite new ones. Whatever your justification, you might leave children thinking, "Why did she do that? Mom didn't love me as much." By treating all your children (if not all your descendants) equally, you improve the chances that they will peacefully coexist.

That said, it is reasonable to take note in your planning of children's career decisions, choice of a spouse and all the unforeseeable events that a parent witnesses in a child's life. If you encouraged your son to follow his heart and become a schoolteacher, are you penalizing him by leaving him the same size inheritance as his younger sister, who made a fortune when she sold her company?

Assuming you chose to treat everyone equally, you may want your estate plan to even out certain disparities that have arisen during your life. For instance, if you lent money to one child for a business venture and were never repaid, you could leave that child proportionately less. If one of your children never married or had children, and you have set aside college funds for grandchildren, you could give a larger inheritance to the child who is not a parent (though you should note, and hope all parties recognize, that a child with grandchildren and college costs needs more funds).

Still, some things are hard to equalize. Consider a family business. Company founders often want to pass along the enterprise to family members who are running it, while those who don't work in the business favor cashing out. It is hard to apportion things so everyone comes out equally, or, if not equally, at least feeling that they were treated fairly.

One way to address this particular issue is to find out whether any of your children want to continue in the business. If none do, your estate plan can reflect the expectation that the company will be sold. If one or more children want to continue in the business, you can look for ways the children who will not be involved might receive other, comparably valued assets, such as stocks, bonds and real estate, or the proceeds of a life insurance policy (see Chapter 8).

Summer and vacation homes are another potential source of conflict. Before leaving these assets to more than one person jointly, find out whether they want them and how they might continue using them. Various legal vehicles are available for sharing and running these homes, financing their operation and buying out people who do not want to participate (see Chapter 10).

Some parents, especially those who have created their wealth rather than inherited it, are concerned about the corrosive effect an inheritance might have on their children's work ethic, and act accordingly when they plan their estates. Unfortunately, there is no easy answer to the question, "How much is enough?"

While some people come up with an arbitrary number, others use a more nuanced approach. For example, you can identify the basics you want to provide for your children (say, education, health insurance and a house), give them enough to cover those expenses and have the rest go to charity.

Rather than leaving your children (or grandchildren) guessing about the motives behind all these difficult decisions or feeling slighted, you may want to spell out your reasoning in your estate plan-

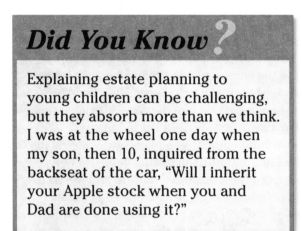

Did You Know?

Explaining estate planning to young children can be challenging, but they absorb more than we think. I was at the wheel one day when my son, then 10, inquired from the backseat of the car, "Will I inherit your Apple stock when you and Dad are done using it?"

ning documents. Having a frank discussion beforehand takes a lot of courage, but it gives all the affected parties a chance to be heard, and can clear up misunderstandings – yours and theirs. The downside, of course, is that it doesn't tend to bring out the best in human nature, and you may be the target of the residual anger.

How you handle this delicate issue will depend on the dynamics of your family and your level of comfort in talking about financial topics.

How much goes to charity? Some people deliberately structure their estate plans to benefit charity and make their wishes clear. Many more think of charity as a sort of default beneficiary. For example, a charity might receive a bequest only if a person has no living relatives when he or she dies. In other cases, people who are afraid of spoiling their children structure their estate plans to benefit family up to a certain amount and leave the excess to charity. Warren Buffett and Bill Gates are two self-made businessmen who have been outspoken about their intentions to give most of their assets to charity, rather than to their children.

Many people with smaller balance sheets also feel an obligation to give back to their community. For them, a crucial question is how much to donate during life and what to leave in an estate plan.

Gifts made during your lifetime – if you can afford them – give you the pleasure of seeing the good works that may result from your generosity, and they can be much more tax efficient: you are able to take an income tax deduction for the year in which the gift was made. For people with more than $3.5 million in assets whose estates may therefore be subject to the 45 percent estate tax, a lifetime gift reduces their net worth, leaving less to tax. In contrast, if you make a gift in your will, your estate can take a charitable deduction against only the estate tax – there is no income tax write-off. Because of the advantages of lifetime gifts, it is a good idea to give the person who holds your durable power of attorney (see Chapter 1) the power to prepay charitable bequests. (Chapter 17 outlines a variety of tools for charitable giving, both during life and through an estate plan.)

Still, for all the advantages of giving while you are alive, some people prefer charitable bequests to lifetime donations because they want to be sure they have enough for a comfortable retirement. For them, a key estate planning issue is how to structure the gift so that it will not shortchange family.

The basic choice is to describe your bequest as a preset dollar amount or as a fixed percentage of your estate. Unless you are relatively sure what your net worth will be when you die (and few people have that degree of certainty), there is a potential pitfall: If your net worth declines – for example, in a stock market meltdown like the one in 2008 – your family may not get as much as you intended them to have.

One alternative, if you want to describe your bequest in percentage terms (for instance, "50 percent to my wife, 20 percent to each of my two children and 10 percent to charity") is to require that family members get at least a certain amount that you specify before anything goes to charity. For example, you could say, "50 percent of my estate, but no less than $500,000 to my wife; 20 percent of my estate but no less than $100,000 to each of my children," with the balance of the estate split according to the percentage formula. Another possibility is to provide for charity to get a fixed amount, but include a circuit breaker, so that it does not exceed a certain percentage of your estate. Any fixed amounts you include can be subject to an inflation adjustment.

Maximizing flexibility. When your finances or the economic environment are uncertain, build as much flexibility into your estate plan as possible, to allow your heirs to make adjustments in how the pie is divided. The primary way of doing that is with an estate-planning technique known as a disclaimer.

Basically, a disclaimer involves saying "no thanks" to an inheritance. People making disclaimers, known as disclaimants, are generally treated as if they had died before the person from whom they are inheriting. Disclaimers can help your heirs implement a variety of tax strategies. They can also be used to give heirs some choices about charitable giving. If you are not prepared to make significant charitable bequests through your estate plan because you are not sure if your heirs will need the money, you can give them the option of shifting assets to a charity through a disclaimer.

In some contexts it does not matter whether your estate plan mentions the possibility of disclaiming. The law gives heirs a right to disclaim, so you don't have to provide for it in your will. But most often there is a person who would be next in line. If you want your heirs to be able to disclaim to charity instead, your will must mention this option and name the specific charity or charities that will receive any assets that are disclaimed – the choice of the charity is not up to the people who would otherwise inherit the assets. Example: "To my daughter Sally, but if she disclaims, to our town public library." The charities you name can include charitable trusts, your own private foundation or a donor-advised fund (see Chapter 17).

Safeguarding an Inheritance

When giving away money and other assets through your estate plan, you have a choice between leaving it to your heirs outright or in trust. Outright transfers give recipients immediate control over their inheritance. Trusts put a person or company in charge of managing the assets and distributing them according to your wishes, and thus play a key role in preserving an inheritance. Trusts are extremely important in a second marriage for people who want to leave assets to children from an earlier one (see Chapter 3).

Not only can a trust achieve substantial tax savings, it can shield assets from two key risks. One is the prospect that heirs who are spendthrifts or inexperienced at dealing with money will fritter away the assets or be vulnerable to financial scams; the other is the growing possibility in our litigious society that funds will be eroded by creditors, such as ex-spouses or someone who wins a lawsuit against your heirs (see Chapter 18).

Disclaimants Beware

Writing a will so that heirs can implement strategies through disclaimers is only half the battle. Anyone disclaiming an inheritance needs to be aware of the potential pitfalls that surround the process. Under federal tax law, your heirs must make their disclaimer within nine months of your death.

Generally a disclaimant may not have accepted an interest in the asset or any of its benefits. (There are special rules for surviving spouses.) Innocent mistakes, like depositing a dividend check in one's own account, could preclude someone from making a disclaimer.

State laws may impose additional requirements, such as giving notice of the disclaimer to the executor (called the personal representative in some states), to estate beneficiaries and to the surrogate's court or its functional equivalent.

The downside, of course, is that trusts restrict your heirs' access to the funds. And by locking up everything in trust, you may undermine the self-confidence of adult children. Without the opportunity to make their own mistakes, struggle and ultimately succeed, children might get the impression that "Dad never thought I was going to amount to anything, and that's why he kept such tight controls over this money." A combination of outright access to some of their inheritance and protection afforded by some assets left in trust can balance the goals of autonomy and your desire to preserve what you leave behind.

Here, too, disclaimers can preserve flexibility for your heirs. Let's say you would ordinarily leave an outright inheritance to your children or siblings but want to protect the assets from potential creditors. In that case, you can provide for an outright bequest, but give your heirs the option to disclaim into a trust. The trust must be set up before you die, and the money must never touch the inheritor's hands. By disclaiming into this trust, the inheritor gives up control over the assets forever but can generally keep them out of the hands of creditors.

Some people try using trusts to influence their descendants' behavior. Consider the incentive trust, which makes distributions for desirable behavior (such as graduating from college) or withholds funds for undesirable actions (like using drugs).

These trusts can be hugely troublesome. One difficulty is that it is easier to punish people when they go astray than it is to reward them when they do something good. And although parents want to inspire their children to do great things, achievement can be hard to define. For example, the so-called "investment banker clause," which provides for payouts from a trust based on how much money a beneficiary earns, seems to penalize the son who decides to teach high school or the daughter who wants to do charitable work.

History includes some notable examples of people who tried to use trusts as a way to control their heirs – even from the grave. One was Leona Helmsley, the billionaire real estate developer and hotel operator who died in 2007. In her will, she specifically disinherited two of her grandchildren, Craig Panzirer and Meegan Panzirer Wesolko, "for reasons which are known to them," but which were not spelled out. She left two other grandchildren, David and Walter Panzirer, $10 million apiece.

Half of the sum was in a trust with substantial strings attached: in order to receive annual distributions from the trust for the rest of his life, each grandson was required to visit the grave of their father (Helmsley's son Jay Panzirer, who died in 1982) every year on the anniversary of his death. The only exception to this requirement was if the grandson had a physical or mental disability that in the trustees' opinion made it impossible to visit.

To show they visited, each grandson had to sign the register kept at the mausoleum where their father was buried (this, too, was described in Helmsley's will). And if they missed a single visit, they would not receive any payouts from the trust in the future.

Basic Documents You Need

The paperwork required to pass assets to your heirs can depend on a variety of factors, including what the assets are, the type of account they are in, how they are titled and which estate planning documents mention them. These are the key documents to know about:

Will or living trust. There is widespread confusion about the differences between these two documents, and when you need one rather than the

Will or Living Trust?

Both a will and a living trust can be used to transfer assets, but each also has other unique uses.

	Will	**Living Trust**
Uses besides transferring assets	Name guardians for children who are minors, create trust that takes effect after death	Hold assets for your benefit while you are alive – for example, in case of dementia
When it takes effect	Not until death	During life or at death
Privacy	None: it's a public record	Private
Procedure for creating and amending	Must be signed with certain formalities, which vary from state to state (for example, requirements for witnesses, and whether it can be handwritten)	Signature usually is sufficient; depending on state law, may be desirable to have it notarized
Steps necessary after death	Must be submitted for probate – court's approval	Probate usually not necessary
Who distributes property	Executor or personal representative	Trustee

other. A common misconception is that revocable trusts avoid estate taxes, which is not true. Both a will and a living trust can be used to transfer assets, but each has unique uses (see chart on page 21). For example, only a will can be used to appoint a guardian for a child.

In some states, revocable trusts are also used to eliminate probate – the process through which a court makes sure a will is legally valid. Whether probate is costly or burdensome will depend on the state. Still, there are

Tie Up Loose Ends

Charles Kuralt, the CBS News correspondent and anchor who died in 1997, could have saved his loved ones a lot of heartache and legal expenses if he had used a will or living trust to transfer certain property to Patricia Elizabeth Shannon, his secret, intimate companion for 29 years.

Among other things, that might have avoided or at least curtailed a six-year, public court battle between Shannon and Kuralt's family. Shannon claimed Kuralt had left her 90 acres and a renovated schoolhouse near the Montana fishing retreat where they spent time together; his will left everything to his family.

During the course of the lawsuit, details of the relationship, said to be a surprise to Kuralt's wife, Susan Baird Kuralt, who lived in New York, and her daughters spilled into court papers. Kuralt posthumously became the subject of scandal and talk show banter.

The outcome of the case turned on a court's interpretation of a handwritten note that Kuralt sent Shannon several weeks before he died, saying he would arrange to give her the land. The court ruled in Shannon's favor, though it remained unclear whether the note was a valid amendment to Kuralt's 1994 will or simply a promise to revise the document that Kuralt never carried out.

After the court awarded Shannon the property, valued at $600,000, several more rounds of legal battles followed over who was responsible for paying the federal estate taxes on it. The Montana Supreme Court ruled in 2003 that the taxes should come out of the daughters' share. Kuralt's wife died in 1999 while the dispute was pending.

times when you might want to use a revocable trust to limit how much of your estate goes through probate or to avoid it altogether. For example, if you are concerned about publicity over your net worth or the identity of your beneficiaries, you might transfer assets through a trust – which, unlike a will, is not a public document. Someone with a domestic partner might choose to leave assets to that partner through a revocable trust, because it is harder for family members to challenge a trust than a will.

A living trust is also useful if you own real estate in a state that is not your primary residence. Real estate is governed by the probate rules of the state in which it is situated. Unless the property is in a revocable trust, an Illinois resident who has a home in Florida, for instance, would need to probate the property separately there.

Personal property memorandum. This indicates whom you want to receive jewelry, art and other personal possessions that are not described in the will. You should keep these two documents together.

Why might you want to use a personal property memorandum, rather than a will? The main reason is privacy. Your will, which is a

> # Did You Know?
>
> Today using "last will and testament" is like wearing a belt and suspenders, but it wasn't always so. Historically, a will was used to pass along real estate to heirs, while a testament covered personal property. The distinction no longer applies, although the phrase lives on.

public record, identifies who got what, for all to see. With a personal property memorandum, strangers don't need to know that you left your Picasso to your sister or your collection of autographed guitars to your high school buddy, for instance. And if you have a change of heart, you can modify this document without the formalities needed to amend a will.

Still, there's a catch: depending on where you live, your executor – the person or institution you appoint to put your will into action – may not be required to follow the wishes you express in an independent document. In some states, these memos are considered binding on the executor. Elsewhere they are only treated as guidance, meaning your executor can consider your stated preferences – but need not follow them unless you make the personal property memorandum part of the will, which largely defeats the purpose.

Providing for Fido

Although you cannot give assets directly to pets, you can leave money and instructions to provide for them after you are gone.

The tobacco heiress Doris Duke, who died in 1993, included a paragraph in her will with detailed instructions about who should become the owner of whatever dog lived at her Beverly Hills home when she died (her first choice was the caretaker of the house). Duke also created a $100,000 trust to cover her pet's food, medical bills and other expenses.

Such trusts have become increasingly popular, and the law on them is evolving – about 40 states now permit them. Creating and administering pet trusts involves many of the same issues that arise with other types of trusts (see Chapter 6), including how to fund the trust, whether it should take effect while you are still alive (for example, if you are no longer able to care for your pet), and whom to choose as trustee. You will also want to identify the caregiver (include alternates in case the person you have in mind cannot do it), ideally someone other than the trustee. Include care instructions, and indicate what should happen to the funds after your pet dies.

Still, these trusts are not airtight. Heirs can challenge them, and if a court finds you allocated too much for your pet's care, it can whittle down the amount in trust. That's what happened with the $12 million trust Leona Helmsley set up to benefit her dog, Trouble. After Helmsley died in 2007, two of her grandchildren, whom she had disinherited (see page 20) challenged the arrangement. They persuaded the court to reduce the trust to $2 million and walked away with $3 million apiece. The other $4 million went to a charitable trust that Helmsley and her husband Harry had set up.

If you live in a state that does not allow pet trusts, you need a different approach. The simplest is to designate in your will the person to care for your pet, and leave that individual enough money to carry out the responsibility. This raises two potential pitfalls: the amount could be subject to estate tax and there's no legal mechanism for making sure things go as you planned.

Payable on death provisions and beneficiary designation forms. Certain types of assets do not usually pass through a will or living trust. These include savings bonds, and certain bank accounts or certificates of deposit, which can be made automatically payable on death to the person you name. Retirement accounts are distributed according to beneficiary designation forms that you complete when you open an account and can later amend (see Chapter 7). Similarly, when you apply for life insurance, you are asked to choose a beneficiary, and the proceeds are paid out according to those instructions (see Chapter 8).

Joint title. By jointly titling assets in a certain way, you may enable them to pass automatically to your co-owner, outside your will or living trust (see Chapter 4). Joint accounts are commonly used for aging parents and their adult children, siblings, spouses and domestic partners. But it is essential that you trust each other completely. With a joint bank account, for instance, either person can withdraw all the money without the other's consent. Depending on the form of joint ownership, you could also expose each co-owner to the other's potential liabilities (see Chapter 18).

Joint accounts have other significant disadvantages. Unless the joint tenant is a spouse, you must consider the potential gift-tax costs of adding someone's name to an account (see Chapter 3). When you are dealing with real estate, stock certificates or bonds, you have technically made a gift by setting up a joint account. For bank and brokerage accounts, there is no gift until the person withdraws money from the account.

Other drawbacks apply uniquely to spouses. Joint accounts can complicate the division of assets in a divorce. And by having the property go directly to the surviving spouse, you may lose the opportunity to take advantage of various estate planning strategies (see Chapter 3).

Who Implements Your Wishes

Your estate plan expresses your wishes, and you entrust your executor to carry them out. This is the person or institution that administers your estate after you die and remains in charge until it is legally closed. Before that happens, the will must be admitted to probate. Any creditors need to be paid, the taxes need to be paid and the beneficiaries named in your will

Mapping Out the Executor's Role

A will is a road map to the responsibilities of the executor or personal representative, and you need to tailor it to your particular circumstances. Typically the personal representative is expected to:

- Gather the assets and take title to them – the personal representative is the legal owner of the property until it is distributed to the beneficiaries named in the will.

- Inventory the assets and determine what they are worth (some states require that these lists be filed with a local court), getting appraisals as necessary.

- Safeguard the assets by prudently managing and investing them.

- Collect any debts owed to the estate.

- Pay medical bills and present claims to the insurance company for reimbursement.

- Respond to any other creditors' claims that may be filed.

- File your final income tax return and pay any taxes owed.

- File the estate tax return and submit any taxes that are due.

Other powers may relate to the specific assets you own or the dynamics of your family. For example, to prevent family feuds you might want the will to include guidelines about how the personal representative should divide tangible personal property (see "Personal Possessions: A Lightning Rod for Conflict," page 14). Some people include the power to borrow and lend money. Business owners might authorize a personal representative to operate, sell or make changes in the company. And if you own significant real estate, you might want the personal representative to be able to sell, lease or mortgage it.

should receive their share of what is left. If there is an estate tax audit or a will contest, the executor will oversee that process, too.

Being an executor is a huge responsibility. Depending on the complexity of the estate and subsequent events, the job might last for a couple of years and sometimes many more. Whom you choose as executor or executrix (a woman who serves this role) can make the difference between an estate that is settled harmoniously and efficiently, and one that gets bogged down in a legal and financial quagmire.

The best executor is honest, efficient, has sound financial judgment and gets along well with people. Estate administration can get complex, and executors should know enough to call the experts when their own knowledge falls short.

An executor, called a personal representative in some states (the terms are used interchangeably here), is a fiduciary, which means that certain legal obligations automatically apply. These include a duty to act always in the best interests of the beneficiaries and to avoid conflicts of interest when handling the estate. Specific functions need to be outlined in the will (see "Mapping Out the Executor's Role," page

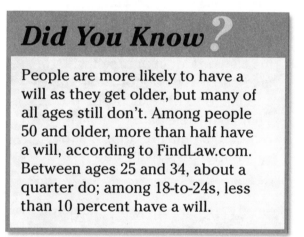

Did You Know?

People are more likely to have a will as they get older, but many of all ages still don't. Among people 50 and older, more than half have a will, according to FindLaw.com. Between ages 25 and 34, about a quarter do; among 18-to-24s, less than 10 percent have a will.

26). If you do not name a personal representative and an alternate, and your first choice is not able to serve, a local court will appoint one instead.

Choosing family. Most people think first of naming a family member, especially a spouse or child, as executor. The advantage of this is that your next of kin presumably understands your intentions better than anybody else and can readily find the assets that need to be inventoried.

This can also save the family money. Many states set caps on the fees that executors may charge, but they vary widely. While some are framed simply in terms of what's reasonable, others are based on a percentage of the estate value. For a large estate, the executor's fee can get expensive. When family members who are also beneficiaries serve as executors, they often waive the fees. Other times, families are happy to have this money go to one of their own, rather than paying an outside executor. In that case, those who find the paperwork and complications overwhelming can hire professionals to guide them through the process.

But putting family members in charge has several drawbacks. When they are also beneficiaries, as is typically the case, conflicts of interest can arise and be difficult to navigate. What's more, mishandling a potential conflict or a particular task with financial implications can lead to ill will among beneficiaries. Ultimately they may hold the executor liable for a wide variety of missteps.

In an effort to be fair, some people name all their children as co-executors. When that happens, sibling rivalry and trouble reaching a consensus can make it hard to get things done. Likewise, naming a spouse along with children from a previous marriage, or even those children alone, can lead to friction. Making the right choice in a particular situation is a matter of knowing the individuals and how they would react.

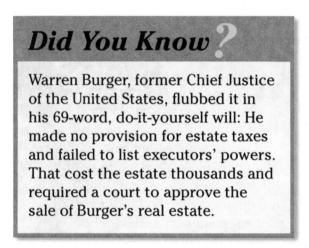

Did You Know?

Warren Burger, former Chief Justice of the United States, flubbed it in his 69-word, do-it-yourself will: He made no provision for estate taxes and failed to list executors' powers. That cost the estate thousands and required a court to approve the sale of Burger's real estate.

Reaching outside the family. For all these reasons, it may be helpful to name a professional who knows the ropes either as the sole executor or co-executor with family members or a trusted friend. The options include an individual adviser or a corporate fiduciary, such as a bank or trust company. If you choose an individual, designate at least a couple of alternates in case that person is unwilling or unable to serve when the time comes. You do not have that concern with a corporate fiduciary, which provides institutional longevity. It is also more likely to carry enough insurance to cover any potential liability.

Either way, meet the professionals you have in mind to be sure they are able to provide the services you require. Inquire about their experience with similar matters and ask about fees – subject to the maximums set by state law, they are typically based on the size and complexity of the estate.

To-Do List

Prelude to Planning

The estate planning process starts with complex personal choices. Before meeting with a lawyer, give some thought to:

❧ Whom do you want to benefit through your estate plan?

❧ Are you concerned that once your heirs receive their inheritance, they will no longer have an incentive to work?

❧ Do you want your estate plan to treat all your children equally?

❧ If you have a family business, and only some children are involved in the company, how do you want to address this in your estate plan?

❧ Do you prefer that heirs receive their inheritances outright, or should some of your assets be left in trust?

❧ For assets left in trust, at what ages do you want beneficiaries to receive distributions?

❧ If you have a summer or vacation home, do you want to keep it in the family?

❧ Are there charitable organizations that you would like to mention in your estate plan?

❧ Whom do you trust to serve the following roles: make medical decisions if you cannot act for yourself; act as your attorney under a power of attorney; be the trustee of a living trust; serve as executor of your will.

Chapter 3

Beware
The Tax Bite

*Read this chapter if you have
more than $3.5 million in assets –
or might someday.*

Once you're worth more than a certain amount, federal taxes could shrink your estate. Right now, $3.5 million is the sum each of us can pass on tax-free before the 45 percent federal estate tax kicks in. That figure is called the exemption amount or the applicable exclusion. Unless you're leaving everything else to your spouse or to charity, the federal government takes 45 cents out of every dollar after that.

The potential tax bite doesn't end there. If you leave more than $3.5 million to grandchildren and more remote descendants, another 45 percent levy kicks in. This is the generation-skipping transfer tax, and it applies in addition to any estate tax (see Chapter 14). Let's say you have a $5 million estate and leave everything to your grandchildren. They would receive $3.5 million without having to pay either tax. But of the remaining $1.5 million, the total of these two taxes would consume roughly 62 percent, reducing that $5 million inheritance to about $3.96 million (see "The Back of the Envelope," page 41).

In This Chapter...

- ⚜ *The Special Estate Tax Break For Spouses*
- ⚜ *The Estate Tax Break for Everyone*
- ⚜ *Quick and Easy Ways to Cut Federal Estate Tax*

Depending on where you live or own real estate, you may also have state estate tax to contend with. Arizona, California, Florida, Texas and some other states have no estate tax (one reason they're popular places to retire). But nationwide about half the other states impose an estate tax apart from the federal tax. (For more about state estate tax, see Chapter 4.)

Tally up these three taxes and you can easily see how your family could wind up with a lot less than you anticipate.

Even if $3.5 million sounds like more than you ever expect to have, it's good to think ahead, and to allow yourself some optimism. Fortunes have been made through hard work, smart saving and shrewd investments. Why not you? Your estate plan should anticipate these possibilities.

Various strategies are available to reduce the government's take. Many involve spending money while you are alive. Assuming you can afford to do that, another issue arises: Will a particular estate planning technique require you to pay gift tax? This tax, of up to 45 percent, applies to certain transfers that exceed the $1 million lifetime gift tax exemption. Gift tax is a backstop to the estate tax. It inhibits people from giving away so much while they are alive that there will be nothing left for the government to tax later.

While it's true that the more money you have, the more could potentially get eaten up by estate tax and generation-skipping transfer tax, it's also true that the greater your net worth, the more ways that are available to cut the tax bite while paying little or no gift tax.

Subsequent chapters discuss many different tools for minimizing all these taxes. Some achieve goals that may be a high priority for you anyway – like preserving retirement assets (see Chapter 7), educating children and grandchildren (Chapter 9) and benefiting charity (Chapter 17). Others, designed purely to shift wealth to younger generations, are aimed at people whose heirs will be saddled with an enormous estate tax bill if they did not do careful planning (Chapters 15 and 16). No matter what your situation, the rest of this chapter will cover some basic rules and strategies you need to understand.

The Special Estate Tax Break for Spouses

For better or worse, the law gives spouses a big tax advantage – but with complications. Assets inherited from a spouse are not taxed. This is the unlimited marital deduction (if your spouse is not a U.S. citizen, see "What If You Married an Alien?" on page 35).

The marital deduction doesn't avoid estate tax – it just postpones it. If assets inherited from a spouse remain when the survivor dies (say the wife inherited money from her husband and never spent it), those assets would be taxable as part of her own estate. By delaying the tax on these assets, the spouse is left more to live on. And of course, any or all of this money used before your spouse dies escapes tax altogether.

You can leave assets to your spouse directly (outright) or have them go into a trust, called a marital trust. While a trust creates more paperwork and gives your spouse less control over the funds (see Chapter 6), it can also protect the assets from creditors (Chapter 18), prevent a spouse with unwise spending habits from disbursing everything too quickly and preserve the funds for your children in case your spouse remarries (Chapter 4).

The marital deduction doesn't apply to all trusts, however, but only if you take one of two approaches to make it apply. Which you use will depend on your answer to this question: "Do you want your spouse to decide who gets the trust assets next?" (Remember, he or she might choose a future spouse, rather than the children you had together.)

You don't want your spouse to decide. Use a qualified terminable interest property, or QTIP, trust. This trust must require the trustee to pay all income to the surviving spouse for life (the trustee can also make distributions of principal) and not permit distributions to anyone other than the spouse while he is alive. After that, the assets can go to whomever you specify in the trust.

It's okay for your spouse to decide. In that case you could give your spouse a power of appointment – the right to decide who will get the assets after he dies.

What If You Married an Alien?

I f your spouse is not a U.S. citizen, your ability to use the marital deduction is much more limited. Congress was concerned that foreigners married to U.S. citizens would take inherited assets out of the country and never pay estate tax on them. So, in 1988, it passed a law to prevent that from happening. This law applies even if your spouse has a green card and is a permanent resident.

You can still use your estate tax exemption and leave your spouse $3.5 million tax-free. But anything above that gets taxed immediately unless it goes into a special kind of trust, called a qualified domestic trust, or QDOT. Any time this trust distributes principal, it must withhold estate tax – at the rate that was in effect when you died. (If the spouse receives distributions of income, they are subject to income tax, but not estate tax.)

How does this put aliens at a disadvantage? First, the marital deduction applies only if assets are in a trust (with citizens it applies to outright inheritances as well), and for all their advantages (see Chapter 6), trusts can be cumbersome. In addition, while a surviving spouse who is a U.S. citizen can postpone estate tax until he or she dies, a non-citizen could be forced to pay it earlier. Of course, if the spouse dies without ever receiving principal, the estate tax is delayed until then, just as it would be for citizens.

To be a QDOT, the trust must include certain features. The most important is that your spouse can't be the only trustee. At least one trustee must be a U.S. citizen or company. (For information on choosing a trustee, see Chapter 6.) Ideally, you should set up a QDOT while you are alive, even if nothing goes into it until after you die. You can even leave it up to your spouse to decide, based on financial circumstances at the time, which assets to put into this trust.

All is not lost if you neglect to set up a QDOT. Your spouse can rescue the situation in one of two ways. The best strategy is to become a U.S. citizen before your estate tax return is due (nine months after you die), though it may be hard to navigate the government bureaucracy that quickly. Alternatively, within the same time frame, your survivor can set up a QDOT and fund it with anything that doesn't fit within the exemption amount.

The Estate Tax Break for Everyone

There's no equivalent of the marital deduction for single people, unmarried couples and couples in same-sex marriages. (The federal Defense of Marriage Act of 1996 defines marriage as a "legal union between one man and one woman," and spouse as "a person of the opposite sex who is a husband or a wife.") Still, everyone, regardless of marital status, can use the $3.5 million estate tax exemption.

The exemption applies to each of us personally – it's not something that we share with a spouse or partner. In fact, spouses could inadvertently lose it. The problem stems from a common practice of spouses to leave everything to each other in what is called an "I love you" will. True, the whole pot qualifies for the unlimited marital deduction and is not taxed when the first spouse dies. But after that it becomes part of the survivor's estate and is subject to tax when the surviving spouse passes away.

There's a way around the problem that preserves the exemption amount for both spouses and can be beneficial to other couples as well. Unromantic as it may sound, it starts with each of you holding at least $3.5 million worth of assets (or as much of that as you can afford) in your own name (see "For Richer or Poorer," page 40). Once you've done that, you can get the most mileage out of the exemption with this strategy:

In your will or revocable trust (each spouse or partner needs to have one of her own), divide your estate into two parts. When the first of you dies, an amount up to the federal exemption goes into what's called a bypass or credit-shelter trust. It can distribute income and principal to family members (typically the surviving spouse or partner, although it can also benefit children and grandchildren) for as long as that individual is alive, and after that pass on whatever is left to the people you designate (for example, the children).

Since funds in the bypass trust (often labeled the family trust) are covered by the exemption amount, they will not be taxed when you die no matter how large the trust grows. Putting them in trust, rather than leaving them to your spouse or partner outright, ensures that they will not be considered part of her estate, either. Therefore, they are not subject to tax when she dies. Neither is any increase in the value of the funds after they go into the trust.

The rest of your estate can be distributed anyway you like. For married couples, whatever goes to your spouse, called the marital share, is covered by

How to Preserve the Exemption For Both Spouses

Assume husband and wife each have $5 million of assets held in their own names. When the first spouse dies, divide his or her estate into two parts:

$3.5 million (the federal exemption) goes to a bypass (or credit-shelter) trust. It can distribute income and principal to the surviving spouse and other family members while the spouse is alive, and after that pass on whatever is left to family.

Tax result: Since these funds are covered by the exemption amount, they will not be taxed on the first spouse's death. Nor are they considered part of the surviving spouse's estate, so they will not be taxed when he or she dies either.

$1.5 million (the marital share) goes to the surviving spouse outright or in a marital trust.

Tax result: This part the estate is not taxed when the first spouse dies. But because it is considered part of the survivor's estate, whatever assets remain are subject to tax when the surviving spouse passes away.

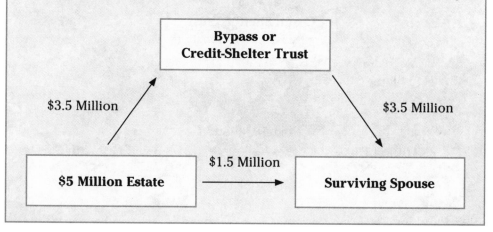

37

How to Maximize the Value of The Exemption to Partners

Assume both partners each have $5 million of assets held in their own names. When the first partner dies, divide his or her estate into two parts:

$3.5 million (the federal exemption) goes to a bypass (or credit-shelter) trust. It can distribute income and principal to the surviving partner and others while the partner is alive, and after that pass on whatever is left to family.

Tax result: Since these funds are covered by the exemption amount, they will not be taxed on the first partner's death. Nor are they considered part of the surviving partner's estate, so they will not be taxed when he or she dies either.

$1.5 million goes to the surviving partner outright or in a separate trust.

Tax result: This part the estate is taxed when the first partner dies.

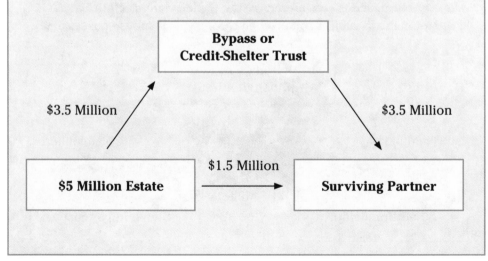

Bypass or Credit-Shelter Trust

$3.5 Million $3.5 Million

$1.5 Million

$5 Million Estate ⟶ **Surviving Partner**

the unlimited deduction, as long as it goes to your spouse outright, through a QTIP or in a trust with a power of appointment. Assuming your spouse doesn't spend all the money, what remains of the marital share will be taxed when he dies. For unmarried couples, anything that exceeds what you put in the bypass trust – whether left to your partner outright or in a separate trust – would be taxed when you die.

The preceding diagrams show how the pieces fit together, depending on whether or not you have a spouse.

These diagrams assume that you will take full advantage of the exemption amount. But that strategy isn't for everyone. Even in these examples a large portion of your spouse or partner's inheritance would be locked up in trust. In smaller estates it could eat up the entire inheritance. While this strategy would save on taxes, unless the trust

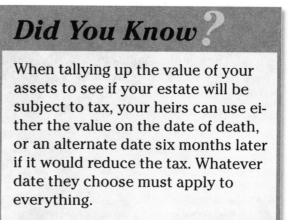

Did You Know?

When tallying up the value of your assets to see if your estate will be subject to tax, your heirs can use either the value on the date of death, or an alternate date six months later if it would reduce the tax. Whatever date they choose must apply to everything.

provides that she can receive distributions liberally for broad purposes, the trust arrangement could limit her access to the funds. Not knowing what you will be worth when you die can make it unwieldy to put such a plan in place.

There are a variety of ways to address these uncertainties. They are covered in the next chapter, which deals more broadly with taking care of your spouse or partner.

Quick and Easy Ways to Cut Federal Estate Tax

One of the best ways to trim estate taxes is to give away assets while you are alive and leave less for the government to tax after you are gone. Without any limits on these lifetime gifts, it would be very easy to avoid estate tax. To prevent that, the law imposes a gift tax of up to

For Richer or Poorer

I n order to use the estate tax exemption, you must have assets of your own. Jointly held property (for example, real estate or bank accounts titled joint tenants with right of survivorship) doesn't count because when one owner dies, full ownership automatically passes to the other (see Chapter 2).

What can couples do if one is richer than the other, and they don't each have enough in their own name to use the exemption amount fully? The simplest solution is for the wealthier person to transfer assets to the other. If spouses don't want to make an outright gift, they can put the assets in a QTIP trust that they set up during life. That way you can be sure the assets will ultimately go to your children, but still use your spouse's exemption.

Unfortunately, this strategy doesn't apply to retirement accounts – you can't give them away while you are alive.

Another consideration: shifting assets may require you to pay gift tax if the recipient is not your spouse. How much you can give away without using your $1 million lifetime gift tax exemption will depend on your marital status and, if you're married, the citizenship of your spouse. These are the rules:

Marital status	Amount of annual tax-free gift
Married couple, both citizens	Unlimited
Married couple, poorer spouse not a citizen	$133,000 (indexed for inflation)
Married couple, richer spouse not a citizen	Unlimited
Unmarried or same-sex married couple	$13,000 (indexed for inflation)

45 percent once you have passed a certain point.

You can give up to $13,000 each year to as many recipients as you would like without incurring a gift tax. Spouses can combine this annual exclusion to jointly give $26,000 to as many people as they want tax-free. You can make these gifts outright to individuals or put the funds into certain trusts for their benefit (see Chapter 6).

Over time, annual exclusion gifts can really add up. Consider a married couple with two adult children, both of them married, and four grandchil-

The Back of the Envelope

Assume you have a $5 million estate and leave everything to your grand-children. Together, estate tax of $675,000 and generation-skipping transfer (GST) tax of $256,034 reduce the inheritance to about $3.96 million.

What's the calculation? You can do the multistep process on the back of an envelope.

Step 1: Apply the $3.5 million estate tax exemption to the $5 million estate. On the remaining $1.5 million, there's a 45 percent estate tax = $675,000

Step 2: Subtract the $675,000 estate tax from the $5 million estate before you compute the generation-skipping transfer tax. The result is $4.325 million.

Step 3: Allocate or apply the $3.5 million generation-skipping transfer tax exemption (see Chapter 14) to $4.325 million. The amount that isn't covered, $825,000, is your base for GST tax.

Step 4: With a little algebra, subtract the tax from the tax base before you calculate the 45 percent tax (so you don't pay GST tax on the tax).
   x (GST tax) = 45 percent ($825,000 minus x)
   GST tax = $256,034
   Total tax = $256,034 + $675,000 = $931,034

dren. If the grandparents together make annual exclusion gifts of $26,000 to each child, each child's spouse, and each grandchild (a total of eight people), they can reduce their taxable estate by $208,000 a year.

There are also strategies that benefit family without using your annual exclusion, and, in effect, reduce the size of your taxable estate. They include paying for tuition, dental and medical expenses (see Chapter 9) and converting traditional retirement accounts to Roth accounts (Chapter 7).

Did You Know ?

Joe Robbie, an entrepreneur and lawyer who owned the Miami Dolphins, didn't plan for a $47 million estate tax bill. To cover it, his family had to sell the team and its stadium in 1994, and missed out on the huge surge in the value of pro football teams in recent years.

Gifts that exceed the annual exclusion (which is indexed for inflation) count against the $1 million lifetime gift tax exemption, and gift tax applies once you have passed the limit. When you die, the estate tax exemption available to you is reduced by the amount of the gift tax exemption you have used.

Other chapters will cover the many ways to use the annual exclusion and the lifetime exemption amount. Some, like subsidizing family members who are less fortunate (see Chapter 13), paying life insurance premiums (Chapter 8) and funding college savings accounts (Chapter 9) can be very simple and require little, if any, involvement by a lawyer. Other, more complex tools enable you to leverage the limits to make them go further (Chapters 15 and 16). Because of the transaction fees needed to implement them, these sophisticated techniques tend to be used primarily by people with a net worth of at least $10 million or by forward-thinking business owners or investors who think they are about to strike it rich.

With all estate tax strategies, it's best to start with the least complicated approach that will achieve your goals. You can accomplish a great deal while keeping it simple.

To-Do List

Take Advantage of Tax Breaks

An annual estate planning checkup can flag tax saving opportunities occasioned by changes in the law, the economy and your personal circumstances. Consider the following issues:

❧ Update basic estate planning documents to make sure they use current exemptions to best advantage.

❧ Put assets in your own name to take full advantage of the $3.5 million estate tax exemption. Look over your balance sheet to determine whether any property should be transferred from one spouse or partner to the other or out of joint ownership into the name of one of you individually.

❧ Plan ahead for annual tax-free gifts. Although many people wait until year-end to make these gifts, there are distinct tax advantages to doing these transfers earlier. Not only can the assets begin to grow outside of your estate, but in the year when you die you will have already made your gift.

Chapter 4

Protect
Your Spouse
Or Partner

*Read this chapter if you are
involved in any
committed relationship.*

For most people involved in a committed relationship, leaving a spouse or partner well provided for is the No. 1 goal in estate planning.

Depending on your situation, two competing concerns may lurk in the background: how to structure an inheritance for children from a previous relationship and how to save on taxes.

These goals need not be mutually exclusive. Sometimes you can build enough flexibility into your estate plan so your executor – the person who puts your will into action – can resolve these issues.

In This Chapter...

- ❧ *Sources of Cash*
- ❧ *What to Do About the Roof Overhead*
- ❧ *Passing Retirement Assets*
- ❧ *How to Fund the Bypass Trust*
- ❧ *Planning for State Estate Tax*
- ❧ *Providing for Children of a Previous Relationship*

One impediment to estate planning for unmarried and same-sex married couples is the federal Defense of Marriage Act of 1996, which defines marriage as a "legal union between one man and one woman." Most state laws, which also have an impact on estate planning, take the same approach. As a result, other couples (also referred to in this book as "partners" or "non-spouses") do not enjoy most tax breaks and other rights that spouses rely on in estate planning.

All this makes it harder for partners to save on taxes and provide for each other. So they must be vigilant in their planning. Some have tried to compensate through adoption – one adult adopting the other to create inheritance rights. How well this works will depend on state law and how courts interpret it. More often, couples must rely on estate planning tools that are not limited to spouses.

Sources of Cash

T he death of a key breadwinner can leave heirs strapped for funds to meet current expenses, including funeral costs. To avoid the need to liquidate assets, perhaps at fire-sale prices, these are some steps you can take:

Buy life insurance. Using life insurance as a source of cash could be even more important for partners than it is for spouses. They don't have the benefit of the unlimited marital deduction, which permits the tax-free transfer of assets to a spouse who is a U.S. citizen (for the rules on non-citizen spouses, see Chapter 3), postponing any tax on the assets until the second spouse dies. In contrast, a person in an unmarried relationship can get saddled with immediate estate tax when the total assets that he or she inherits from the other partner are worth more than $3.5 million.

Another advantage of life insurance for non-spouses has nothing to do with taxes, but rather with confidentiality. Life insurance passes outside your will. Therefore, nobody but the beneficiary, the insurance company and the Internal Revenue Service need to know about it.

No matter what your reason for wanting life insurance, beware a common pitfall: If you are both the insured and the policy owner, the proceeds would be considered part of your estate. If your spouse is the beneficiary, there would be no tax when you die because of the unlimited marital deduction, though what remains will be taxed when the surviving spouse dies (assuming all the money had not been spent). But if your partner is the beneficiary and your total assets, including the life insurance proceeds, are worth more than $3.5 million, the 45 percent estate tax could immediately eat into the inheritance, leaving less for him to live on. The best way to avoid the tax in both cases is to set up an irrevocable life insurance trust, which can buy the policy and, when you die, hold the proceeds for whomever you have named as beneficiary (see Chapter 8).

Create a grantor retained income trust, or GRIT. This is one of the few estate planning tools that a spouse and close family members cannot use. But it's great for other couples (and can also work well with nieces and nephews). With a GRIT, you put assets into an irrevocable trust and retain the right to get income from the trust for a specific number of years. When that term expires, all the trust assets, including any appreciation, go to the remainder beneficiaries you've named tax-free. To maximize what they get, you can invest the

GRIT in property that you expect to grow in value.

For gift tax purposes, you've made a taxable gift when you set up the trust, but the value of that gift is deeply discounted. The discount reflects the value of the right to get the assets a certain number of years from now, reduced to reflect the probability that you will live that long. The chief drawback of a GRIT is that if you don't survive the trust term, the entire property is includable in your estate.

When setting up the trust, you should also consider the possibility of a breakup in your relationship. Since the trust is irrevocable, you can't retain the right to change the beneficiary. However, the trust can stipulate that if you are no longer living together (unless, perhaps, one of you needs to go into a nursing home or relocate for work) the remainder interest goes to another person named in the trust document.

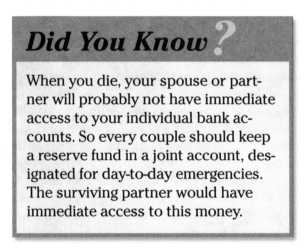

Did You Know?

When you die, your spouse or partner will probably not have immediate access to your individual bank accounts. So every couple should keep a reserve fund in a joint account, designated for day-to-day emergencies. The surviving partner would have immediate access to this money.

Keep money in the bank. If like many couples your assets are divided into "yours," "mine" and "ours," make sure there is enough money to cover immediate expenses. These reserve funds can be held in each of your separate accounts or in a joint one. Just be aware that when you die, your spouse or partner will probably not have access to your individual account right away, and you will each need the discipline to keep the fund flush. A better approach is to maintain a joint account designated for emergencies that can also be available for this purpose.

How should that account be titled? This is just one of various contexts in which titling is relevant to estate planning. Title affects how rapidly assets become available to your heirs, how those assets are taxed and whether they are protected from creditors' claims. Each option has pros and cons, and the best choice for one purpose might not be the best choice for another. (This subject is also discussed in Chapters 2, 3 and 18, in each case focusing on the aspects of titling for the topic covered.)

With bank and brokerage accounts, the most frequent form of joint ownership is joint tenancy with rights of survivorship (it appears on some joint statements abbreviated JTWROS). It is available to any two people who want to own assets together. Both owners have access to the assets during life, and when one joint tenant dies, the survivor immediately becomes the sole owner of the whole property, regardless of what the will says, or whether there is a will. These features make this type of ownership appealing both to spouses and other couples.

Immediate access provides secure funds in case there is a will contest. For example, let's say you plan to leave everything to your second spouse but are worried that the children from your first marriage might challenge your will. If that happens, you don't want your spouse to be short of funds should a battle drag on. So you might set aside a certain amount in a bank account, naming your spouse as joint tenant with right of survivorship. When you die, he will have access to the funds right away.

For all these advantages, joint tenancy has a serious drawback: it exposes each owner to the other's potential liabilities. (This risk is discussed in detail in Chapter 18.) Unmarried couples also need to be aware that state laws on joint tenancy for non-spouses may vary. Consult a lawyer who is familiar with the rules of the state where you live.

What to Do About the Roof Overhead

If you own a home together you must determine the best way to hold title to it. Again, your choice can affect taxes and creditor protection.

Joint tenants with rights of survivorship. The advantage of this form of ownership is that a co-owner automatically inherits the whole property when the other owner dies, so his right to live in the house is secure. However, it could be used to satisfy a judgment against either of you unless you live in a state with a homestead law that protects a personal residence from creditors' claims (see Chapter 18).

Still, you need to consider taxes. For spouses, half the property is automatically included in the estate of the first to die, but is covered by the unlimited marital deduction. Non-spouses get less favorable treatment. For them, the tax law presumes that the entire property is included in the estate of the first to die, which could trigger immediate estate tax on the whole thing. You can avoid that result by showing in an estate tax audit how much the survivor contributed to buying the home. In that case, the portion allocated to the estate would be reduced.

Tenancy in common avoids some of these problems. With this form of title, you own just part of the property, known as an undivided interest. Typically your share would equal whatever you kicked in, though if someone gave you the asset – say an interest in land – as a gift or bequest, it would equal whatever percentage of the property you received. As a rule, creditors have access only to the portion owned by the person who owes them money, rather than to the whole thing. When one owner dies, just that person's share gets included in his or her estate; if you want that share to pass to your spouse or partner, you should provide for it in your estate plan. This form of title may interest spouses who want to fund a bypass trust with their home (see page 57).

In approximately 30 states, spouses – but not other couples – also have the option of holding real estate in tenancy by the entirety. As with joint tenants, each spouse automatically inherits the other's share. As noted in Chapter 18, the key advantage of tenancy by the entirety is that, at least in non-community property states, only the couple's joint creditors have access to the asset. Creditors of just one spouse cannot collect on their lien unless there is a divorce or the non-debtor spouse dies. (Here, too, homestead laws offer protection in some states.)

What if you live in a home that only one of you owns – for example, you bought the house before the start of the relationship? If both spouses are U.S. citizens or the spouse who does not own the home is, a half ownership interest can be transferred tax-free (see Chapter 3). Everyone else must consider the gift-tax rules that would apply to the transfer. You can give up to $13,000 each year (adjusted for inflation in $1,000 increments) to your partner – and as many other recipients as you like – without incurring gift tax. Any gift that's more than this annual exclusion counts against the lifetime gift tax exemption – what each individual can give away during life without triggering gift tax. Once you have passed the limit, which is $1 million, a gift tax of up to 45 percent applies.

The simplest way to fit more into each of these amounts is to transfer partial interests in the home to your partner. Whether you do this all at once or by successive gifts over time, you can reduce the value of each interest substantially (see Chapter 10).

But beware of potential complications. You will want your partner to be a beneficiary of your homeowners' policy. If you're dealing with a co-op apartment, you may need approval from the board of directors. (With condominium properties, this is not a concern.) And whenever there's an existing mortgage, you will probably need the lender's permission. Also check the fine print to be sure the transfer of a partial interest doesn't give the bank the right to cancel the loan and require you to pay up.

For spouses, there are times when a smart tax strategy might be for just one of you, rather than both of you, to own the house. One scenario is when you want to use it to fund a bypass trust (though, as noted on page 58, this has pros and cons). The other involves the sad situation when, because of health issues, you are fairly certain which of you will die first. In that case, when the home has appreciated significantly in value, it might make sense to have it owned solely by the spouse whose death will occur sooner.

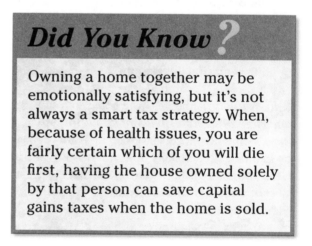

Did You Know?

Owning a home together may be emotionally satisfying, but it's not always a smart tax strategy. When, because of health issues, you are fairly certain which of you will die first, having the house owned solely by that person can save capital gains taxes when the home is sold.

This strategy could result in a substantial income tax saving for the surviving spouse. Here's why: Inherited assets are entitled to an adjustment in basis to their value on the date of death. If the property has appreciated, there will be a step-up in the cost basis, which could reduce or eliminate the capital gains tax your heirs have to pay if the property is sold.

One important condition applies: If your spouse transfers the assets, you die within a year, and your spouse inherits the same assets back, there is no step-up. This provision in the Internal Revenue Code, which applies to non-spouses too, prevents a healthy spouse from transferring everything to a dying spouse (with no gift tax) and getting it back with a basis step-up (and no estate tax).

Consider how effective this tool can be for spouses if the less healthy one survives the required year. Let's say Harry and Sally bought a rambling old Victorian long ago for $100,000, and it is now worth $1 million. A romantic couple, they like knowing that they own it jointly. Then, Harry is diagnosed with a degenerative illness and is expected to live only two years. The children are grown and Sally expects to sell the house after Harry dies. Compare the tax consequences of the following:

Leave the house in joint name and sell it after Harry's death for $1 million, its date-of-death value. Since the house is joint property, half is included in Harry's estate and is entitled to a step-up in value, from $50,000 to $500,000. (The result is different in a community property state – see "How Community Property Affects Your Estate Plan," page 53.) On Sally's half, there is a $450,000 capital gain ($500,000 minus $50,000). Since Sally lived in the house for two of the last five years, she doesn't have to pay taxes on $250,000 of that gain, a special tax break on the principal residence. On the balance of the gain, which is $200,000 ($450,000 minus $250,000), Sally must pay 15 percent capital gains tax, or $30,000. Assuming Sally is a U.S. citizen, she won't have to pay estate tax, since the house (along with everything else she inherits) is covered by the unlimited marital deduction.

Sally transfers her share of the house to Harry, inherits it when he dies two years later and then sells it for $1 million, its date-of-death value. At Harry's death, the cost basis of the house gets stepped up from $100,000 to $1 million. As a result, there is no capital gain and Sally does not need to pay income tax on the sale of the house. Here, too, there is no estate tax because of the unlimited marital deduction.

(For a further discussion of estate planning when bad health is a factor, see Chapter 19.)

Passing Retirement Assets

Money in individual retirement accounts or employer-sponsored retirement plans, such as 401(k)s and 403(b)s, cannot be covered by a will. Instead, the money is distributed according to beneficiary designation forms that you fill out when you open the accounts or later amend. It's extremely important that you complete these forms and keep them up to date, and have your lawyer coordinate them with the rest of your estate plan. (For a detailed discussion of estate planning with retirement assets, see Chapter 7.)

How Community Property Affects Your Estate Plan

Most states leave it up to married couples to separate their assets into "yours," "mine" and "ours." The law imposes a framework for spouses in the nine community property states: Arizona, California, Idaho, Louisiana, Nevada, New Mexico, Texas, Washington and Wisconsin.

If you are domiciled in one of these states, meaning that you call it home, you are subject to the rules of community property. According to these rules, anything you have going into the marriage or individually receive by gift or inheritance during the marriage is considered separate property. Most of what you acquire once you are married and living in a community property state is considered community property, and you are each considered a one-half owner. That includes your house, regardless of how it is titled, your salary and even your IRA. Commingling separate and community property often results in the entire property being treated as community property. The law in most community property states allows you and your mate to enter into an agreement – either before or after you're married – specifying that certain property that would otherwise be considered community property should be treated as separate property, and the reverse.

The distinction between community and separate property affects how you calculate your federal income tax, the degree to which your assets are protected from creditors and how they are divided in divorce. A complete discussion of the subject is beyond the scope of this book. IRS publication 555, "Community Property," provides a primer and can be downloaded at www.irs.gov.

For estate planning purposes, keep in mind a couple of things. One is that the total value of your assets when you die includes both your separate property and half the value of any community property. There's also a huge tax advantage associated with community property: When the first spouse dies, both halves of the property get a step-up in basis. This enables you to minimize capital gains tax if the surviving spouse sells the property – such as a house. In contrast, in other states couples who jointly own a home only get a step-up in basis on half the house, belonging to the spouse who has died.

How to Fund the Bypass Trust

C hapter 3 described how the bypass or credit-shelter trust can preserve the $3.5 million exemption amount for both spouses and maximize its value for other couples. To review: Because funds in the bypass trust – often labeled the family trust – are covered by the exemption amount, they will not be taxed when you die. Putting them in trust, rather than leaving them to your spouse or partner outright, ensures that they will not be considered part of her estate, either. Therefore, they are not subject to tax when she dies. Neither is any increase in the value of the funds after they go into the trust.

To get the full benefit, however, you must fund the family trust with the entire $3.5 million exemption amount. What if you don't have $3.5 million? One possibility is that you never will – and won't ever need one of these trusts. On the other hand, if your fortunes improve, you might not be as diligent about updating your estate plan as you should be (most people aren't). It's better to put a system in place that can grow with you – at least until you get around to changing it if the need arises.

In the process, you need to address some difficult questions:

If I set up a bypass trust, how much should go into it? One possibility, which is available to both partners and spouses, is to put a cap on the amount going into the bypass trust. For instance, you can limit it to a specific sum or a certain percentage of your estate. Although this might forgo part of the exemption, presumably the welfare of your spouse or partner is more important.

Spouses can put a more flexible plan in place that builds upon the qualified terminable interest property, or QTIP, trust discussed in Chapter 3. You may recall that assets inherited by a spouse who is a U.S. citizen are not taxed so long as they go to your spouse directly (outright) or through a certain type of trust that qualifies for the marital deduction. A QTIP is one such trust.

To apply the marital deduction to the QTIP, there's a formality that must be observed: Your executor, who signs the federal estate tax return, Form 706, must elect to treat the trust property as if it has passed to the surviving spouse. This is called a QTIP election. There have been plenty of malpractice lawsuits against executors, as well as the lawyers and accountants they hired to prepare the estate tax return, who neglected this detail.

With that background, here is one strategy that spouses can use to keep options open: Fund the bypass trust with the full federal exemption but give the executor the option of making the QTIP election over some of these funds when the first spouse dies. To make this strategy possible, the bypass trust must be "QTIP-able," meaning that it provides (or could provide, as the result of the election), that the spouse will get all the income and nobody else is entitled to any distributions from the QTIP portion of the trust. Depending on the election, the executor can turn the entire bypass trust or just a portion of it into a QTIP trust.

This is sometimes called a one-lung trust, because instead of setting up both a marital trust to provide for the spouse and a separate bypass trust, as described in Chapter 3, your estate plan starts with just a single trust. After the QTIP election has been made, the trust can be divided into two separate trusts – one for the portion over which there has been a QTIP election, and a separate trust for the rest.

There is one potential pitfall if the executor making a QTIP election is the surviving spouse. Shifting what otherwise would have been her right to receive distributions from the trust may be considered a taxable gift. (The law on this point isn't entirely clear.) You can avoid that risk by giving the power to make a QTIP election to a co-executor or, if the spouse is the sole executor, to an independent party.

> ## *Did You Know* ?
>
> Carroll Rosenbloom, who owned the Los Angeles Rams football team, groomed his son Steve as his successor. By leaving 70 percent of the ownership to his wife, Georgia Frontiere, Rosenbloom gave her free rein. Within months of his death she fired her step-son.

Another approach for spouses, which also relies on the QTIP election to make the necessary adjustments after the first spouse dies, is to start by funding a marital trust with a specific amount that you expect will provide adequately for the surviving spouse, and creating a bypass trust that can be funded with anything more than that, up to the exemption amount. Here, too, you would give the executor the option of making the QTIP election over only a portion of the assets, and then putting the rest into the bypass trust if it was not already fully funded. This strategy takes care of the spouse first and relies on a bypass trust to shelter any excess. (Again, the person making the election should not be the surviving spouse.)

A more controversial option that looks much simpler on paper is to leave everything to your spouse or partner outright, but give him the right to disclaim (turn down) all or part of the inheritance and have it go into a bypass trust. When it comes to disclaimers, the world of estate planning lawyers is divided into two camps: those who like the flexibility a disclaimer affords, and those who think there are so many ways to mess up a disclaimer – especially for non-spouses – that it should be avoided.

If you use a disclaimer your will should incorporate several important caveats – not for legal reasons, but to educate your survivors. One is that your spouse or partner must take this step within nine months of your death. Another, trickier, rule is that the Internal Revenue Code prohibits someone who disclaims, known as a disclaimant, from accepting an interest in the asset or any of its benefits. Heirs have fouled up by making such innocent mistakes as depositing a dividend check in their own account, changing the way an IRA is invested or collecting life insurance proceeds.

One exception to this particular rule applies for surviving spouses. A spouse is allowed to receive income and principal, for example, from property disclaimed into a bypass trust. But a non-spouse is not. Therefore, a partner who disclaims into a bypass trust cannot be a beneficiary of that trust. So it would be extremely unusual for unmarried couples to use this method of funding the trust.

Did You Know?

Rock Hudson, a leading man in Hollywood, was gay – and his death from AIDS at age 59, raised awareness of the disease. In his will, he originally left his tangible personal property to a longtime companion, Tom Clark. But months before Hudson died, he struck Clark from the will.

Although a spouse can be a beneficiary of a trust funded by disclaimer, federal regulations, which say disclaimants can't have control over the property, bind her hands in two other ways. If she is the trustee, she must follow specific or ascertainable standards in making distributions, rather than having total discretion. And she can't be given what's known as a power of appointment – the right to determine who gets the property after her interest ends. If the tax efficiency of your estate plan depends on your spouse exercising the power to disclaim, make sure someone else has the power to disclaim on her behalf if she becomes mentally incapacitated (see Chapter 1).

Finally, keep in mind that as useful as disclaimers can be in this context and others (see Chapter 17), estate planners joke about the five-word lie spouses routinely tell each other: "Honey, I promise to disclaim."

Will my spouse or partner have as much cash as he needs? Assuming you want to set up a bypass trust, or at least leave open the possibility, you can arrange things so the spigot can be turned on and off, but you must think about this issue in advance. (For basic information about how trusts work and why flexibility is desirable, see Chapter 6.) Here are some issues to ponder before you have a lawyer prepare a bypass trust:

❧ Does income have to be distributed to the surviving spouse or partner, or are payments at the trustee's discretion?
❧ Should the trustee be able to distribute principal?
❧ If so, should that power be completely discretionary, or subject to preset standards included in the trust?
❧ Should the surviving spouse or partner be the only current beneficiary, or should children be, as well?
❧ Should the surviving spouse or partner have a power of appointment? *This power should not be included if the trust might be funded through disclaimer: a disclaimer isn't valid if the asset being disclaimed is still subject to the individual's direction about how it passes at death.*
❧ If the spouse or partner will have a power of appointment, should he be limited to exercising it in favor of the children you had together?
❧ Should the surviving spouse or partner have the power to remove and replace trustees?

Which assets should be used to fund the trust? The ideal assets are cash, bonds or marketable securities. But for many people, their home and retirement accounts are their most valuable assets or the only ones available to fully fund a bypass trust. Each presents its own challenges because of special rules that apply.

If you use retirement assets to fund a bypass trust, you may lose certain income tax benefits (see Chapter 7). Therefore you need to weigh the potential estate tax savings against the income tax cost.

Using a home to fund a bypass trust is also an imperfect solution. The way to do this with a jointly owned home is for the surviving spouse to disclaim the one-half interest in the property he has inherited. That part of the house then becomes a bypass trust asset, although the spouse could buy it out of the trust and replace it with cash, either all at once or over time.

The trouble with this approach is that unless the spouse is a trustee of the bypass trust, you take away the survivor's sense of ownership. Depending on the arrangement, the trust may need to share the cost of maintenance and repairs, and it can't deduct property taxes.

To leave open this option, some couples put the house in just one of their names rather than holding it jointly, anticipating that the home will ultimately go into a bypass trust. But those who take that step don't get the creditor protection available to them in states that permit couples to own real estate as tenants by the entirety.

Given the complications and disadvantages of funding a bypass trust with a home or with retirement assets, you will want to look for alternatives. If you don't have any, you can forgo the bypass trust and buy second-to-die life insurance, which covers both members of a couple and pays off only when both of them have died. The proceeds can be used to pay the estate taxes.

Planning for State Estate Tax

If you live in a state that has a separate estate tax (about half do) or own real estate in one of those states, you need to consider the effect of this additional tax. That's especially true in states where the state exemption is less than the federal one. This poses a dilemma for spouses who have divided their estates between a bypass trust and a marital share, a classic estate-planning tool discussed earlier in this chapter and in Chapter 3.

For example in New York, where the state exemption is only $1 million, fully funding the bypass trust in order to take advantage of the federal exemption would leave your estate to pay state tax when you die on the $2.5 million that is not covered by the state exemption.

This situation poses a tough choice. If you allocate more to the marital share, your estate avoids both federal and state estate tax when you die but could get stuck paying more federal tax (if the assets appreciate), as well as the state tax, when your spouse does. If you put more in the bypass trust, there's no federal tax on this sum when you die but your heirs must immediately pay state estate tax.

Because the federal tax rates are higher than the state ones, in most situations it will be best to make sure that as much property as possible is not subject to federal estate tax – either at the first or second death – even if that means paying some state tax. But you don't need to decide now. Instead, you can postpone the decision about how to allocate the estate between the bypass trust and the marital share until the first spouse has died.

There are several ways to do that. Here, too, you could give your spouse the option to disclaim into the bypass trust. Other approaches rely on the QTIP election, which (for reasons noted above) should not be done by your spouse.

Some states, including Massachusetts, Rhode Island and Washington, offer an easy way for married people to address the problem. In these states, it's possible to make a separate state QTIP election when the first spouse dies. This enables the first spouse to preserve his or her entire federal exemption and delay the state estate tax that would otherwise apply to some funds in the bypass trust until after the second spouse dies.

For instance, if the state exemption is $1 million, as it is in Massachusetts, and the bypass trust is funded up to the federal exemption of $3.5 million, the executor could make a state QTIP election for $2.5 million ($3.5 million minus $1 million) of the funds in the bypass trust. As a result, that part of the estate would be exempt from federal estate tax and would not be subject to state estate tax until the second spouse dies.

Elsewhere, you can use the same strategy that you might use if you weren't sure you would need a bypass trust: Fund the bypass trust with the full federal exemption but give the executor the option of making the QTIP election over some of these funds when the first spouse dies.

Providing for Children of a Previous Relationship

In a functional relationship, spouses and partners share a common interest in their children's well-being. In second marriages or partnerships, this dynamic is hard – often impossible – to replicate, and sometimes with good reason. For example, there might be residual anger from a messy divorce that children witnessed, grief for a parent lost or concern that the surviving parent's new, much younger, spouse will inherit everything.

Therefore, it's best to make arrangements for your children that don't require any help or cooperation from your new mate. Similarly, don't create a plan that your new spouse could foil. For example, don't make your children's inheritance dependent on your spouse's disclaimer into a bypass trust for their benefit.

There are a number of ways to structure your children's inheritance. You can leave them specific sums or a percentage of your estate, subject to inflation adjustments. You can make them the remainder beneficiaries of your QTIP and beneficiaries of various trusts, including a bypass trust.

It also pays to discuss these issues frankly with your spouse or partner. When the stakes are high, some people cover them in a prenuptial agreement that specifies not only what happens in the event of divorce but also how assets will be divided if the couple is still married when one of them dies.

That's what Peter Jennings, the ABC News anchorman, did when he married Katherine Freed, his fourth wife, in 1997. A 21-page prenup, which pegged the size of Freed's inheritance to how long they were married, provided that once they reached the eight-year mark, her share of the marital estate would double, from 25 percent to 50 percent. Most of the rest would go to Jennings's two children from his third marriage. Freed gave up her right as spouse to claim an elective share of Jennings's estate, a minimum portion spouses are entitled to under state law (in New York it's one-third when there are children; one half when there aren't).

Jennings's 10-page will, signed three months before he died of lung cancer in 2005, not only incorporated the prenup but also stipulated that no matter when he died, the couple would be deemed to have been married for more than eight years. It was fortunate for Freed that Jennings took that step, as he passed away several months short of their eighth anniversary. According to Jennings's estate tax return filed in New York Surrogate's Court, Freed received more than $21 million, including the couple's Manhattan co-op apartment valued at $10.5 million.

To-Do List

Cover All the Bases

Providing for the financial security of your spouse or partner requires you to do much more than have your lawyer prepare the standard legal documents. Here are some other steps to take:

❧ Keep enough funds in joint accounts to cover immediate expenses.

❧ Based on all relevant factors, determine the best way to hold title to your other assets, especially your home.

❧ Figure out whether you have enough assets apart from your home and retirement accounts to use at least part of the $3.5 million estate tax exemption.

❧ Make sure you are not the owner of a life insurance policy that names you as an insured. If you are, the proceeds could be subject to estate tax. (For ways to remedy this situation, see Chapter 8.)

❧ Fill out beneficiary designation forms for all retirement accounts and ask your lawyer to coordinate them with the rest of your estate plan.

Chapter 5

What if? Provide for Young or Disabled Children

Read this chapter so you can anticipate their needs and make sure they will be nurtured.

W ho would raise your children if something happened to you? For most people, few prospects are more wrenching. Often, parents put off writing a will because this particular thought is unbearable. Some assume – incorrectly – that it is enough just to ask a relative or trusted friend to step in if the need arises.

But not formalizing the arrangements and doing some estate planning along the way could leave your children in a vacuum. For ex-

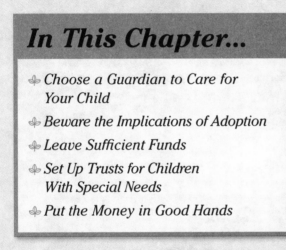

In This Chapter...

- ♣ *Choose a Guardian to Care for Your Child*
- ♣ *Beware the Implications of Adoption*
- ♣ *Leave Sufficient Funds*
- ♣ *Set Up Trusts for Children With Special Needs*
- ♣ *Put the Money in Good Hands*

ample, if you are a single or surviving parent and do not have a written document outlining your wishes, a court usually decides who will fill your shoes. A custody battle might erupt or, awful as it sounds, no one may want your children. And without financial planning, there may not be enough money for your child's support.

In families where a child has special physical, emotional or cognitive needs, the issues are even more complicated. In the past, special needs children, as they are now called, frequently might not outlive their parents. Now, medical advances have greatly extended their life expectancies. So it is essential for parents to make provisions for the care, custody and financial needs of disabled family members.

Addressing this issue requires that you talk openly about the subject, something not so often done a generation ago. Lawyers have learned to ask if there are special needs children because clients might not mention them otherwise.

Choose a Guardian to Care for Your Child

A guardian's responsibilities range from the mundane to the monumental: everything from tying shoelaces and drying tears to selecting schools and medical care. You should designate more than one person, so if your top choice is not available, your second preference is clear. Depending on the financial arrangements you make, the person in charge of caring for your child may not be the same person who controls the child's assets – as discussed on page 75, there are good reasons for assigning each role to a different person. In some states, if you have not made arrangements for both functions, the court will appoint a separate person to deal with the child's money.

When choosing a guardian in case their child is orphaned, people typically look first to relatives, starting with their own siblings – the child's aunts and uncles. Especially if these siblings already have children of their own, the idea is that your children would be raised with their first cousins. A second choice for some people is their own parents, if they are young enough. When there is a big age gap between children (for instance, if a parent has been married more than once and has offspring from both unions), older siblings sometimes serve as guardians for younger ones. How well this works depends on the family dynamics.

Even if certain family members seem like obvious candidates, take into account all the factors involved. For example, it may not be good for a child who has lost his parents to suddenly have to relocate, losing contact with friends and the world he lives in. Put some thought into the lifestyle and values, as well as the location, of the person you're thinking of choosing.

You should consider, too, whether the prospective guardians can incorporate your children into their households. If they have their own children, can they handle more? If they have none, are they prepared to accept a ready-made family? Think back to when you became a parent and how it changed your world; would you want someone who has never played that role to start with your child?

Ideally, couples should agree on the choice of guardian to care for their children, and each of their wills should appoint the same person. Unmarried couples take note: if you are not both biologically related to the child, it is especially important for your estate planning documents to cover all the issues. The rules on adoption of children by unmarried couples vary enormously from state to state, and though the law is evolving, it lags behind current practices. If you and your partner have a child, it's important to consult a lawyer who is familiar with the rules of your state, and to

---

Factors to Weigh in Choosing a Guardian

Appointing a guardian for your children is an agonizing decision, and few parents find someone who meets all their criteria. More often, the choice involves a process of elimination or deciding which qualities are most important. Here are some questions to ask:

- Do I have a relative or close friend who would be willing to take on the role?
- Would that person love my child and provide the attention that he or she would need?
- Am I comfortable with the individual's lifestyle and values?
- Does the person have children about the same age as mine?
- Can the prospective guardian incorporate my children into his or her household?
- If I have more than one child, would the guardian be able to keep them together?
- Does my child already have a relationship and a good rapport with the person?
- Would my child have to relocate?
- Can the person handle any special needs, including medical or behavioral issues, my child may have?

---

revisit the subject if you move to a different one.

For many parents, an important goal is keeping their children together. The actress Natalie Wood included provisions in her will to accomplish that. First, she named her husband, Robert J. Wagner, as guardian not only of Courtney Wagner, their own child, but also of Natasha Gregson, Wood's daughter by a previous marriage to the film producer Richard Gregson.

Wood's second choice, if both she and Wagner died, was to have her housekeeper, Willie Mae Worthen, move into their Beverly Hills home and raise both daughters there. The actress indicated in her 1980 will that the two daughters were growing up together and that it would be in "the best interest of each of them" to continue that way.

Ordinarily in a divorce, if the parent with custody dies, the other biological parent automatically becomes the guardian. However, when Wood drowned in 1981, Wagner took custody of Natasha, then 11, and Courtney, 7. Gregson consented to the arrangement.

You will want to have heart-to-heart talks with the people you have in mind before you name them as guardians. You can discuss your goals and theories of parenting in as much detail as you like, but including these specifics in the will is short-sighted. It's great to say, "I want you to live in the Northeast and send the child to private school," but circumstances change. You don't want to tie the hands of the person whom you are trusting with your child's future.

Instead, you can supplement the will with a letter or memo outlining your wishes (for one example, see "The Mummy Manual," page 69). This might cover everything from your prefer-ences about religion, educa-tion and allowance to the name of your pediatrician. It could also ask the guard-ian to consult with specific friends or family members who know your children well but who, for whatever reason, would not be appro-priate as guardians. Though not binding the way a will is, this document provides the guardian with a clear, written record of your preferences. It

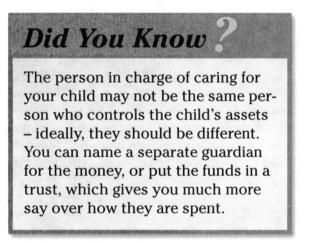

Did You Know?

The person in charge of caring for your child may not be the same per-son who controls the child's assets – ideally, they should be different. You can name a separate guardian for the money, or put the funds in a trust, which gives you much more say over how they are spent.

also sends a message to your children about how much you cared.

Still, try not to micromanage or create a moral obligation for the guardian to follow very precise instructions. Sometimes it's better to express broad goals rather than precise tactics – for example, to help build your child's indepen-dence and confidence; encourage her to pursue interests that come naturally and maintain relationships with family and friends. Being a parent is full of surprises and requires constant judgment calls and adaptation. Try as you might to cover all the bases, ultimately you need to choose the people whom you really trust to do the right thing, and hope for the best.

Given the complexities of providing for minor children, you should review your arrangements at least once every five years. Revisit the subject sooner if something changes – say, your aging parents suddenly cannot handle a ram-bunctious toddler, or the sister you've named as guardian relocates.

If you have a special needs child who will require a guardian on a continuing basis, you will want to put a more long-lasting plan in place. You should name an alternate guardian, in case the original one becomes unable to play that role, and create a backup plan for choosing successors.

Beware the Implications of Adoption

F rom an estate planning perspective, adoption brings potential pitfalls, as well as benefits. For example, while it is possible to become entitled to an inheritance through adoption, quirks in the law could also cause adoption to wipe one out.

With the growing number of blended, or nontraditional, families, these issues arise more frequently, but the law has not kept up. One impediment is the federal Defense of Marriage Act of 1996, which defines marriage as a "legal union between one man and one woman" and spouse as "a person of the opposite sex who is a husband or a wife." Most states take the same approach. These laws can have an enormous effect on the inheritance rights of out-of-marriage children, including the rights they gain or lose through adoption.

Being aware of the rules, which vary from state to state, can help you steer clear of the pitfalls and take advantage of the opportunities. Here are five different adoption scenarios that could affect inheritance rights. A will or trust could change any of the results described below by including or excluding specific individuals or categories of people. For example, some people cut off inheritance rights of individuals who are older than a certain age when they are adopted – primarily as a deterrent to adults adopting each other. (For the rules on one adult adopting another, see Chapter 4.)

A single person adopts a child. The child can inherit directly from this parent, and receive the parent's share of assets left by others – for example, if the child is next in line for all or part of the parent's inheritance under a will or trust (see Chapters 2 and 6).

A married couple adopts a child who is not biologically related to either of them. The child has all the same inheritance rights as those of a child of a single parent, only those rights derive from both parents.

'The Mummy Manual'

After she was diagnosed with incurable breast cancer, Helen Harcombe began to prepare her family for the inevitable. One of her chief concerns was how her husband Anthony, a builder, would raise their daughter Ffion, who was 7 at the time.

Harcombe, a consumer advocate in South Wales who died in 2004 at the age of 28, left behind a three-page, handwritten list that the British press dubbed "the Mummy Manual." The main focus is near term – the sort of detailed information, complete with shorthand wording and abbreviations, that a mother might compile before embarking on a lengthy business trip. Some items are mundane, like instructions about eating fresh, rather than processed, foods, how often to change the bedding and checking her daughter's hair for lice. It covers school, with reminders to rummage through her daughter's book bag for notices, attend parent-teacher conferences and look out for signs of bullying by classmates. There are also suggestions for Christmas stocking fillers and back-to-school shopping.

In the most moving part of the manual, Harcombe projects into the future and imagines a world without her. As her daughter matures, there will be a need for a lock on the bathroom door, she notes. And without elaborating, she includes a reference to her husband taking down her photos. She simply asks that he put them away for Ffion.

The list concludes with an effort to leave her family laughing – Harcombe clearly understood that death is hardest for those who are left behind. She asks her husband to keep in touch with her own friends, her parents and Ffion's godparents. And she threatens to haunt him if he doesn't.

(At the time of this book's publication, the full text of "the Mummy Manual" was available at www.dailymail.co.uk/news/article-346306/The-mummy-manual.html.)

In a second marriage, one spouse adopts the other's child from a previous marriage. Here, too, the child can inherit from both these parents. But what about the former spouse who was the child's other biological parent? Whether adoption extinguishes that right will depend on state law.

Let's say Jill marries Jack, the heir to a software fortune, and they have a child named Brandon before Jack tragically dies. Then Jill remarries and her new husband wants to adopt Brandon, who is still a minor. In this situation, Brandon may no longer be considered Jack's descendant. Depending on state law and how Jack's parents set up their own estate plans, Brandon could lose his right to inherit part of the software fortune.

One partner in an unmarried couple adopts the other partner's biological child. It's important to determine whether, under state law, the adoption will cut off inheritance rights that stemmed from the biological parent. If so, the parent could still make provisions for the child in her own estate plan, but if the child is not considered her descendant, any associated inheritance rights would be cut off.

An unmarried couple wants to adopt a child who is not biologically related to either of them. As in the example above, the result would depend on state law.

Leave Sufficient Funds

Except for the wealthy, raising a child is a pay-as-you-go proposition. You may gradually set aside money for large future expenses, such as college, but most funds for day-to-day costs come from current earnings. A premature death ends that income stream. Unless the person you are naming to care for your child is willing and able to pay for raising him, you need to leave enough money to cover everything your child will need.

As discussed on page 75, you can name a guardian for the money, or put the funds in a trust and designate a trustee to spend the money on your child's behalf. While financial guardianships are a matter of state law and require court supervision in some states, trusts are a private matter.

A trust also gives you much more say over how the funds are spent (see Chapter 6), and a chance to address lifestyle differences between the guardian's family and your own. Say the people caring for your child have more limited means than you do. You could give them permission to move into your house, or leave money in trust for a larger house – perhaps to ensure that your child has her own room – and set aside funds for maintenance and repairs. To avoid

What Heath Ledger Taught Us

One of the first things you should do when you become a parent is to create an estate plan or revise an existing one. By not tending to that detail, Heath Ledger, the actor, nearly disinherited his daughter, Matilda Rose, who was 2 when Ledger died of a prescription drug overdose in 2008.

Ledger's three-page will, signed five years earlier when he was 24, probably seemed sufficient at the time. It called for the bulk of his estate to be put into a trust and divided into two parts. Half would go to his parents, Kim Ledger and Sally Bell, and the other half would be split equally among his three sisters – Kate and Olivia Ledger and Ashleigh Bell.

But Ledger's life changed. He was nominated for an Academy Award for his role as a gay cowboy in the 2005 film "Brokeback Mountain" and had a child with the actress Michelle Williams (who played his wife in the film). They never married and split up shortly before he died. Ledger had not amended his will to mention either Williams or their child.

The situation raised a thicket of legal issues about whether his child was entitled to an inheritance. The answer depended on where Ledger's domicile, or legal home, was. He was a citizen of Australia and signed his will there, often worked in California and died in his New York apartment. His domicile would determine which law applied.

In most states, Matilda would have a right to inherit at least part of her father's estate, because the law protects children from disinheritance if a parent forgets to update the will. In other words, it is possible to disinherit a child, but you must do it purposely, not accidentally.

Fortunately, Ledger's parents and siblings avoided what could have been years of courtroom wrangling. Nine months after Ledger died, they relinquished their whole inheritance, reportedly as much as $20 million, to Matilda, who was approaching her third birthday. That may or may not be precisely what Ledger would have wanted. By updating his will after Matilda was born to make his wishes clear, he could have eliminated the guesswork and set up a trust for his daughter's benefit. Under many state laws, the child's mother could petition the court to put the inheritance in a trust, which would achieve a variety of benefits discussed in Chapters 6, 9 and 18.

situations where your children have privileges the guardians can't afford for their own children, you can authorize payments from the trust to cover certain extras for all the children. These might include private school tuition, summer camps or family vacations.

Life insurance is the obvious vehicle to supplement whatever assets you have accumulated. Just do not make the mistake (as many people do) of owning a policy that insures your life. If you do, the entire sum could be taxable as part of your estate even though you have named your children as beneficiaries. The alternative is to set up a life insurance trust that buys the policy, owns it and when you die holds the proceeds for whomever you've named as beneficiary. As long as the trust is properly administered (see Chapter 8), the money is then free of estate taxes.

Special considerations apply when making provisions for a child with special needs. To qualify for Supplemental Security Income (a welfare program) and Medicaid, which they may someday need, disabled people cannot have more than $2,000 ($1,600 in some states) of assets in their own names. This affects the way you set up and fund life insurance trusts (see Chapter 8), as well as other strategies for covering the child's future expenses.

Many people wind up disqualified for these benefits because well-intentioned parents and grandparents did not know the rules. For example, putting money in a custodial account for the child under the Uniform Transfers to Minors Act can easily disqualify the recipient. Potentially, so can Section 529 college savings plans, which allow you to set up for each child a separate account earmarked for higher education (see Chapter 9).

🌿

Set Up Trusts for Children With Special Needs

A common misconception is that planning for children with special needs requires families to disinherit them so they will qualify for public assistance. A much more attractive alternative is to set up a special needs or supplemental needs trust to provide for each such child. As long as the trust meets certain federal requirements, the child can still be eligible for public assistance upon reaching age 18, or sooner in certain cases, such as when the family is indigent.

This is desirable not only for the Supplemental Security Income (SSI) benefit, which is $700 a month, but also because qualifying for SSI is a prereq-uisite to receiving Medicaid. Once they turn 18 most children are no longer covered by their parents' health insurance unless they are full-time students or disabled. For people who qualify, Medicaid picks up many health care expenses, pays for supervision in a group home and foots the bill for job training.

Although some very wealthy people choose to cover all these expenses themselves, those who do lose access to various public services, including case management, which can be hugely beneficial to disabled people and their families. Instead, most families use their own funds to supplement what is available through public assistance. Like other trusts, special needs trusts also protect assets from claims of creditors (see Chapter 18) and people who may prey on the beneficiary.

Depending on your circumstances, you should consider two basic types of special needs trusts. The most common is what is known as a third-party trust, set up and funded by someone who is not a beneficiary – typically a parent or grandparent. These tend to be put in place while the older generation is still alive, but not funded until their death. For instance, the trust may be named as the beneficiary of a will, a retirement plan or a life insurance policy.

The Secret Son

When Arthur Miller, the playwright, died in 2005, most newspaper obituaries did not mention his son Daniel, who has Down syn-drome, and was then 39. Daniel had spent most of his life in state-run institutions and programs in Connecticut, while his father kept his exis-tence a secret. Shortly before Miller died, he revised his estate plan and made Daniel an heir through a trust of 25 percent of the estate, equal to the shares left to each of Miller's other three children, according to published reports about the family.

The inheritance made Daniel wealthy and disqualified him for govern-ment aid. It also resulted in a reimbursement claim by the state, resolved privately, for the care he had received. There were ways to avoid that, but Miller did not take advantage of them.

The second trust to consider is an OBRA '93 trust (a reference to the Omnibus Budget and Reconciliation Act of 1993 that permits it). These are generally self-funded trusts created for people younger than 65 to shift assets out of their control so they will qualify for public assistance. Often, OBRA '93 trusts are funded with inheritances or recoveries from personal injury or medical malpractice lawsuits.

OBRA '93 trusts can also be useful for elderly parents or grandparents who have a disabled family member and want to qualify for Medicaid themselves. Normally, moving property out of the parent's name would not make the parent eligible for Medicaid. But the 1993 law enables parents to transfer all their assets to an OBRA '93 trust to benefit the disabled person. In this limited context, both parties could then receive Medicaid. Although this technique is rarely used right now, as the longevity of children with disabilities increases, more people may want to consider it in the future.

While third-party trusts may not have money to spend right away, OBRA '93 trusts sometimes start out with millions of dollars in funding. And these assets can be spent even while the parents are still alive. For example, they have been used to build houses and swimming pools, install an elevator in an existing home, redo kitchens to make them wheelchair accessible and buy vans.

Under federal law, all OBRA '93 trusts must include a payback provision, giving the state or states that have been providing Medicaid services to the individual the right to get reimbursed after the beneficiary dies for any expenditures made on her behalf. The payback requirement applies only when you are dealing with the beneficiary's own money – not funds in third-party trusts. With third-party trusts, when the disabled beneficiary dies, whatever is left goes to any other beneficiaries designated in the trust document.

Some families have both a third-party trust and an OBRA '93 trust. When that is the case, it is best to deplete the OBRA '93 trust first since only this trust has a payback provision.

Anther restriction to be aware of is the monthly limit on earned income for people who may be eligible for Social Security Disability. Unlike Supplemental Security Income, which is a welfare program, Social Security Disability is an insurance program for disabled workers who can no longer work and their family members. There are no asset or unearned income limits for receiving Social Security Disability, but the benefit is limited based on earnings. Eligibility rules are technical, but an individual may earn approximately $980 a month ($1,640 a month if blind) without losing Social Security Disability benefits.

On top of the federal rules, a crazy quilt of state laws can affect the formation and administration of special needs trusts. Since Medicaid is a federal-state program, states have the power to regulate these trusts and inevitably there are differences from state to state. State laws can affect trust terms, administration and how they are funded.

For both special needs trusts and OBRA '93 trusts, rules on how the money can be spent are roughly the same. Ideally the trust shouldn't be used for food, clothing or shelter – the purpose is to supplement, rather than to supplant, public benefits. If the trust is used for the necessities, the beneficiary could lose up to one-third of the Supplemental Security Income benefit.

Within these parameters, it is possible to greatly improve the beneficiary's lifestyle. These trusts have paid for cable TV, computers, telephones, vacations, medical benefits that Medicaid doesn't cover or a higher quality of care, like a dentist or psychotherapist of the beneficiary's choice.

Generally speaking, the trustee – the person or institution in charge of the trust – should have full discretion about how much to distribute and when to make those payouts. And the funds should be sent directly to the provider of the goods or services, such as a travel agent, a home health agency or a store. Distributions to the beneficiary, even for pocket money, would be considered unearned income and could reduce the Supplemental Security Income benefit.

Put the Money in Good Hands

Just as your will should appoint a guardian for your children, it is crucial to leave instructions about who should manage the assets you leave.

As noted earlier, setting up a trust that requires a trustee to follow your instructions is much better than a financial guardianship arrangement, even one in which you have hand picked the guardian. Worse yet, if you do not name a specific person for the guardian's role, the court takes over supervision of any money left to children younger than 18, the age of majority in most states. This includes not just the assets that pass under the will – such as stocks, bonds, and the family home – but also payments from life insurance policies, retirement accounts and custodial accounts. The person caring for your child may have to go through an onerous process to get any expenditures approved. And you will have given a court one more chance to decide issues for you, rather than having things done your way.

To avoid various undesirable financial consequences, you should use a trust in conjunction with life insurance policies and when leaving funds for children with special needs. Other times you may be tempted to rely on much simpler and less expensive custodial accounts, which name an adult to oversee the funds until the child reaches majority (18 or 21, depending on the state).

Custodial accounts, however, have a number of disadvantages (see Chapter 9). One is that children are legally entitled to the money when they reach the specified age, even if they lack the maturity or experience to manage it. Another drawback, when you are providing for the support of a child who is still a minor, is that you have much less say over how the money will be spent.

> ## Did You Know?
>
> If you are setting up a special needs trust for a child with a disability, let other relatives know. That way, if a grandparent wants to help, she can indicate in her will that the trust should receive the inheritance. Money left outright to the child could disqualify him from public assistance.

In contrast, by putting assets in trust for minor children, you can direct that income and principal be paid any way you like. Until your children reach a certain age (say 25), you might leave distributions entirely up to the trustee. After that, you may select two or three ages at which portions of the principal will be distributed (for instance, one-third at 25, another third at 30 and the balance at 35).

Compared with the emotionally charged issue of choosing someone to care for your child, deciding who will manage her money may seem relatively easy. But proceed with caution. Much as you would like to believe, "If I'm going to trust someone with my child, I might as well trust him with her money," it's much better to keep the two functions discrete and select another person or financial institution to manage the money (see Chapter 6).

To-Do List

Coordinate Elements of an Estate Plan

When parents die prematurely, a lot of loose ends can be left behind. The following precautions can help avoid potential legal and economic pitfalls:

❧ *Review all accounts for which you are a custodian for your child.* Include those at banks, mutual fund companies or brokerage houses, as well as 529 college savings plans; verify that there is an alternate custodian. You should not be the custodian of an account that you set up.

❧ *Determine whether children are named as primary or backup beneficiaries of retirement accounts, such as IRAs and 401(k)s – either your own or accounts set up by the child's grandparents.* Discuss with financial advisers the possibility of creating a trust to receive the child's share (see Chapters 6 and 7).

❧ *For a child with special needs, do not create custodial accounts or 529 college savings plans for that child if she may become dependent on public benefits.* If you or a relative have already set up such an account, spend the funds on your child before she will be eligible for public assistance. If a 529 plan is in place, consider changing the beneficiary to another family member in the same generation.

❧ *Make sure life insurance policies are owned by a trust and that it is named as the beneficiary of the policy (the child, in turn, is a beneficiary of the trust).* This should be a special needs trust if your child has a disability that would ultimately qualify him or her for public assistance.

❧ *Examine any existing trusts that name your child as a beneficiary.* If you have a special needs child, the trust should not give him or her a Crummey power – the right for a limited time, usually 30 or 60 days, to withdraw from the trust the contribution to the trust during the current year (see Chapter 6).

❧ *Suggest that relatives update their estate plans.* By not amending wills and trusts, grandparents, in particular, might have inadvertently excluded new family members, including your child.

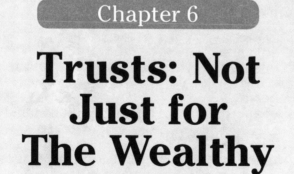

Chapter 6

Trusts: Not Just for The Wealthy

*Read this chapter even if you think
you don't need this very useful tool.*

You may think trusts are just for the super-rich. In fact, they are enormously useful – and sometimes essential – for people of more modest means. There are numerous situations when a trust is the best way to achieve your goals.

A trust can safeguard your assets and provide for your own care should you no longer be able to handle your affairs.

In This Chapter...

- ❧ *What Is a Trust?*
- ❧ *How Do You Create a Trust?*
- ❧ *What Are the Key Issues to Cover?*
- ❧ *Whom Should You Choose as Trustee?*
- ❧ *What Checks and Balances Are Available for Long-Term Trusts?*
- ❧ *What Does It Cost to Set Up And Use a Trust?*

A trust can prevent payouts from life insurance policies being subject to estate tax.

A trust can avoid tax on an inheritance when one spouse is a U.S. citizen and the other isn't.

A trust can provide for children from a previous marriage.

A trust can hold money for minors and ensure that they can't spend it all the minute they reach majority.

A trust can prevent funds from being eroded by family members whom you consider spendthrifts.

A trust can protect assets from creditors and former spouses, whether your own or those of your heirs.

A trust can save estate taxes on both assets put into the trust during your life and on any future appreciation of those assets.

A trust can help you avoid or minimize generation-skipping transfer taxes on money destined for grandchildren or future generations.

A trust can benefit family and charity through one tax-efficient vehicle.

What Is a Trust?

One thing that makes trusts hard to conceptualize is that you can't see them or touch them. They are an invisible legal wrapper for holding assets, such as cash, real estate, an insurance policy, shares in a closely held company or publicly traded securities. A trust is created by a document that looks like a contract and is called the trust instrument. The person who sets up the trust and funds it is known as the grantor or the settlor. Briefly, here's what happens next:

Step 1: Title to any assets you put into the trust passes to the trustee. This is the person or company that you have chosen to carry out your wishes. You can have one trustee or several.

Step 2: The trustees manage the assets, either by themselves or by hiring investment managers. Legally, a trustee is a fiduciary, which means the trustee has a duty to always put the beneficiaries' welfare first.

Step 3: Following your directions in the trust instrument, the trustees make distributions or payouts to the people or charities you have named as beneficiaries.

How Do You Create a Trust?

You can set up a trust during your lifetime (an inter vivos trust) or with your will (a testamentary trust). Lifetime trusts may be either irrevocable, meaning that you can't change them or undo them, or revocable, meaning that you can. Unfortunately, trusts set up to save estate taxes usually have to be irrevocable. You will need a lawyer's help with the paperwork, which might run 20 pages or more.

What Are the Key Issues to Cover?

One advantage of a trust is that it can designate someone to fulfill your goals when you are no longer around. The more clearly you spell out those goals, the easier it will be for the trustee or trustees to follow your wishes. These are some issues to sort out:

Who are the beneficiaries? A trust can benefit one person or many – known as a pot trust. Often they have both current beneficiaries who are entitled to assets immediately and future (remainder) beneficiaries, who will not receive distributions until some event occurs – such as when they reach a certain age or the current beneficiary dies.

Trusts that pay income to current beneficiaries and preserve principal for future ones pit one set of interests against the other. Legally, trustees must be impartial, but in real life they can get caught in the middle of the two sets of beneficiaries. Lifetime beneficiaries generally want the largest possible payout, while future beneficiaries prefer trust assets to accumulate and increase in value. These conflicting priorities are affected both by the choice of investments and by decisions about when to make distributions.

What is the timetable for distributions? Often trusts start making payouts at specific ages – for example, with income to people in their 20s and distributions of principal staggered at ages 30, 35 and 40, to encompass the high-spending years when many people are getting married, starting families and buying homes.

What are the trustee's responsibilities? Traditionally, their primary obligations are to:
- Interpret the trust document
- Make distributions of income or principal and keep records of these payouts
- Invest and maintain investments in an ever-changing market
- Send annual Crummey notices, when required (see "Crummey Fundamentals," page 83)
- Prepare the trust tax return.

Depending on the purpose of the trust and who the beneficiaries are, trustees may serve a variety of related functions. Some people rely on trustees to help educate younger generations about financial matters. When trusts are set

Crummey Fundamentals

A popular way of funding many types of trusts is to use the annual exclusion – the $13,000 ($26,000 for spouses who make joint gifts – a process known as gift-splitting) that you can give each year to as many people as you would like without having to pay gift tax. One condition for the annual exclusion is that the gift must be a present interest, meaning something the recipient can use right away, rather than a future one.

The most common way to satisfy this requirement is to give beneficiaries Crummey powers: the right for a limited time, usually 30 or 60 days, to withdraw from the trust the yearly gift attributable to that beneficiary. Each year, the trustees must send a notice, called a Crummey notice, to the beneficiaries (or the parents, if the beneficiaries are minors) letting them know about their right to withdraw their portion of the annual gift to the trust.

Although there's nothing difficult about preparing these notices – some lawyers will even give you a template – many people neglect to send them and to keep copies with the trust documents. This could come back to bite your heirs later if your estate is audited. In the worst-case scenario they could get stuck paying back gift taxes for the money you put in the trust.

up for minors, the trustee may step into the shoes of a parent who dies prematurely and become the child's financial guardian (see Chapter 5).

How should the trust assets be invested? Without specific directions to do otherwise, trustees have a legal obligation to invest in a diversified portfolio – in other words, not put all the eggs in one basket. The precise asset allocation should reflect the needs of beneficiaries. That will determine if the portfolio is invested for growth or value, or to generate income, for example.

Will the trustee have broad or narrow powers to make distributions? With narrow powers, the trustee can pay out income and occasionally principal only for very specific reasons, such as "health, education, maintenance or support," "college education" or "medical emergencies." Narrow powers are commonly used in situations in which the creator of the trust wants to control and tightly define the use of trust property.

Broad powers to make distributions – with or without a specific standard – allow for more subjective decisions. These trusts call for the trustee to exercise independent judgment to "maintain reasonable comfort" of a beneficiary, to preserve the person's "accustomed manner of living," or "for any purpose." Often these powers show up in trusts for the benefit of a surviving spouse or children where the grantor is comfortable that the trustee won't abuse the broad guidelines.

Giving a trustee broad powers is a good idea if you want the trust to last for multiple generations. The more flexibility the trustees have, the better they will be able to react to unanticipated situations. Some people even make the trust fully discretionary – giving trustees the last word over payouts. But that doesn't mean the trustees should apply their own values to a given situation. Instead, they're supposed to react the way you would if you were handling the situation yourself. That's all the more reason to explain your intentions as clearly as possible in the trust document – and to be sure that you are comfortable with the trustees you designate.

Should beneficiaries be able to remove and replace trustees? More and more trusts include this power. For example, in a marital trust, which initially benefits the surviving spouse, that individual – assume it is the wife – might have the power to remove a corporate trustee unilaterally if she is not satisfied with its services. If the children are beneficiaries after she dies, the trust might give them the power by majority vote to remove and replace a trustee.

In longer-term trusts, the document could designate as trustee one person, a group of people (such as a committee of family members or beneficiaries) or a business (such as a bank or law firm) to appoint the successor.

If you plan to include powers to remove and replace trustees, the trust document should clearly define the circumstances under which removal may occur and the type of successor trustee you prefer.

How long should the trust last? Trusts can last for a finite term or, in states that permit dynasty trusts, continue for many generations. Some trusts are set up to end at the time of a specific event, such as when an income beneficiary dies or reaches a certain age. But in our litigious society, having a trust continue for longer offers this distinct advantage: It can protect a beneficiary's assets from someone who wins a lawsuit against the beneficiary (see Chapter 18).

Whom Should You Choose as Trustee?

The ideal trustee is objective, a careful record-keeper and either experienced with taxes and investing or capable of retaining others who are. You will want a fiduciary who is able to give your trust as much attention as it requires, over a prolonged period, if necessary. These are the options.

Family, friends and business colleagues. One attraction of such trustees is that they presumably understand the family dynamics and can balance the needs of various beneficiaries when making decisions about distributions. But even assuming they have the background, training and objectivity, these individuals, who often serve as trustees without compensation or for a nominal charge, may not have time to handle a trustee's numerous responsibilities.

Another consideration is the potential legal liability. A fiduciary can be found liable for negligence, as well as for intentional misdeeds. If they mishandle trust investments or distributions, trustees could be the target of a lawsuit by disgruntled beneficiaries. They may not have the financial resources and insurance protection to cover their errors nor the desire to put themselves in this position.

> ## *Did You Know?*
>
> Paul Newman, who died in 2008, flourished in the spotlight, but kept his estate plan offstage. His will directed that "airplanes and all race cars" be sold and most tangible property go to his wife, Joanne Woodward. Everything else went into a trust, a private document.

Professional advisers (such as lawyers and accountants). A key question is whether they are equipped to field the day-to-day questions that can come up. Although you may be pleased with their other services, when acting as fiduciary they may not have the resources, the time or the knowledge base of a large organization. So you had better question them closely on these issues before designating them. They typically charge their standard hourly fee for the service (in some states, a maximum is set by law).

Corporate trustees. Institutional services are available through banks, trust companies and some law firms. On the whole, corporate trustees have a depth of experience that most individuals can't match. They are more likely to keep up with changes in the law that affect investment returns or the tax efficiency of the trust. And they understand the complexities and potential pitfalls of certain types of trusts. Corporate fiduciaries also provide continuity through multiple generations and an institutional memory, which is especially helpful in long-term trusts.

A common criticism of corporate trustees is that they are rigid and bureaucratic. Not all corporate fiduciaries operate this way, but you do need to perform your due diligence (see "Interviewing Corporate Trustees," page 87). Because distribution decisions are often made by committee, you want to be sure it meets frequently enough (and on an emergency basis when necessary) to implement the trust terms.

A combination of individual and corporate trustees. Some people find the most flexible arrangement is to appoint co-trustees: an individual who knows the family well and a corporate fiduciary with extensive experience in trust administration. This might be appropriate when something comparable to parental authority is necessary to protect the interests of children or grandchildren. In that case, you might want to limit the individual's role to making the kind of decisions that would normally fall to a parent, such as deciding how much money to distribute to the beneficiaries. As co-trustee, the corporate fiduciary could have sole responsibility for asset management and legal compliance.

In recent years it has become increasingly popular to appoint beneficiaries as co-trustees for their own trusts, which are primarily overseen by a corporate fiduciary. This fosters a sense of involvement that beneficiaries might not feel when all the control resides elsewhere, and this structure can be a tool for educating the next generation about money.

One potential pitfall, however, is that giving beneficiaries of the trust authority over discretionary distributions could have adverse consequences, such as causing the property to be included in their estates or exposing it to their creditors. It is much more common – and sensible – to have family co-trustees participate only in decisions that do not involve distributions to themselves.

Many long-term trusts that start out with individual trustees ultimately end up with corporate fiduciaries, which are more enduring. Over time, corporate trustees may be better suited to deal with events and people that you cannot anticipate when establishing the trust.

Especially when individual trustees are involved, it is crucial that your

Interviewing Corporate Trustees

If you are considering a corporate trustee, look for an organization with decades of experience in the business, a track record for integrity and a presence in your community. Here are some questions to ask:

❧ What do you charge? (If they are managing an investment portfolio, their fees will be higher than if they are simply making distribution decisions.)

❧ Do you require the trust to have at least a certain monetary value before you will serve as trustee?

❧ How do you plan to invest the assets?

❧ Will you be delegating investment decisions? (If so, to whom?)

❧ If the trust has unique assets (such as art, real estate, water rights, oil and gas interests, or shares in a family owned business), how will they be managed?

❧ If you do not have expertise in managing these kinds of assets, what process will you use to hire the right experts?

❧ Who will have custody of the assets?

❧ How will you balance the interests of current and future beneficiaries?

❧ What process do you use to make decisions about discretionary distributions?

❧ If beneficiaries live in different geographic areas, how do you plan to communicate with them?

❧ Do you have offices in various locations?

document include a succession plan – so a mechanism is in place for choosing subsequent trustees if the initial ones become unwilling or unable to serve. Some grantors allow individual trustees to choose their successors. Others provide that when a trustee's tenure ends, for whatever reason, that power shifts to a successor, perhaps a corporate fiduciary.

What Checks and Balances Are Available For Long-Term Trusts?

One challenge when setting up long-term irrevocable trusts is to come up with a framework that will achieve your goals many years in the future. Problem is, neither a family's needs nor the state and federal tax laws are constants. Will those angelic toddlers grow up to be black sheep? That's always possible. A less obvious, but hugely important, factor, is whether federal law and, perhaps even more significantly, state law may change.

The rules that govern a trust depend on its situs (location), and state laws are evolving. Among the key areas currently in flux are the extent of creditor protection for certain trusts, whether a trust can be a dynasty trust that continues forever, and whether it is possible to decant the trust – that is, to pay out funds from one trust to another. Over time, it might be desirable to change the situs of a trust so that it can take advantage of strategies in states with the most favorable laws.

To address these issues and others, a growing number of people are designating a trust protector, sometimes called a special trustee or trust adviser. This is someone, independent of the trustee, whom you assign to make certain key decisions and adapt various trust terms as circumstances change. Obvious choices for the role include friends, personal advisers who know the family, close business associates or family members who are not beneficiaries.

Although trust protectors have been common in other countries for decades, they're something of a recent phenomenon in the United States. American lawyers first started using protectors 50 or more years ago in offshore trusts aimed at asset protection (see Chapter 18). More recently, trust protectors have showed up in domestic trusts. Though most common in irrevocable trusts, they also can be useful to oversee the trustees of revocable, or living trusts set up to safeguard assets for those who no longer have the faculties to manage funds themselves (see Chapter 1).

Trust protectors are especially helpful with two other kinds of trusts. One is a trust that will not be funded until the grantor dies. With the grantor gone, someone must be entrusted with tough personal decisions. Professional trustees may prefer not to make judgment calls about when to accelerate payments of principal, for instance. You might want them to deal with technical matters such as managing money, keeping records and preparing taxes, while putting personal decisions in the hands of a trust protector.

Trust protectors can also perform a key function with irrevocable trusts funded during life in order to get property out of the grantor's estate. Much as the grantor might like to be able to add beneficiaries, for example, doing so would cause the trust property to be included in her estate for federal tax purposes. But let's say the grantor has named her brother as protector. The brother may be able to take that action instead.

The flexibility a protector provides can be useful for other reasons. Given all the recent mergers and changes at financial institutions, you may want the freedom to switch trustees after familiar trust officers have been replaced. A protector can be given the power to remove and replace a corporate trustee if you have not given that power to the trust beneficiaries.

A trust protector's powers can be broad or limited. Initially, grantors gave protectors only the power to remove or replace trustees or to veto distributions – for instance, in a trust authorizing fiduciaries to make discretionary payouts to beneficiaries. More recently, the menu of options has expanded. Some trusts authorize the protector to veto or direct investment decisions, to split a pot trust into multiple trusts, so that each beneficiary has his or her own trust, and even to end the trust and distribute the assets.

Increasingly, lawyers recommend that protectors be able to change the situs of the trust to implement various tax strategies. For example, you might give the protector the power, when appropriate, to switch a trust to a state that's more favorable for creditor protection or that permits dynasty trusts.

A word of caution: The more expansive a protector's list of powers gets, the greater the potential for problems. Not only must you choose someone you can trust, but the protector should have some understanding of how a trust works and the pitfalls to avoid. For certain kinds of trusts, the protector needs to be careful that exercising his or her power doesn't ruin the tax advantages that go with that trust. For example, with a Crummey trust (see "Crummey Fundamentals," page 83), denying the holder of a Crummey power the right to make withdrawals during the specified period each year could result in certain gifts to the trust being taxable, rather than eligible for the annual exclusion.

Another issue to consider is whether you want to provide for successor protectors and a mechanism for choosing them, just as you would provide for successor trustees. The broader the protector's powers, the more seriously you must undertake every decision concerning one.

What Does It Cost to Set Up and Use a Trust?

For all the benefits and tax savings that trusts can achieve, significant costs can be incurred in establishing and overseeing them. These include:

Set-up costs. The legal bill to prepare a trust can run $2,500 to more than $15,000, depending on the type of trust, its complexity, where you are situated and the size of the law firm doing the work (see Chapter 19).

Trustee's fees. Fees for corporate trustees or advisers serving that function vary widely and will depend on the services they perform. If trustees are managing an investment portfolio, their charges will be higher (typically a percentage of assets under management) than if they are simply making distribution decisions.

Income taxes. If a trust is distributing all income, the beneficiaries will be taxed. But when a trust has capital gains or is accumulating income, such as interest, dividends, rents or royalties, the trust must pay tax. That includes federal income tax and, possibly, state income tax, depending on where the beneficiaries and trustees live or are based (for corporate trustees). Because taxes can eat away at the trust's investment earnings, they leave less for beneficiaries.

One strategy to address the problem is to make the trust a grantor trust – one in which the person creating the trust retains certain powers. In that case, the grantor, rather than the trust, pays the income tax while she is alive, leaving more for beneficiaries. Attractive as this may be in some cases, you must be able to afford that tax bill annually (see Chapter 15).

Tax preparation. The trust needs to file an annual income tax return whether or not it owes income tax, and submit tax information to beneficiaries. Expect an accountant to charge at least $1,000 for this service.

To-Do List

Look Before You Leap

Trusts can achieve a variety of goals, and other chapters of this book include details about trusts created for particular purposes. The tradeoff is that trusts can also create complications for you and the people you hope to benefit. So before you go feet first into a trust, discuss all the ramifications with your lawyer and tax adviser. Here are some important questions to ask:

❧ What's the profile of the person who typically sets up this type of trust? (Then ask yourself: "Does it make sense for me?")

❧ Is there a simpler or less expensive way to achieve my goals?

❧ From a tax perspective, what are the best assets to put into the trust? (Then ask yourself: "Am I willing to part with any of these assets?")

❧ Is it possible to contribute these assets without paying gift tax?

❧ Will the trust save more than it will cost to create and operate?

❧ Will the trust tie my hands or restrain the beneficiaries in undesirable ways?

❧ Is there a way to undo or alter any aspects of the trust should I change my mind?

❧ Do the individuals or institutions I plan to name as trustees or the people I plan to name as beneficiaries live in high-tax states? If so, how will that affect the trust's effectiveness?

Chapter 7

Preserve Retirement Accounts

*Read this chapter if you have
any kind of retirement account,
such as an IRA or a 401(k).*

M oney in individual retirement accounts or employer-sponsored retirement plans, such as 401(k)s and 403(b)s, will not normally be covered by a will, an issue not everyone is clear about. Instead, the funds go to inheritors according to beneficiary designation forms that you fill out when you open the accounts or later amend.

These forms, which function as contracts, notify the bank or financial institution (the custodian) about who will inherit your account. This is your beneficiary. You can have as many beneficiaries as you like, including:

– Your spouse or partner
– Other family members
– A trust to benefit family
– Charity

Two types of taxes can shrink the pie for people who inherit retirement accounts. One is the tax that may apply to your estate. The balance in your retirement account when you pass away gets tallied up along with the rest of your assets. If your total estate is worth more than $3.5 million, a 45 percent estate tax can eat into these assets.

In This Chapter...

- ⚜ *Maximize the Stretch-Out*
- ⚜ *Give Your Spouse Options*
- ⚜ *Go Roth, if You Can*
- ⚜ *Use Retirement Assets to Benefit Charity*
- ⚜ *Aim for Flexibility*

The tax bite doesn't end there. Whether or not your heirs have to pay estate tax, if your account is what's called a traditional IRA or employer-sponsored plan (as opposed to a Roth account), your heirs will be required to pay income tax each time they withdraw funds. Depending on their tax bracket, the federal income tax could be as high as 35 percent.

After various deductions, in the worst-case scenario, this is what's left of a $500,000 retirement account inherited as part of an estate worth $4 million:

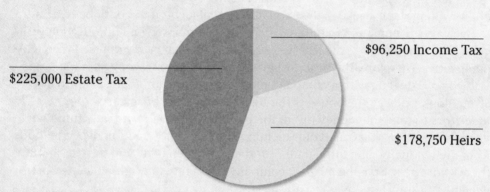

$225,000 Estate Tax

$96,250 Income Tax

$178,750 Heirs

Source: Barry C. Picker, CPA/PFS, CFP

Depending where you live, state income or estate taxes, or both, may also apply.

Fortunately, a handful of strategies are available to minimize the tax bite.

Maximize the Stretch-Out

Generally, IRA inheritors must withdraw a minimum amount each year, starting on Dec. 31 of the year after they inherit the account. The rules for spouses are more lenient (see page 98).

If they choose to, heirs can extend these minimum required distributions over their life expectancy. This is known as the stretch-out, since it stretches out how long the money will last and allows the account to continue to grow.

Because the minimum required distributions are based on life expectancy, the younger the beneficiary, the less he must take out each year. From an income tax perspective, therefore, the best designated beneficiary is a young person.

If you are dealing with a company plan, there is no automatic right to a stretch-out. Unless the spouse is the beneficiary, most businesses require inheritors to take the money out of the plan in a lump sum, often within five years or less. But you can avoid the lump-sum payout if you roll over the funds from the company plan into an inherited IRA. This enables you to stretch out the withdrawals. Starting in 2010, company plans must permit all named beneficiaries (not just spouses) to do this.

Calculating the minimum required payout each year is fairly straightforward: take the account balance on Dec. 31 of the previous year and divide it by the beneficiary's life expectancy, as listed in IRS tables (see page 305). There is income tax on this required payout.

Consider Sally, who leaves part of her IRA, worth $100,000, to her grandson, who is 21 when Sally dies at age 69. He must begin taking distributions by Dec. 31 of the year following Sally's death but can stretch out withdrawals for the rest of his life. Based on an account balance of $100,000, the grandson's first required distribution at age 22 is $100,000 divided by his life expectancy of 61.1 years (from the IRS table), or $1,636.66. If he continues to withdraw just the minimum required distribution each year, and the investments appreciate at a steady rate of 6 percent, this inheritance can provide the grandson with a nest egg for his own retirement.

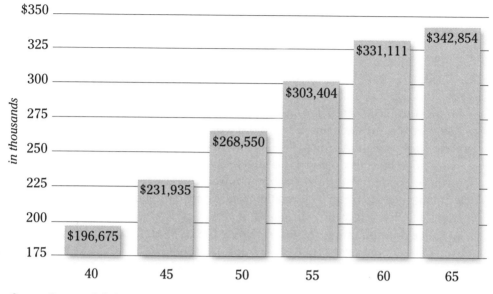

in thousands

Source: Brentmark Software Inc.

Keep a couple of caveats in mind when leaving retirement accounts to grandchildren. One is that if they might be minors when you die, you should name an adult custodian for the assets or, better yet, name a trust for the grandchild's benefit as the designated beneficiary (see "Can a Trust Be a Beneficiary?" page 101). Another is that IRAs left to grandchildren are subject to generation-skipping transfer tax, in addition to estate tax and income tax. This is a levy of 45 percent on the amount of a grandparent's total transfers to all grandchildren that exceeds $3.5 million. As with any other asset, an IRA left to the owner's child could be subject to the generation-skipping tax if the child decides to disclaim (legalese for decline) the inheritance, passing it on to a grandchild. (For more about the generation-skipping transfer tax, see Chapter 14.)

But never name your estate as the beneficiary. If you do, under the worst combination of circumstances, funds might have to be withdrawn within five years of your death, with all the income tax paid as the money comes out of the IRA. This could also happen if you forget to name a beneficiary at all, or if no one can find the beneficiary designation form when the time comes.

Customized Beneficiary Designation Forms

Unlike wills, which provide in detail how property will be distributed, the preprinted form that a custodian gives you to fill out may seem cursory.

Many standard beneficiary designation forms call for account owners to name only a primary and a secondary beneficiary. The better ones go beyond that to provide for per stirpes distributions; that's legal lingo for passing inheritances down to the next generation if one beneficiary dies before the account owner, rather than automatically having that beneficiary's share go to other co-beneficiaries. Some forms offer additional options, like leaving your retirement assets to a trust or to charity.

Ask an estate-planning lawyer to review the form and coordinate your retirement accounts with the rest of your estate plan. The larger your retirement account and the more complicated the estate plan, the harder it may be to cover all the bases with the custodian's boilerplate form.

Depending on how the standard form is set up, you may prefer to have your lawyer prepare a customized, more complex beneficiary designation form. Some lawyers will include a couple of customized beneficiary designation forms as part of the standard estate-planning package. Otherwise, you will need to pay extra for that service, most likely at your lawyer's hourly rate.

Give Your Spouse Options

Most married people start by naming their spouse as beneficiary of a retirement account. In fact, if the account is a qualified plan (a category under federal law that includes a defined-contribution plan, defined-benefit plan, Keogh plan for the self-employed and 401(k) – but not an IRA) the Employee Retirement Income Security Act of 1974 gives your spouse the right to be the sole primary beneficiary of the account. To name anyone else, you need your spouse's written consent.

For IRAs and qualified plans, the law gives special privileges to spouses who inherit the funds. Unlike other inheritors, who must begin making withdrawals by Dec. 31 of the year following the account owner's death, a spouse – let's assume it's the wife – who inherits an IRA or company plan has another option. She can roll the assets into her own IRA and postpone required minimum distributions until the year after she turns 70½.

Despite this potential advantage, making your spouse the beneficiary can wind up costing more in both income taxes and estate taxes. Here are the dilemmas that arise, and the steps you can take to address them.

The income tax dilemma. Unless your spouse is much younger than you are, the potential stretch-out is somewhat shorter than if you named a child or grandchild as the designated beneficiary.

Sometimes there's no alternative – for example, your spouse might need the money. If you cannot be sure ahead of time, keep your options open: make your spouse the primary beneficiary and name a younger person as the contingent or alternate beneficiary. (Again, you must do this on the beneficiary designation form.) When you die, your spouse can decide whether to inherit the IRA directly and roll it over into her own IRA, or disclaim the inheritance and let it pass to the younger beneficiary (see Chapter 2).

The estate tax dilemma. This is an issue for people who do not have enough other assets to fully fund a bypass trust, a planning tool used to preserve the $3.5 million estate tax exemption for both spouses (see Chapter 3), without using retirement accounts.

If you use IRA assets to fund the trust, your spouse may lose the special income tax treatment that would otherwise apply to those funds. If you don't, your other heirs could ultimately wind up paying more estate tax down the line.

To review how the bypass or credit-shelter trust works: You arrange to fund the trust with up to $3.5 million of assets when you die. The trust distributes income and principal to your spouse or other family members while the surviving spouse is alive, then passes on whatever is left to family. Since funds in the bypass trust are covered by the exemption amount, they will not be taxed when you die. Nor are they considered part of your spouse's estate, so they are not subject to tax when she dies either.

But making a bypass trust the beneficiary of a retirement account accelerates the income taxes and draws down the assets more quickly than if the spouse inherited them directly. Here's why. A spouse who inherits the IRA directly can roll over the IRA to her own IRA, postpone withdrawals until reaching age 70½ and take minimum distributions based on the Uniform Lifetime Table, which applies in most cases (see page 307). The table is based on the joint life expectancy of the beneficiary and a hypothetical person 10 years younger.

Spouses get less generous treatment if the benefits are payable to a typical bypass trust, which provides income to the surviving spouse for life and leaves the remainder to children. Under that scenario, ordinarily withdrawals would be based on the life expectancy of the surviving spouse as the oldest beneficiary. But the trust would have to start taking payments the year after the IRA owner's death and base those withdrawals on the Single Life Expectancy table that applies to inheritors (see page 305).

Assuming you cannot fully fund the trust without tapping retirement accounts, the choice, then, is whether to save income taxes (no bypass trust) or estate taxes (bypass trust). For many people, the best course of action is to leave the decision to their heirs. You can do this by naming your spouse as primary beneficiary and the bypass trust as secondary beneficiary. (Again, you must do this on the beneficiary designation form.) When you die, your spouse can decide whether to inherit the IRA directly and roll it over into her own IRA, or disclaim the inheritance and activate the trust as secondary beneficiary (see Chapter 2). At the same time, you can be sure you are not shortchanging your spouse by diverting money to the trust that she might need for living expenses.

Go Roth, if You Can

If you are concerned about estate taxes and do not plan to use all the retirement assets yourself, the simplest, best tax-saving strategy is to create a Roth account, rather than a traditional one, or convert existing retirement accounts to Roth IRAs. What is the difference?

With traditional accounts, including IRAs and employer-sponsored plans such as 401(k)s and 403(b)s, you can take a tax deduction as you make contributions, and there is no need to pay tax as investments in the account grow. The downside of these tax-deferred plans comes when you or your heirs withdraw the money. At that point, every cent coming out of the account is subject to income tax at whatever rate happens to be in effect.

Can a Trust Be a Beneficiary?

The short answer is yes, and you may have good reasons for naming a trust as the beneficiary of a retirement account. For example, it might be worth considering a trust if the intended beneficiaries are minors, or if you want to control the cash flow to heirs you regard as spendthrifts. The trust can essentially force them to take advantage of the stretch-out.

However, complex rules govern this strategy. If the trust qualifies as a designated beneficiary, as the tax code and the Internal Revenue Service use the term, it can take withdrawals based on the life expectancy of the oldest beneficiary. If the trust does not qualify as a designated beneficiary, it will still receive the money but may be required to take the payout within as little as five years.

To qualify as a designated beneficiary, a trust must meet various criteria contained in IRS regulations. Pitfalls abound, so ask your advisers to design a trust that meets your goals as well as the government criteria. Then make sure you name it on the beneficiary designation form on file with the financial institution that holds your retirement account.

With a Roth, you pay tax when you put money into the account, or when you convert or roll over a traditional account to a Roth. The payoff is that, subject to certain restrictions, no tax is assessed when the money is withdrawn.

But you need to keep the restrictions in mind because, depending on the situation, withdrawals could result in income tax, a 10 percent penalty, or both. You're home free if you have had a Roth account for at least five years and are 59½ or older. In that case none of the withdrawals will be subject to income tax or a penalty. Your heirs are home free if they inherited a Roth IRA and you have had the account for at least five years. They can withdraw the money any time without paying tax or a penalty. The table on the next page summarizes the tax consequences of some other common scenarios.

Even more significantly, with a Roth IRA there is no requirement for you to take yearly minimum distributions once you reach age 70½. That gives you a lot of flexibility. You can take money out of the account if you need it, or let it continue compounding tax-free. This can leave more for your

Rules for Roth Withdrawals

Depending on the situation, withdrawals from a Roth IRA could result in income tax, a 10 percent penalty, or both.

	Income Tax	10 Percent Penalty
You invested directly in a Roth		
• You withdraw contributions before age 59½	No	No
• You withdraw account income before age 59½	Yes	Yes *(certain exceptions apply)*
You converted a traditional IRA to a Roth		
• You withdraw converted funds within the first five years of the conversion	No	Yes *(certain exceptions apply)*
• You withdraw account income within the first five years of the conversion	Yes	Yes *(certain exceptions apply)*
• Beneficiaries withdraw converted funds within the first five years of conversion	No	No
• Beneficiaries withdraw account income within the first five years of the conversion*	Yes	No

*Measured from the year of your opening a Roth account, not from when the beneficiaries inherited it.

Source: Barry C. Picker, CPA/PFS, CFP

beneficiaries if you don't use the money yourself.

Owners of 401(k)s, whether Roth or traditional, must start taking distributions at 70½ unless they are still working for the company. But you can easily avoid this requirement once you leave the company by rolling over the account into a Roth IRA before you reach 70½, or when you retire, if you work past age 70½.

Estate planning benefits of a Roth. By leaving your heirs a Roth account rather than a traditional one, you eliminate the income tax, though not the estate tax. But a Roth can also indirectly save estate taxes, for several reasons.

One is that your money has the potential to continue to grow untaxed and untouched for as long as you live, which may increase the amount that your beneficiaries inherit. And by essentially prepaying the income tax for your heirs, you have in effect made them an enormous gift – and one that the government will not tax.

Finally, the money spent on income tax reduces your overall net worth. Theoretically, then, there will be less money outside of your retirement accounts for the government to tax when you pass away. The bottom line: when you leave your heirs a Roth, you do them a big favor.

Five routes to a Roth. Whether you have the option of a Roth will depend on your personal circumstances. There are five possibilities:

1. Open or invest directly in a Roth IRA. To contribute to a Roth IRA, you must have earned income, not just income from investments. The maximum you can put into the account is $5,000 a year if you are less than 50, and $6,000 if you are 50 or older (annual contributions to traditional IRAs and Roths together can't exceed these limits). You can make these contributions whether or not you participate in a company plan, but income limits apply. At higher income levels, which vary from year to year, the amount you can contribute gets reduced and is ultimately eliminated.

2. Contribute to a Roth 401(k) or 403(b). Although Roths within company plans have been permitted since 2006, it took employers a while to install them. But studies by employee benefits firms show these plans are gaining ground. Your choice of a Roth or a traditional contribution can vary from year to year – you make the election when you fund the plan. Unlike a Roth IRA, no income limits restrict your ability to fund these accounts. Here, too, though,

The Power of a Roth

How much you or your heirs benefit from a Roth conversion will depend on how the investments perform and how long they remain in this tax-free account. The potential is great.

Let's say Harry converts a $100,000 IRA to a Roth. See how much the account could be worth in the future, assuming he lives at least 35 more years and does not make any withdrawals during that time.

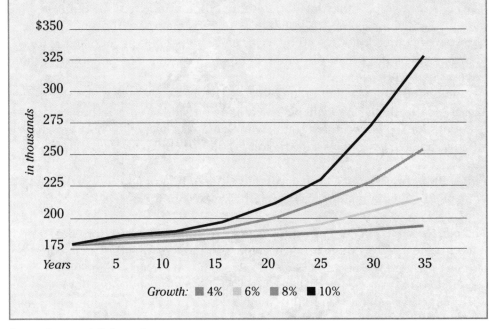

Source: Brentmark Software Inc.

the contribution limits are adjusted for inflation, and vary from year to year.

If you can't foot the whole tax bill, you can make part of your retirement contribution to a Roth and the rest to a traditional account. But you should not do a Roth at all if, for budgetary reasons, it reduces what you can save for retirement. For example, if you have allocated $10,000 for a retirement contribution this year and have a choice between putting $7,000 after-tax dollars into a Roth 401(k), or $10,000 before-tax dollars into a traditional one, you should opt for the latter. Whether you have chosen tax-free or tax-deferred growth, it is better to have $10,000 in a retirement account than $7,000.

3. Convert a traditional IRA to a Roth account. Until recently, you were shut out of this option if your adjusted gross income, modified by adding back in excluded foreign income, foreign-housing deductions and other items, was more than $100,000. Starting in 2010, all taxpayers, regardless of their income or filing status, can do a Roth conversion.

The most painful aspect of the conversion is the price tag. When converting from a traditional IRA to a Roth, you owe income tax on the amount you convert (this can be the entire account balance or part of it). However, if you do the conversion in 2010, the tax law offers two additional benefits. First, you do not have to pay any tax on the conversion for the first year after you make it. Instead, you can choose to pay the tax in two installments – half with your 2011 income tax return and the remainder with the 2012 one.

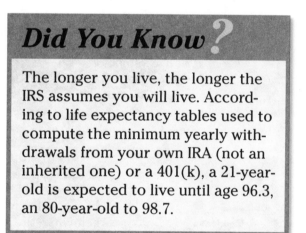

Did You Know ?

The longer you live, the longer the IRS assumes you will live. According to life expectancy tables used to compute the minimum yearly withdrawals from your own IRA (not an inherited one) or a 401(k), a 21-year-old is expected to live until age 96.3, an 80-year-old to 98.7.

4. Roll over your traditional company plan into a Roth IRA. This is a strategy to consider if you are about to change jobs or are approaching retirement. At that point, you can roll the assets directly into a Roth IRA, but you must pay income tax on the account balance. The key question is whether you can afford that toll charge. It is better not to pay those taxes with funds withdrawn from the IRA or other retirement accounts, especially if that would generate yet more tax. And ideally the conversion shouldn't push you into a higher tax bracket.

5. Roll over an inherited traditional company plan into a Roth IRA. Doing the rollover avoids the need to take the money out of the company plan in a lump sum, as most businesses require non-spouses to do – often within five years or less. By rolling the money into an inherited Roth and paying the income tax now, inheritors also avoid income tax on later withdrawals.

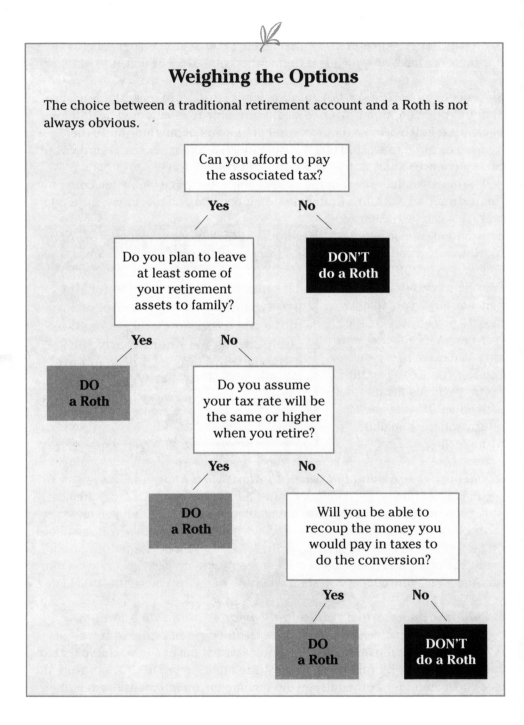

Weighing the Options

The choice between a traditional retirement account and a Roth is not always obvious.

Can you afford to pay the associated tax?

Yes — Do you plan to leave at least some of your retirement assets to family?

No — **DON'T do a Roth**

Yes — **DO a Roth**

No — Do you assume your tax rate will be the same or higher when you retire?

Yes — **DO a Roth**

No — Will you be able to recoup the money you would pay in taxes to do the conversion?

Yes — **DO a Roth**

No — **DON'T do a Roth**

Note that when an estate is subject to federal estate tax, beneficiaries are entitled to an income tax deduction for the portion of the estate tax attributable to an inherited IRA. They can take this deduction whether or not, under the will, they are personally responsible for paying the estate tax. With a traditional IRA, heirs can use the deduction only to offset funds withdrawn in a given year. Those who roll over a company plan into a Roth IRA can take the entire deduction in the year of the conversion. This can greatly reduce the out-of-pocket cost of doing the rollover.

When doing the rollover, spouses have a choice not available to other inheritors. They can either roll the account over into an inherited IRA or into their own IRA. The difference is when they must start making withdrawals. With an inherited IRA, Roth or traditional, distributions must begin by Dec. 31 of the year following the account owner's death unless the spouse who died was younger than 70½. In that case, distributions do not have to begin until the year the spouse would have reached age 70½. In contrast, when you have your own Roth IRA, there is no requirement for lifetime distributions.

Non-spouses who want to do the rollover only have the option of rolling over the inherited company plan into an inherited IRA – not into their own IRA. Therefore, they must begin taking distributions by Dec. 31 of the year following the account owner's death, although they can stretch out these withdrawals over their life expectancy.

The bottom line is that because of the mandatory distribution requirements, you don't get as much benefit from converting an inherited company plan to a Roth IRA as you would from converting an IRA you had set up yourself.

On the other hand, people who inherit retirement assets from a traditional company plan may be better off than those who inherit a traditional IRA from anyone other than a spouse. Why? Because of a quirk in the law, non-spouse beneficiaries of an IRA cannot convert it to a Roth IRA, but those who inherit a company plan can.

❦

Use Retirement Assets to Benefit Charity

Given a choice about how to divide up the assets in their estates, some philanthropically inclined people find it more tax-efficient to give retirement assets to charity and leave their heirs other property. This strategy saves both income taxes and estate taxes. A charity, which is tax-exempt, can draw the funds without paying income tax, and the estate can take a charitable deduction for the amount left to charity.

The simplest way to make the gift is by directly naming the charity on the beneficiary designation form. You can either make the charity a 100 percent beneficiary of the account or indicate that the charity is a beneficiary of a specific percentage of the funds and have the rest go to other beneficiaries.

In certain years, it has also been possible for people 70½ and older to give as much as $100,000 directly from their IRAs to charities during life. This option, known as a charitable IRA rollover, was available during 2006 and 2007. After a nine-month hiatus, Congress extended the law allowing lifetime gifts of IRA assets through Dec. 31, 2009. Under the law, the sum going to charity is not subject to income tax, and the donor may not take a deduction for the donation. Whether the charitable IRA rollover will be extended again is not clear as this book goes to press.

To find out whether these donations are currently allowed, and how to make them, check the updates section of the *Estate Planning Smarts* Web site, www.estateplanningsmarts.com.

So far, IRA funds donated while you are alive cannot be used for contributions to donor-advised funds, supporting organizations or private non-operating foundations. But with donations though an estate plan, you have a wider range of choices when choosing the charitable entity to receive the gift: it can be any organization to which you can make a gift that would qualify as a charitable deduction on your tax return.

Aim for Flexibility

Many people find it difficult to resolve all these issues. Small wonder – it's complicated! A highly effective way to address the situation is to leave your heirs the option of shifting assets after you die through a disclaimer (see Chapter 2). The property would then go to the next person or entity (such as a trust) in line to inherit it.

The key, in all these cases, is to plan whom the primary beneficiary might disclaim to and name those parties as contingent beneficiaries on the beneficiary designation form. Inheritors will be limited by the terms of this form – they can't disclaim to whomever they please.

To-Do List

Give Your Retirement Plan A Checkup

An annual review of your retirement plan can help you spot estate-planning oversights as well as tax-saving opportunities. Consider these issues:

❧ Make sure that all beneficiary designation forms are up to date, and coordinate the transfer of retirement assets with the rest of your estate plan. The forms should include primary and alternate beneficiaries, and should not name your estate as beneficiary. If you have named minors as beneficiaries, make sure assets are left to them either in custody or in trust.

❧ If you want a trust to be the beneficiary of your IRA, ask your advisers to design one that meets various criteria contained in IRS regulations. Then make sure you name the trust on the beneficiary designation form on file with the financial institution that holds your retirement account.

❧ If you send a change-of-beneficiary form to your financial institution, use certified mail and request that it return a copy of the form acknowledging, in writing, its receipt of the change.

❧ Keep copies of all beneficiary designation forms with your will and other important papers.

❧ If you recently changed jobs or retired, roll over your company plan into an IRA (it could save your heirs some hassles later).

❧ Check any powers of attorney you have signed to be sure they cover retirement assets (see Chapter 1). They should authorize someone to make rollovers and choose beneficiaries if you become incapacitated.

Chapter 8

Be Smart About Life Insurance

Read this chapter whether or not you have life insurance.

L ife insurance, in conventional wisdom, is associated with income replacement – to pay the mortgage or foot the bill for college education when the primary breadwinner dies. However, its role in an estate plan may go far beyond that. Insurance can be a tool for paying estate taxes, building a charitable legacy and making lifetime gifts to family go further. Death benefits are typically free of federal income tax and, if you set things up properly, not subject to estate taxes.

In This Chapter...

- ⚜ *Estate Planning Goals That Life Insurance Can Serve*
- ⚜ *Avoiding Estate-Tax Traps*
- ⚜ *Minimizing the Gift-Tax Bite When Funding the Premium*

It is not always necessary to spend a lot of money for coverage. Premiums for the simplest form of insurance – term-life policies, which provide a preset death benefit when you die – have fallen sharply in recent years. Permanent insurance, which combines a death benefit and an investment component, known as the cash value, is more expensive.

A variety of permanent insurance products is available. (For more information, see the "Resources and Further Reading" section in the back of this book.) A major selling point for these policies is that if the cash value of the policy does well, it can be accessed tax-free. But, of course, these investments can also do poorly, just like any other investment. In fact, many of them tanked in the 2008 stock market downturn (and had plenty of company).

The two most important lessons that we can draw from that sorry episode are: don't buy a product that you can't understand and if it sounds too good to be true, it probably is. (Of course, that covers a lot more than life insurance.)

Estate-Planning Goals That Life Insurance Can Serve

The conventional wisdom is that as you get older, it no longer makes financial sense to carry life insurance. The big spending years are behind you, so your expenses are lower. And if you're shopping for a new policy it can be expensive because the premiums are so high – either because of your age or because your medical history makes it hard to qualify for the most favorable rates.

While this may be true, even older people who can afford the premiums buy large amounts of life insurance. No matter what your life stage, insurance provides a source of ready money for a variety of purposes. These include:

Covering the family's living expenses. The death of a key provider can radically alter the financial life of a family. Heirs need cash for current expenses, and raising the necessary funds is not always easy. The estate may be left with such assets as art, restricted stock, family business interests or real estate that can't be readily liquidated. And whatever the assets, there's always the risk that market conditions may not be favorable at the time your family needs the cash. Life insurance avoids the need to liquidate assets simply to pay the bills.

Paying the estate taxes. If your estate is big enough to be subject to state or federal estate tax, the tax is due nine months after you pass away. This is an issue especially for estates made up of illiquid or hard-to-sell assets.

Protecting your business. The death of a business partner or key employee can be devastating to a small business. Life insurance proceeds can be used to meet payroll, fund retirement benefits or cover other expenses until the company bounces back.

Financing buy-sell agreements. Life insurance can also be used in a small business setting to finance buy-sell agreements. In these contracts, partners or co-owners decide in advance what would happen to each of their business interests should various contingencies, including death, occur. This avoids situations where a surviving owner becomes an unwilling partner with the co-owner's heirs.

Instead, partners can agree that the surviving owner has the obligation to buy out the other's share from the estate (a cross-purchase agreement) or that the shares of the owner who died will be sold back to the business (a redemption agreement). With a redemption agreement, the company buys the policy on the owner's life. With a cross-purchase agreement, the owners insure one another individually. Either way, the policy proceeds provide the resources to settle at least part of the purchase price.

Equalizing inheritances. When a business interest accounts for a large portion of an owner's estate, dividing it equitably requires careful planning. Most likely, the owner will want heirs who are actively involved in the business to inherit it but will not want to short-change other family members. If the owner doesn't have other, comparably valued assets (such as stocks, bonds or real estate) to give those who are not involved in the business, life insurance can equalize inheritances.

Did You Know ?

Unmarried couples don't have the benefit of the unlimited marital deduction, which postpones estate tax on assets inherited from each other until the second spouse dies. Life insurance can make up for the tax, which applies to estates worth more than $3.5 million.

Financing charitable giving. You can enhance your philanthropic efforts by donating new or existing life insurance policies to charity. As with most other charitable donations, this entitles you to an income tax deduction for the fair market value of the policy. How you calculate that deduction will depend on whether the policy is new or older, whether it has cash value and whether it is paid up, meaning no further premiums remain to be paid. For tax reasons, if a policy still requires premium payments, it's best to donate funds to the charity and let it pay the premiums.

A tax-efficient way of financing the premiums is to contribute appreciated securities to the charity, which can liquidate them to pay the premiums. In this scenario, you get an income tax deduction, and you avoid the capital gains tax you would have to pay if you sold the assets and donated the proceeds.

Sometimes donors use life insurance to back up a large pledge – for instance, a gift that will be acknowledged with the naming of a building, an endowment or a school within a university. That way, if the donor dies before the pledge is fulfilled, the life insurance proceeds can be used to carry out the donor's intentions.

Funding dynasty trusts. In the growing number of states that permit dynasty trusts – which are designed to pass wealth through multiple generations without incurring estate, gift or generation-skipping transfer taxes (see Chapter 14) – life insurance proceeds can be owned by and payable to the trust, so the proceeds flow into the trust at the insured's death. Typically the trust would pay income to current beneficiaries and allow the principal to grow tax-free for future generations.

Leveraging annual exclusion gifts. Currently, you can give up to $13,000 each year (indexed for inflation) to as many recipients as you would like without incurring a gift tax. Spouses can combine this annual exclusion to jointly give $26,000 to any person tax-free – a practice known as gift-splitting. One way to make these gifts go further is to use the money to buy life insurance. Individual family members can buy the policy directly, using your gifts to pay the premiums. Or, you can make the gift to a trust, which in turn can buy the life insurance. To make such a gift to a trust qualify for the annual exclusion requires special planning and special drafting of the trust.

How does this leverage your gift? Only the money you give your family or put into the trust counts against the annual exclusion – the face value of the policy doesn't matter. And the payoff could be substantial. For a 55-year-old male who qualifies for the most favorable rates, a 20-year term policy with a $2 million death benefit costs approximately $7,000 per year.

Avoiding Estate-Tax Traps

One mistake many people make is to buy a life insurance policy and name themselves as the owner. If you do that, the proceeds will be part of your estate. In that case, those funds are added to everything else you leave behind. If the total is more than $3.5 million, and you've left it to anyone except your spouse or to a charity, it will be subject to estate tax.

Naming your spouse as the beneficiary of a policy you've bought doesn't necessarily solve the problem. True, no estate tax applies when you die because of the unlimited marital deduction – assets inherited from a spouse are not taxed. However, if the total estate, including the insurance proceeds, is worth more than $3.5 million when the surviving spouse dies, the money could be taxable at that time. Special rules apply to spouses who are not U.S. citizens (as noted in Chapter 3).

The best way to avoid estate tax on life insurance proceeds is to have the policy owned by an irrevocable trust. You must not retain any ownership over the assets or the power to change the trust terms. The type of trust used for this purpose is an irrevocable life insurance trust, or ILIT. Typically the ILIT buys the policy and, when you die, holds the proceeds for whomever you've named as beneficiaries. These beneficiaries can be anyone you choose, including your spouse, your partner and children.

Using an ILIT has a number of advantages in addition to saving estate taxes. It can benefit minors, who are not allowed to own the policy directly but only through a custodianship or a trust, and can protect the assets from creditors, ex-spouses and spendthrifts.

Minimizing the Gift-Tax Bite When Funding the Premium

The major challenge when using an ILIT is to figure out how to get money into the trust so it can pay the premiums without your having to pay gift tax. How you do this will depend on the number of beneficiaries, the annual cost and how much you have to contribute. Here are some ways to fund the policy, minimize taxes and leave more money for your heirs.

You have plenty of money and many heirs among whom you want to divide it. Oddly, the more beneficiaries you designate for your ILIT, the easier it is to fund a policy. By using the annual exclusion, you and your spouse can put in $13,000 apiece every year for each trust beneficiary.

If you plan to fund an ILIT with annual exclusion gifts, the trust must give the beneficiaries what are called Crummey powers, and the beneficiaries must receive an annual Crummey notice, sent by you or by the trustee at the time you add the gift to the trust. This gives them the right for a limited time (usually 30 or 60 days) to withdraw from the trust the yearly gift attributable to them. Without providing the beneficiaries Crummey powers, your gift to the trust would be considered a future interest (something beneficiaries can't use right away) rather than a present one and would not qualify for the annual exclusion.

Note that when a beneficiary is disabled, the right of withdrawal – even if unexercised – may cause a reduction or loss of public benefits, because the person may have access to more money than he or she is allowed to have to qualify for state and federal assistance (as noted in Chapter 5). Therefore, when a special needs trust is the beneficiary of an irrevocable life insurance trust or when an irrevocable life insurance trust is written as a special needs trust, you should not give Crummey powers to the disabled beneficiary.

Your choice of trustee is also crucial. It's better not to take on this responsibility yourself, even as a co-trustee, because that might look as though you still own the policy. Even while you are alive, when the main responsibilities are paying the premiums and sending Crummey notices,

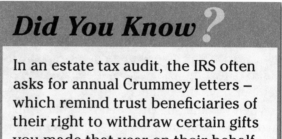

Did You Know?

In an estate tax audit, the IRS often asks for annual Crummey letters – which remind trust beneficiaries of their right to withdraw certain gifts you made that year on their behalf. Without these letters, contributions that might have qualified as tax-free gifts could be subject to tax.

it is better to have professional advisers – such as lawyers, accountants or financial planners – serve as trustees (as noted in Chapter 6). If you start with an individual trustee, you might want to make provisions to involve a corporate fiduciary as co-trustee to invest the proceeds and administer the benefits after you die.

You don't have a lot of heirs, and paying that premium will trigger the gift tax. If the trust owns a large policy, annual exclusion gifts may not be enough to fund the premium. In that case, you can avoid gift tax by lending the money to the trust, rather than making a gift of it. This loan must be documented, and the trust must pay interest at the applicable federal rate, set each month by the Treasury (or interest must accrue at that rate and be paid with the principal at the insured's death). If you have the cash, you can lend it directly. If you don't, you can borrow from a bank and then lend that money to the ILIT. The difference between the interest rate you pay the bank and the IRS-approved rate you get from the trust amounts to a tax-free gift to the trust.

You don't have a lot of cash, but your privately held business is flush.
This is a common situation among entrepreneurs. In this case, your business
can lend money to the trust so it can pay the premium. You can arrange the
loan so that the principal is not due until your death and can be paid out of the
policy proceeds. To help the ILIT finance the yearly interest payments, you can
make annual gifts to the trust.

You have only enough cash to pay part of the premium. Get someone in
the family to share the cost in what's called a split-dollar arrangement. Split
dollar is typically used with permanent insurance. Here's how the arrangement works: you give enough money to the ILIT to pay a portion of the premium, reflecting what a term life insurance policy would cost. Then a family
member pays the balance.

When you die, the trust and the family member typically share the proceeds. The family member, who gets repaid first, must get back either what
was paid out or the cash value of the policy, whichever is greater. Otherwise,
the arrangement would be considered an interest-free loan subject to gift tax.

You are setting up other trusts anyway. This is a terrific opportunity to use
payouts from those trusts to fund the ILIT, with the goal of making it self-sus-
taining. For instance, suppose you place appreciating assets, such as stocks,
into an irrevocable trust and retain the right to receive an annual income for
a preset period. If you're alive at the end of the period, any property left in
the trust (known as a grantor retained annuity trust, or GRAT) could pass to
the insurance trust. (For more about GRATs, see Chapter 16.) For technical
reasons it is not a good tax strategy to fund an ILIT that is a dynasty trust with
this GRAT remainder interest.

Before using a family deal to finance costly life insurance, ask advisers
whether the arrangement can be undone if your circumstances change.
Remember, too, that with any loan transaction, at the end you have to repay
the debt – most likely out of the policy proceeds.

To-Do List

Take an Ounce of Prevention

Certain precautions can help you avoid future hassles or tax pitfalls with life insurance policies.

❧ *Make sure you are not the owner of a life insurance policy that names you as an insured.* If you are, the proceeds could be subject to estate tax. To avoid that situation, set up an irrevocable life insurance trust, or ILIT and have it buy the policy. If you already are the owner of the policy, there are several potential remedies. You can transfer an existing policy to the trust, but if you die within three years of switching it over, the proceeds would generally be included in your estate and would potentially be subject to tax. Another option, with a term policy, is to let the original policy lapse and have the ILIT buy a new one. A third is to create a ILIT and make it a grantor trust (see Chapter 15). Then sell the policy to that trust.

❧ *Examine existing policies to make sure the coverage is adequate and will last as long as necessary.* You will want to be sure the payout is enough for your heirs to meet current expenses and to pay any estate taxes.

❧ *Send Crummey notices to beneficiaries of life insurance trusts funded with annual exclusion gifts each year when you make your annual gift to the trust.* This gives them the right for a limited time (usually 30 or 60 days) to withdraw from the trust the yearly gift attributable to them. Without giving beneficiaries these Crummey powers, your gift to the trust would be considered a future interest (something beneficiaries cannot use right away) and would not qualify for the annual exclusion.

❧ *If a special needs trust is the beneficiary of an irrevocable life insurance trust, or an irrevocable life insurance trust is written as a special needs trust, make sure that you have not given Crummey powers to the disabled beneficiary.* Doing so may cause a reduction or loss of public benefits, because the person may have access to more money than he or she is allowed to have to qualify for state and federal assistance.

Chapter 9

Pay for
Health Care
And Education

Read this chapter if anyone you love
could use help with these expenses,
now or in the future.

With health care and education costs ever on the rise, you'll do your heirs (and anyone else you love) a favor by helping to foot the bills. Fortunately, there are various ways to do this while minimizing income, gift and generation-skipping transfer (GST) taxes.

If your estate could be subject to tax, and you can afford to spend the money now, taking some of these steps can be a highly effective planning tool, because any assets contributed will not be part of your taxable estate. And you may have the pleasure of seeing people benefit from your gifts.

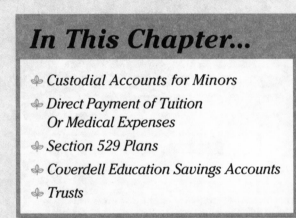

In This Chapter...

- ♣ *Custodial Accounts for Minors*
- ♣ *Direct Payment of Tuition Or Medical Expenses*
- ♣ *Section 529 Plans*
- ♣ *Coverdell Education Savings Accounts*
- ♣ *Trusts*

Should you plan to offer such help on a continuing basis, rather than just temporarily, you will need to put in place a more long-lasting arrangement for those people who may come to depend on your assistance. This provides a safety net in case something happens to you. There are even ways to continue funding these expenses for generations to come.

Some strategies are available either for health or education. Others are limited to education. This chapter will cover both, starting with the least complicated tools that apply to everyone and moving on to more sophisticated methods that require a lawyer's help. You can use these techniques alone or in combination with each other.

Custodial Accounts for Minors

This is the first savings fund that many parents and grandparents set up for young children, typically at a bank, mutual fund company or brokerage house. What makes them appealing – and hugely popular – is that they are simple and inexpensive to open. You put the money in an account for the person you want to benefit, and name an adult as custodian to oversee the funds.

But beware of a common trap associated with these accounts: If you fund the account and also make yourself the custodian, the money plus any appreciation could be subject to estate tax down the line. That could happen if you die before the minor is old enough to take control of the funds. Then, whatever is in the account would be tallied up with everything else you own. If your estate is subject to tax, this account would be, too.

The simplest solution is to make the custodian someone who won't be making contributions to the account. This could be another person whom you trust – one parent might name the other, for example, or a grandparent could name the child's parent. Another possibility is to name a financial institution to act as custodian. Whomever you name, the custodian is a fiduciary, legally obliged to invest the funds wisely and put the child's welfare first.

Under the Uniform Transfers to Minors Act (UTMA), the law that most states have adopted to regulate custodial accounts, the child owns the money as soon as it goes into the account but cannot withdraw it until reaching the age specified under state law. The age generally depends upon whether the funds were placed in the custodial account by gift (see "Gift Tax Basics," page 125) or by some other mechanism (for example, the settlement of a lawsuit). Generally, the age for withdrawal of contributions made by gift is 21.

At that point, these accounts can provide the child, now an adult, with disposable funds. Whether the recipient spends the money on books, a car or a spring break trip to Florida, the responsibility for the money will give her some experience handling her own funds – which is, after all, an important part of growing up. Those who manage well may have cash for larger expenses like the downpayment on a house, seed money for a start-up company or a subsidy for a low-paying first job. Those who deplete the fund by managing it poorly may learn, you may hope, valuable life lessons.

How much is enough for this purpose? That depends on your philosophy about money and lifestyle, as well as your assessment of what the child might need. The larger the balance in a custodial account and the closer children get to the age when they can take control of the funds, the more parents tend to wring their hands about the influx of cash their offspring are about to get. Perhaps they're concerned that instead of using it for tuition, the child will buy a sports car, finance a drug habit or take an extended vacation. Or maybe the pot has grown so large that the young person doesn't have the financial acumen to handle it.

It might be tempting to just take back the money or invest it all in savings bonds with the hope that the child won't find out. But that would violate the UTMA. Children are legally entitled to the money when they reach the specified age. At that point they can claim it – or sue for it if the custodian won't give them account information, for example.

But other strategies can deal with an abundance of riches. Depending on your situation, you might use one of them or a combination, by dividing the custodial account into various buckets.

Did You Know ?

When putting money into a custodial account for a minor, do not name yourself as custodian. If you do name yourself and you die before the minor is old enough to take control of the funds, the money would count as part of your estate and could be taxed.

Spend it down. You can't use these accounts for support obligations (basically food, clothing and shelter), but it's generally safe to apply the funds to what might otherwise be unaffordable extras, such as private school, dance lessons and summer camp.

Invest in a Section 529 plan (see page 127). Although this designates the money for higher education, it does not remove it from the UTMA rubric. Therefore, after reaching the age specified by state law, the child can still take out the money and use it for something else. There is a financial drawback to doing this, though: As with any 529 account, if the money is not used for college, graduate or vocational school, the earnings portion of the withdrawal is subject to income tax and a 10 percent penalty.

Before moving custodial funds into one of these plans, you must create a "custodial 529" – the money can't go into a regular 529 account that may already exist for that child's benefit. In addition, since only cash can go into 529 accounts, it may be necessary to liquidate custodial assets first, which could mean paying tax on any gains.

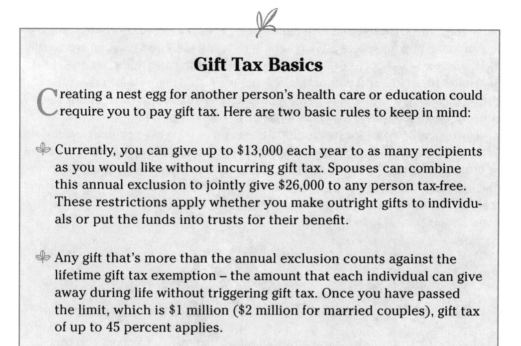

Gift Tax Basics

Creating a nest egg for another person's health care or education could require you to pay gift tax. Here are two basic rules to keep in mind:

❧ Currently, you can give up to $13,000 each year to as many recipients as you would like without incurring gift tax. Spouses can combine this annual exclusion to jointly give $26,000 to any person tax-free. These restrictions apply whether you make outright gifts to individuals or put the funds into trusts for their benefit.

❧ Any gift that's more than the annual exclusion counts against the lifetime gift tax exemption – the amount that each individual can give away during life without triggering gift tax. Once you have passed the limit, which is $1 million ($2 million for married couples), gift tax of up to 45 percent applies.

Invest in an asset that can't readily be converted to cash. Although this maneuver sounds clever, it's potentially fraught with legal problems. Typically it involves a limited partnership that some families use, both for investment and estate planning purposes (see Chapter 16). Here you put property – assume it's publicly traded stock – into a partnership, and then give or sell shares of that partnership to family members. In effect, those shares are illiquid because few people outside the family would want to buy them.

By using custodial funds to buy shares of a family partnership, you make it difficult, if not impossible, for the account holder to liquidate the partnership interests when reaching majority. But you may also subject yourself to a claim that you have breached your fiduciary duty as custodian. Don't try this without good legal advice, and even then be aware of the risks.

Transfer some or all of the money to a Section 2503(c) trust. Some states allow the custodian to do this before the child reaches age 21. Note, however, that a Section 2503(c) trust (discussed more fully on page 132) must still give the child the right to withdraw at age 21 – at least for some reasonable period of time, such as 30 days.

Distribute the UTMA to the child and have the child contribute the money to a trust. If at some point after reaching majority the child is receptive to the idea, the custodian could distribute the assets to the child and have the child distribute them to a trust. Usually the trust is drafted so that until reaching a certain age (say, 30) the child cannot amend or revoke the trust without the consent of someone else (such as a parent).

Gentle persuasion – for instance, "a trust is a good way to protect assets from creditors" (see Chapter 18) – is sometimes enough. Alternatively, a parent or grandparent may agree to add additional funds to the trust if the child complies, so that ultimately the child will get more when the trust ends. Requiring that the trust begin to make some modest annual distributions to the child immediately may also help.

❦

Direct Payment of Tuition or Medical Expenses

This is a terrific estate-planning tool that costs nothing in taxes and that you can easily do yourself. Without using your annual exclusion (see "Gift Tax Basics," page 125), you can pay for tuition, and also for dental and medical expenses of whomever you choose, with no limit on how much you spend. The only condition is that you make the payments directly to the providers of those services (for example, the school, doctor or dentist) and that the expenses not otherwise be reimbursable (for example, by health insurance). For more about the rules as they apply to medical expenses, see Chapter 13.

The tax break only applies to tuition, not to fees, books, supplies, room or board. When financing tuition, you can pay annually or prepay for multiple years, as long as the money goes directly to the educational institution for a particular student and is not refundable or transferable. The risk of prepaying, of course, is that the payments could be forfeited if the student winds up not going to that school or completing his or her education there.

Direct payments can be greatly facilitated by creating an agency account for the purpose. Here's how it works: you open a bank account in your own name and put in enough money to cover the expenses for an extended period of time. Then you give another person a power of attorney (as discussed in Chapter 1) to pay certain bills, such as health and education expenses, from the account. If, because of a physical or mental disability, you are unable to make the payments, that person now has the power to write checks in your name directly to a qualified provider.

Grandparents, in particular, may find this approach more convenient than having bills channeled to them through the child's parents. Instead they can give one of the parents a power of attorney and relieve themselves of the paperwork.

Of course, direct payments can only continue while you are alive. Therefore, as discussed below, it's best to choose an additional funding strategy that can serve as a safety net if you pass away before the individuals you wish to benefit finish school, or if you want to subsidize their health care after you're gone.

Section 529 Plans

Qualified state tuition programs, which can be used for higher education, are available in all states and the District of Columbia. You need not use the program offered by your home state, although sometimes there are benefits to doing so, such as the ability in some states to take a state income tax deduction for your contributions. (No matter which 529 program you choose, there is no federal income tax deduction for your contributions.)

Named for the Internal Revenue Code section that permits them, these plans allow you to set up a separate account for each family member whom you want to benefit. A private money manager chosen by each state typically manages the funds but you can select among different investment options. Withdrawals from a 529 account are federal-tax exempt provided the money is used to pay for college or graduate school. Other details of the plans, including the maximum amount you can contribute, and the investment options, vary by state.

Federal law allows you to contribute to these plans up to the annual exclusion amount (see "Gift Tax Basics," page 125). The law also permits lump-sum deposits of as much as $65,000 per person at once ($130,000 for married couples), but you must file a gift-tax return electing to treat the gift as if it had been spread over five years. During this five-year period, you cannot make additional annual exclusion gifts to the person you are benefiting with the 529 plan. If you die before the five-year period is up, part of gift, reflecting the number of years still to go, will be included in your estate.

An attractive feature of these plans (which makes them different from UTMA accounts) is that you can be the account owner and retain some con-

Simple Ways to Help Out

Without any fancy estate planning, or even a lawyer's assistance family members can help each other enormously with medical and tuition expenses. Imagine a well-off couple with two adult children, both of whom are married, and four grandchildren. Here are some simple steps they can take in a single year without having to pay gift tax.

Type of gift	Amount	Total recipients	Total, this type of gift
Lump-sum deposit in 529 plan for each grandchild	$130,000*	4	$520,000
College tuition for grandchildren (paid directly to school)	$50,000	2	$100,000
Private school tuition for grandchildren (paid directly to school)	$25,000	2	$50,000
Health insurance for each family (paid directly to insurer)	$15,000	2	$30,000
Total tax-free gifts:			*$700,000*

Counts as an annual exclusion gift (see "Gift Tax Basics," page 125), spread over five years. During this time, the couple can't make any additional annual exclusion gifts to these grandchildren.

trol over the funds. For example, if the family member you initially planned to benefit can't use the money (perhaps because he or she received a scholarship), you can easily change the beneficiary to someone who is a family member of the original beneficiary. However, if the new beneficiary is in a subsequent generation to the old one, there may be gift-tax consequences.

128

Federal rules limit how frequently the account owner can change beneficiaries and investment options.

Should you end up needing the money yourself, any earnings that are withdrawn are subject to income tax and a 10 percent penalty.

These single-purpose vehicles can work well both for parents and grandparents (contributions are exempt from generation-skipping transfer tax because they qualify for the annual exclusion), but some people find them too restrictive. A key disadvantage is that you must contribute cash. If you need to sell investments to obtain that cash, you may have to pay capital gains tax. Also, while you can choose among several investment alternatives when you set up the plan and alter the strategy once a year, you'll have far more latitude if you set up a trust that gives a trustee investment authority.

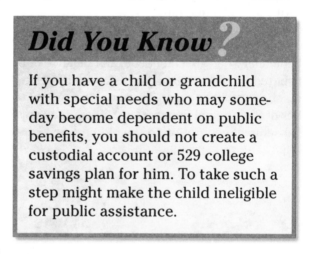

Did You Know?

If you have a child or grandchild with special needs who may someday become dependent on public benefits, you should not create a custodial account or 529 college savings plan for him. To take such a step might make the child ineligible for public assistance.

How well do these 529 accounts perform? That depends on what the manager has invested in, the overall markets and the fees charged. Fees can vary dramatically from plan to plan and can be difficult to understand. Generally, the fees are lower for plans you can invest in directly, without going through a broker or financial planner.

❧

Coverdell Education Savings Accounts

These accounts, sometimes referred to as education IRAs, can pay for any level of schooling. You can set up a separate account for any family member younger than 18, even if you also fund a 529 plan for that person. A beneficiary can have more than one Coverdell account, but total yearly contributions for his or her benefit can't be more than $2,000.

Income limitations may restrict your ability to fund these accounts, however. Allowable contributions are phased out for single people whose adjusted gross income (AGI) is $95,000 to $110,000 and for married couples filing a joint return with an AGI of $190,000 to $220,000. Parents or grandparents who don't meet the income requirements can give $2,000 to each family member they want to benefit so those relatives can each set up their own Coverdell account.

Funds in the account are not taxed if they are used to pay for education expenses, including tuition, books, supplies, and room and board. Unless the beneficiary has special needs, any balance in the account must either be distributed (subject to income tax and a 10 percent penalty) when the individual reaches age 30 or rolled over into an account to benefit another family member of the original beneficiary. Gift tax may apply if the new beneficiary is in a subsequent generation to the old beneficiary.

Trusts

Although trusts are more complicated than other methods for financing health care and education, generally speaking they offer more flexibility. The table on the opposite page summarizes some key differences between trusts and other education funding tools.

Still, from a tax perspective two hurdles must be overcome when funding a trust:

❧ Unless you plan to use part of the $1 million lifetime exemption, make sure any contributions to the trust qualify for the annual exclusion, so they will not be subject to a gift tax of up to 45 percent (see "Gift Tax Basics," page 125).

❧ Plan for the onerous 45 percent generation-skipping transfer (GST) tax that could apply (on top of any gift tax) if the trust benefits grandchildren.

Overcoming hurdle No. 1

To come within the annual exclusion, a gift must be a present interest rather than future interest (something beneficiaries can't use right away). There are two ways that gifts to trusts can meet this requirement. By far the

Trusts and Other Funding Tools – Key Differences

Direct Payments	529 Plans	Coverdell Accounts	Trusts
Assets that can be used/Maximum funding			
Cash/ No limit	Cash/Varies by state	Cash/$2,000 per year per beneficiary	Many types of assets/ No limit
Who can benefit			
Any person	Initial beneficiary or certain family members*	Initial beneficiary or certain family members*	Any person covered by the trust
Expenses you can pay			
Tuition, and medical, dental and other health expenses, cost of health insurance	"Qualified higher education expenses," including tuition, fees, books and supplies and, under certain circumstances, room and board†	Tuition, fees, books, supplies and other "qualified education expenses" for elementary, secondary and higher education	Expenses permitted under the trust document

These relatives of the beneficiary are: spouse, son, daughter, stepchild, foster child, adopted child, or a descendant of any of them; brother, sister, stepbrother or stepsister, and father or mother or ancestor of either; stepfather or stepmother; son or daughter of a brother or sister; brother or sister of father or mother; son-in-law, daughter-in-law, father-in-law, mother-in-law, brother-in-law or sister-in-law; spouse of any individual listed above; first cousin. For Coverdell accounts any new beneficiary must be under age 30 unless she has special needs.

†*For 2010, certain costs for computers, software and internet access qualify.*

most popular is to give beneficiaries Crummey powers: the right for a limited time, usually 30 or 60 days, to withdraw from the trust the yearly gift attributable to that beneficiary (see "Crummey Fundamentals," page 83). Any trust that includes this power is called a Crummey trust, although depending on the type of trust it may be named for its other distinguishing features.

To avoid these potential pitfalls, some lawyers take another tack – meeting the present interest requirement through a Section 2503(c) trust. This irrevocable trust is relatively straightforward and inexpensive to set up (maximum cost: $3,000 to $5,000), but it has some of the same drawbacks as an UTMA account. These trusts must have only one beneficiary, the trust must give the beneficiary the right to withdraw the assets at age 21, there must be no restriction on the right of the trustee to make distributions of principal and interest before that, and the trust must be includable in the beneficiary's estate if the beneficiary dies.

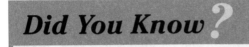

Did You Know?

You can't use custodial accounts for support obligations (basically food, clothing and shelter), but it's generally safe to apply the funds to what might otherwise be unaffordable extras for the child whom it benefits, such as private school, dance lessons and summer camp.

Although this type of trust may sound no better than a custodial account because minors can gain access to the trust assets at 21, lawyers have added an embellishment that reduces the problem: they give the child a window of opportunity – usually 30 or 60 days – to terminate the arrangement, and if the beneficiary doesn't withdraw the funds at 21, the trust continues for a preset number of years.

With this provision, the money is less accessible than it would be with an UTMA account. In other words, a child who doesn't act within the limited time frame must wait for the money. In contrast, with a custodial account, once they have reached the magic age they can claim it any time.

What's more, as a beneficiary approaches 21, you can encourage this young person to leave the money in the trust, with the understanding that he or she will probably get something in your will besides. A smart child will take the hint.

Overcoming hurdle No. 2

Another tax issue comes up when making gifts to trusts that could benefit grandchildren or more remote descendants. Right now, each of us can give away $3.5 million during life or at death without paying generation-skipping transfer tax. The tax applies, on top of any gift or estate tax, once this exemption is used up.

Ordinarily, when putting money into the trust, you would need to apply or allocate your GST exemption to whatever the gift amount was. But you can avoid that requirement if all contributions to the trust qualify for the annual exclusion, and you are putting the money into a special kind of trust that generally does not give rise to GST tax.

Section 2642(c) of the Internal Revenue Code describes the requirements for this trust. It must be irrevocable, can benefit only one grandchild and the trust document must specify that if the grandchild dies before the funds have been fully distributed, the remaining funds become part of the grandchild's estate (making them potentially subject to estate tax at that point).

Trusts created under this section of the code and funded with annual exclusion gifts let you save the GST exemption to use in other ways. But because these trusts can only benefit one grandchild per trust, they are not appropriate for people who want the grandchild's parents to receive benefits under the trust before the funds get distributed to the grandchild. They are also not suitable when you want to shift assets among your grandchildren.

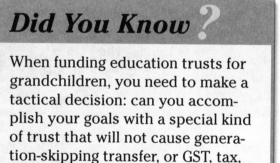

Did You Know?

When funding education trusts for grandchildren, you need to make a tactical decision: can you accomplish your goals with a special kind of trust that will not cause generation-skipping transfer, or GST, tax, so you can save the $3.5 million GST exemption for other gifts?

For a discussion of using the GST exemption to set up a trust for multiple grandchildren, see Chapter 14.

If you want to benefit multiple generations without using up GST exemption, there is another option, but it's considerably more complex and expensive. It's called a Health and Education Exclusion Trust, or HEET (minimum cost: $3,000 to $5,000).

To escape the GST, the HEET must incorporate two features. First, the trust must make payments directly to the schools (or, in a less common use of these trusts, to health care providers). The second requirement is rather quirky. A HEET must have a charity as a co-beneficiary. There's a technical reason for this arrangement. If grandchildren were the only beneficiaries of the trust, eventually it would be subject to the GST. By including a charity as a beneficiary, you make sure that doesn't happen.

No law spells out the terms of a HEET. Lawyers craft it based on their interpretation of tax law, and the Internal Revenue Service has not challenged it in court. One gray area is how much of the trust distributions the charity should get. Some lawyers think half the trust's annual income is a reasonable amount.

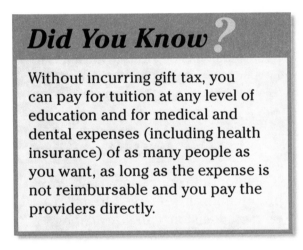

Did You Know ?

Without incurring gift tax, you can pay for tuition at any level of education and for medical and dental expenses (including health insurance) of as many people as you want, as long as the expense is not reimbursable and you pay the providers directly.

Within this basic framework are many variations. In states that permit dynasty trusts the trust can go on in perpetuity (see Chapter 14). If there's extra money and no one left to educate, the trust can authorize that the remaining balance be divided between family and charity. At that point, distributions to grandchildren and their descendants would be subject to GST, since the funds are no longer directly paying for education. Conversely, to avoid a shortfall in a growing family, principal can be used to pay tuition, and assets could be added to the trust as long as charity continues to receive its distribution each year.

While you are alive, the simplest way to help with health and education expenses – and avoid gift and generation-skipping transfer taxes – is to write a check directly to the school or medical provider. By relying on trusts and other tools you can leave a more lasting legacy.

To-Do List

Mix and Match Education Funding Techniques

Which education funding tools you choose will depend on a variety of factors. Here are some questions to ask, and action to take if you answer "yes":

❧ *Do you have a lot of cash on hand – perhaps because you just sold a business or investment?*
Action: Use some of those funds to prepay tuition and make a five-year lump-sum contribution to a 529 plan.

❧ *Are the people you want to help already in school?*
Action: Make direct payments of tuition, and consider setting up trusts or 529 plans in case you pass away before they graduate.

❧ *If the nest egg you're creating isn't needed for education (perhaps because the beneficiary gets a scholarship), would you like the money to be available to cover post-graduation expenses?*
Action: Set up a trust that leaves open the possibility.

❧ *Is there so much money in your child's custodial account that it might reduce his or her motivation to get an education and work?*
Action: Take various steps, within the framework of the law, to spend down or divide the account.

❧ *Do you want to set up a Coverdell Education Savings account but can't because your income is too high?*
Action: Give $2,000 to family members you want to benefit so each can set up his or her own Coverdell account.

Chapter 10

Home Base: Factoring In Real Estate

*Read this chapter if you own your
primary residence or vacation home
or might move to a different state.*

Our homes provide the setting for much our lives. We've watched children grow from toddlers who could barely stand to young adults who tower over us. We've endured renovations to make homes more our own, dug in the garden, solved problems at the dining room table, whispered in the darkness. Letting go or moving on can sometimes tug at our heartstrings. And passing along real estate to heirs poses financial challenges as well. Often a primary residence or a vacation home is one of the largest assets in an estate. It may be difficult to use the $3.5 million estate tax exemption without applying it to the roof overhead. This poses special concerns for couples (as

In This Chapter...

- ❧ *Giving Away Partial Interests*
- ❧ *Putting Your House in a Trust*
- ❧ *Passing Down a Vacation Home*
- ❧ *Donating a House to Charity*
- ❧ *Choosing a State of Residence*

discussed in Chapters 3 and 4). Different complications arise when you are dealing with any valuable real estate that you plan on leaving to family members. An important question is whether they want to keep the property. If not, and it's promptly sold, the cost basis will be adjusted to its value on your date of death (or in some cases an alternate date six months later). This can reduce or eliminate the need to pay capital gains tax. But if a sale would bring your estate above the exemption amount and trigger tax you might have been better off using various lifetime tools to reduce the tax bite.

How you incorporate this asset into your estate plan will depend on a variety of factors, including the type of property, your finances and whom you want to benefit. If you're contemplating a change of residence in the near future, that, too, should enter into the equation.

Giving Away Partial Interests

This very simple way of transferring real estate during life can make the most of the annual exclusion – the $13,000 ($26,000 for married couples) that we can each give every year to as many recipients as we would like without incurring a gift tax. The strategy also packs more value into the $1 million lifetime exemption from gift tax that applies to gifts above the annual exclusion.

How does giving away partial interests make the gift limits go further? These interests are considered fractional shares. Since the gift recipient gets just a partial interest, the value of what's transferred can be substantially discounted, because the partial interest is not a controlling interest: The recipient can't act unilaterally and is yoked together with other interest holders.

You can make gifts of fractional shares all at once (for example, if you were giving various people an interest in the same property) or over time (the most likely approach if there was only one recipient). Meanwhile, each part-owner must pay his or her share of property taxes, insurance and repairs on the property.

This approach can work well in a variety of situations. Suppose you and your spouse bought an inexpensive place for your son to live in while he was in college, and he plans to stay on after graduation. Through a series of combined annual exclusion gifts worth $26,000, the two of you can gradually make him the owner of the property without having to pay gift tax.

Just remember that you need to get a professional appraisal at the time you make the first transfer, with follow-up appraisals if the value of the property has changed when you make subsequent gifts. But if you straddle two years by making your annual exclusion gifts in December and again in January, you can rely on the same appraisal for both.

If you want to benefit various people you can avoid squabbles by making your gifts to a trust that will benefit all of them, and choose a trustee (as discussed in Chapter 6) to oversee the property management. Under this arrangement, you and your spouse together can contribute an interest worth up to $26,000 per year for each trust beneficiary. Another possibility is to put the real estate into an entity such as a family limited partnership or limited liability company, and sell or give away shares in the entity that holds the property – not in the real estate itself (see Chapter 16). You can make these transfers to individuals directly or to a trust that benefits them.

One thing you should *not* do is put your home into such an entity or give away a partial interest in the house and continue to live in it rent free. The tax code says that if you give something away but retain the right to use it, the property is still considered part of your estate. Therefore, it could be subject to tax.

Putting Your House in a Trust

The qualified personal-residence trust, or QPRT, is a tool to consider if you are still living in a house, but plan to leave it to your heirs, either for their own use or so they can sell it. The QPRT (pronounced "CUE-pert") removes part of the value of a costly home from the estate and shelters future appreciation. You just have to win a bet that you can escape the grim reaper for a specified time: the longer the period, the greater the potential tax savings.

Here's how the arrangement works: You put your primary residence or vacation home into an irrevocable trust, retaining the right to live there rent-free for a specified number of years. During that time the trust, of which you could be trustee, owns the property. When the period ends, ownership can pass to the beneficiaries, usually children, or go into another trust, often called a dropdown trust, for the rest of your life. Meanwhile, the QPRT has removed both the property and any future appreciation from the estate. Because the trust freezes the house at its fair market value when it's transferred to the QPRT, no additional tax is due after that.

The immediate attraction of the QPRT is that it discounts the value of the gift and makes the $1 million lifetime exemption from gift tax go further, or produces a lower tax bill if you have exceeded that limit (there's a gift tax of up to 45 percent). For gift-tax purposes, the value of the QPRT reflects the value of the right to acquire the personal residence (the remainder) a certain number of years from when it is set up (the trust term), discounted by the probability that the person setting up the trust (the grantor) will live that long.

Because of the discount, the QPRT can work well even if the property does not increase in value. For example, if you put a $1 million house in a QPRT and the value of the gift is $600,000, but the house later drops in value to $800,000, you will have still removed $200,000 in value from your estate.

Figuring the discount involves a complex actuarial calculation based on a rate set each month by the U.S. Treasury called the Section 7520 rate (named after a section of the Internal Revenue Code). The latest Section 7520 rates are available at www.tigertables.com. The higher the rate and the longer the term, the bigger the discount and the more savings associated with the QPRT.

Let's say Sally, who is 60, has a net worth of $5 million, including a $1 million home that she wants to put into a 10-year QPRT. Assuming a Section 7520 rate of 4 percent, the transferred property would be valued at $576,840 for gift-tax purposes. Extend the term to 15 years and the discounted value drops to $409,250.[1]

The discounted value of the house in the trust will count against Sally's lifetime limit. Say she makes the transfer and still has at least $576,840 ($409,250 for a 15-year trust) of her credit left. In that case, she won't have to pay any federal gift tax.

Who might want to do a QPRT? This estate-planning tool could work well for a healthy homeowner who plans to retire to a different location in 10 or 15 years. Another possible trust candidate is someone with a vacation retreat that she wants to keep in the family (more about that on page 144). Note, by the way, that in the eyes of the Internal Revenue Service, a boat or a recreational vehicle counts as

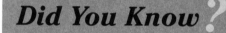

Did You Know?

State tax authorities are on the lookout for people who leave their home state for long-term medical or geriatric care. Even if you keep a house in the place where you have been living and hope to return, if you go into a nursing home, certain states will pursue income and estate taxes.

a personal residence and can be put into a QPRT provided it has cooking and toilet facilities and you've used it for more than 14 nights in a year or more than 10 percent of the time you rent it out (whichever is greater).

The QPRT is especially attractive for people with a significant portion of their wealth tied up in a personal residence. Someone with a home worth $1 million and other investments totaling $4 million might not want to give away investment assets to reduce the taxable estate: she needs to live on the income. A QPRT enables her to reap a substantial estate-tax savings without disturbing her portfolio.

[1]*Lawrence P. Katzenstein, Tiger Tables Actuarial Software*

There is one big catch, however: For a QPRT to work, you must outlive the trust term. If you don't, the property is included in your estate, at its value on your date of death, and is potentially subject to estate tax. If you used part of your $1 million lifetime gift tax exemption to make the gift to the trust, that exemption gets restored, so that the $3.5 million estate tax exemption will not be reduced by the amount of that gift (it would be if you survived the QPRT term). If you exceeded your lifetime exemption and paid gift tax when setting up the trust, your estate can deduct whatever federal gift tax you paid.

One way to hedge your bets is to form multiple qualified personal-residence trusts with staggered terms, just as you might fill a portfolio with bonds of different maturity dates. As long as you outlast one of the trust terms, at least part of the property will be removed from the estate. The law allows you to place two residences into separate QPRTs and also to divide each property among an unlimited number of trusts. So one course might be to put your primary home in a 15-year trust and the vacation hideaway in a 10-year trust. Or you could set up four trusts on the primary home, assigning one-fourth of its value to each (or perhaps taking a partial interest discount) and setting the terms at 5, 10, 15 and 20 years.

> ## Did You Know?
>
> The IRS defines a "dwelling" broadly. A mobile home, a boat or a trailer qualify, as long as it provides sleeping accommodations, a toilet and cooking facilities – and you've used it in a year for more than 14 nights or 10 percent of the time you rent it (whichever is greater).

So what happens once the trust ends? One possibility is to lease the house from the family members who will then own it. Another, which is preferable, is to have the property go to a drop-down trust and lease it from that trust.

Either way, it's important that you pay rent at fair market rates, or the IRS might decide after you die that you retained an interest in the property. Should that happen, the house would be included in your estate and taxed at its value when you die. Beware: If rents go up dramatically in the area where the house is situated, you need to be sure you can still afford the tab.

Any trust that picks up where the QPRT ends should be structured as a grantor trust, meaning that the person who sets it up retains certain rights or powers. The attraction of grantor trusts is that they're not treated as separate taxable entities (see Chapter 15). That means the trust pays no tax on the rent it receives from the grantor once the QPRT term ends. And provided the rent is at fair market value, there's no gift tax, either.

In effect, you can use this trust to transfer additional money in excess of the annual exclusion gifts to family members tax-free. It's even possible to use an irrevocable life insurance trust (as discussed in Chapter 8) as the drop-down trust from a QPRT, in which case the rent money could finance the premium on a life insurance policy.

Another huge benefit of this type of trust is that if it sells the property, the transaction is treated as a sale by the grantor. Therefore it qualifies for the same tax break that is available to homeowners if they sell their principal residence: The first $250,000 ($500,000 for married couples) of capital gain is not subject to tax if you have lived in the house for at least two of the five years before the sale.

All these features of the drop-down grantor trust should make the QPRT more palatable for people who have reservations about it. The children don't own the house at this point – the drop-down trust does – and the setup isn't really going to change your lifestyle. The trust can even require that the property be rented back to the grantor, so long as he pays rent at the fair market value. With a trustee at the helm, you don't have to worry about being evicted by your own offspring. In fact, they don't even have to know about the QPRT until after you die.

But be careful about this: A drop-down trust that passes property to children when the grantor dies should contain a specific provision to cover the contingency of a child dying during the trust term. A trust that says grandchildren will get the parent's share could subject the transfer to generation-skipping transfer tax on top of any estate tax (see Chapter 14). This rule doesn't apply if the grandchild is orphaned before the trust is created. Generation-skipping transfer tax – a whopping 45 percent – applies to gifts or bequests to grandchildren of more than $3.5 million. So a better course is not to give grandchildren orphaned during the trust term a share in this particular property but to make it up to them in the will; property can be left through your estate plan without a generation-skipping transfer tax if the grandchild's parents have died.

What if you want to sell the house before the QPRT ends? The easiest course is to roll over all the proceeds into another residence. Things get more cumbersome if you don't buy another home or if you purchase a less costly one. The trust must cover either possibility by providing the grantor an annuity from the sale proceeds each year until the trust expires. (An extensive discussion of the grantor retained annuity trust, or GRAT, appears in Chapter 16.)

Alternatively, the trust could provide that the part that would have gone to the annuity trust will go to the grantor instead. (The trust can give the trustee the power to decide which of these happens.)

Among the situations in which a QPRT might not be appropriate is when the house has markedly appreciated and the heirs plan to sell it right away. In that case they could be hit with a substantial capital gains tax. Here's why: By receiving ownership through the QPRT, the heirs aren't entitled to the adjustment in basis they would get if property passed through the estate. Instead, their cost basis in the property equals what you originally paid for the home plus the cost of subsequent improvements, with an adjustment for any gift tax paid in the transfer. Presumably, that basis is much smaller than the sale price would be.

In such cases, advisers should run the numbers to see whether the 15 percent capital gains tax wipes out any estate tax savings achieved through the QPRT. Children who plan to use the house as a primary residence for at least two of the five years before selling it can exempt $250,000 of the profits from selling ($500,000 for married couples filing jointly).

Passing Down a Vacation Home

Whether it's a cottage on the Pacific or a château in France, the vacation home you think is a dream legacy might turn into a nightmare for your heirs. Find out whether they cherish the idea of keeping the property in the family as much as you do. They're not ingrates if they don't – they just have different interests or priorities and lives of their own.

If you don't get a firm answer, the simplest approach is to leave the property to the estate and give family members a right of first refusal to buy it. You can limit that option to, say, six or nine months, and give a preference to people who want to purchase the house as a group.

Even if younger generations are enthusiastic about the house, it's better not to make them joint owners. Instead, leave the property to an independent entity, such as a trust, or put it into a limited liability company and give the heirs shares in the enterprise (see Chapter 16). For tax reasons, property should not be placed in a corporation.

Whatever the vehicle, an even bigger issue than estate taxes is: How is the family going to be able to afford to keep this property intact? Some

Good Housekeeping

If you want to create a qualified personal-residence trust, you have a few housekeeping matters to address first. Because most mortgages have due-on-transfer clauses, it's best to pay off an outstanding mortgage, or, if you can't or choose not to, to get the bank's blessing for the QPRT. Otherwise, the principal portion of each payment made after the trust is in effect will count as a taxable gift, which could be an accounting nuisance and will require you to file an annual gift-tax return (see Chapter 13).

You should also have the house appraised, change the name on the property insurance policy and be sure the insurer will cover the home once it's in a trust. In states with special benefits for homeowners, such as homestead laws protecting a person's house from creditors (see Chapter 18) or tax breaks for the elderly, you may lose those benefits by putting property into a trust.

benefactors set up an endowment funded with cash, securities, business interests or the proceeds of a life insurance policy. If you can't cover the expenses forever, you might just leave enough money to take care of a year or two and permit heirs to buy out each other or sell the property to a third party after that.

The more owners and the longer that family ownership lasts, the more organization that is necessary. You may want to put the basic governing framework in place and leave your heirs to work out day-to-day details like choosing a caretaker, allocating time slots and resolving inevitable disparities in how much people use the house. These are some issues for you to consider:

❧ Who sits on the governing body and what is the mechanism for it to make decisions?

❧ Which decisions rise to the level of requiring a vote by the governing body (perhaps capital expenditures of a certain amount) and which do not and could be made by whoever is in residence at the time, or discussed more informally (emergency repairs, for example, or basic maintenance)?

❧ What will happen if a family owner dies, gets divorced or declares bankruptcy?

The Sedgwick Legacy

A Federal-style house in Stockbridge, Mass. built by Theodore Sedgwick, a senator, congressman and judge, has remained in his family for more than 200 years, and recent generations have creatively funded its upkeep. Several family members bought the house from a cousin in 1940 for a nominal sum and put it in a trust to benefit all Sedgwick descendants.

Since then, bequests and lifetime gifts from family members have supplied its primary endowment, while a member of the Sedgwick family who works in the arts has occupied it. In exchange for a reasonable rent, this tenant is responsible for maintaining the house and the family graveyard nearby, hosting family weddings and funerals, and booking visits by other Sedgwicks who can spend weekends and vacations in the guest wing.

- What is the procedure for selling or transferring shares? (Limiting it to your descendants rules out ownership by people who marry into the family.)
- In a buyout, how will the price be determined? (The possibilities range from having other family members pay the full share of the appraised value to imposing a discount and installment payment plan.)
- How many owners must agree before the entire property can be sold?

Donating a House to Charity

Charities are becoming more flexible about the kinds of donations they will accept, and real estate is the most popular type of gift besides cash and marketable securities. You can make these gifts during your life or through your estate plan.

Most likely the charity will sell the property and apply the proceeds to a philanthropic use. For example, the money could go into a donor-advised fund account so that you or members of your family can recommend grants. Or it could be used to fund a charitable remainder trust that will pay an income stream to you or your family and ultimately benefit charity (both these tools are discussed at length in Chapter 17). Before putting the house in the trust, you must move out, or you would violate the rules against self-dealing.

Donating real estate to charity, rather than selling the property and contributing the proceeds, offers significant financial advantages. Whether the donation is during life or through your estate plan, there is no capital gains tax on any appreciation in the property. If done through your estate plan, your estate is entitled to a charitable deduction that can reduce the tax it owes. With lifetime donations, you can deduct the fair market value of the property donated to a public charity, up to 30 percent of your adjusted gross income. (As discussed in Chapter 17, if you elect to limit your deduction to basis for all contributions made in a given tax year, you can deduct up to 50 percent.) Any deduction that can't be taken in the year of the donation – for instance, if your contribu-

> ## *Did You Know* ?
>
> If you change your home state it's important to pull up roots and establish new ones. Otherwise, if your former state has an income tax or estate tax, it may chase you, or your estate, for taxes. In a worst-case scenario, you could wind up owing taxes to two states.

tion exceeds the limit on charitable deductions – can be carried forward up to five years.

Most charities prefer that the property not be mortgaged because, depending on the nature of the real estate, the term of the note and the charitable vehicle used, the gift could run afoul of various tax law restrictions. In addition, just as if it were purchasing the property, the nonprofit must check for liens and be sure there are no environmental hazards that would carry cleanup obligations under federal law (see Chapter 17 for a discussion of these and other real estate issues). And since the property will generally be sold, the value must be high enough that the charity is willing to devote the effort and resources to marketing it.

Donations of real estate can take a variety of forms and must meet certain requirements. If you are considering a lifetime donation, think about these two key issues:

Do you want to continue using the property? By donating a remainder interest, you and your spouse can reserve the right to use the home for your lifetimes and have it pass to charity when you die. This technique removes the property from your taxable estate, and you get an income tax deduction for the actuarial value of charity's remainder interest, based on the ages and number of the life beneficiaries (the older you are, the larger the deduction), the value of the property and the Section 7520 rate.

Most charities insist that donors who participate in these arrangements pay all maintenance costs, taxes and insurance. Home improvements, like updating a kitchen or renovating a barn, require the charity's consent, but you can get an additional charitable deduction for these enhancements based on a similar actuarial calculation. If need be, you can even sell the house during your life and split the proceeds with the charity according to its actuarial interest at the time of the sale. All these subjects should be covered in a co-ownership agreement.

Another variation on the theme that is attractive to people who can use extra cash is to donate the remainder interest in exchange for a gift annuity. (Charitable gift annuities are discussed in Chapter 17.)

Are you ready to sell the house? If so, selling the house through a charitable remainder trust can be a highly effective diversification strategy. Since the trust is a tax-exempt entity, it doesn't pay tax when it sells the asset, so you save the capital gains tax you would otherwise have to pay on a home that has appreciated. You can structure the trust to pay income to you and your spouse for the rest of your lives or for a term of up to 20 years, before the remainder goes to charity. In addition, you get a current income tax deduction based on the current value of the charity's remainder interest.

The best type of charitable remainder trust to use for this purpose is what's called a flip unitrust. Such a trust can be set up so that there's no requirement for the trust to make any payouts until it sells the property. But beware this potential trap: When you have a binding obligation to sell any noncash asset, including real estate, before giving it to charity, the prearranged-sale rule forces you to pay tax on the gain. Here, too, you must move out of the house before you put it in the trust or you will violate the rules against self-dealing.

Choosing a State of Residence

Your choice of domicile – legal lingo for the place you call home – affects your finances in various ways. For people who divide their time between two or more states, saving income taxes has long been a motivation for choosing one state, rather than the other, as a place of residence. Your choice of residence can also have an impact on financial aspects of your estate plan. While that may not be enough to cause you to move, all other things being equal, you might make your domicile in a more financially friendly state.

Once you have decided where you want to live, you need to sever contacts with the old state and establish ties that bind you to the new one. Otherwise, you may not be able to take advantage of the benefits of the state you are moving to, and your former state may claim you're still a resident and chase you (or your estate) for taxes. In a worst-case scenario, you could wind up owing taxes to two states.

How do people get caught? Having what's known as source income in the former state, such as rent from a piece of property you own there, is one way. Another is by selling a business shortly after moving, say, from a state that has an income tax to one without. Tax authorities could notice that the federal tax return for the year of the departure, which includes the sale, reports much more income than the one from the former state.

Continuing to own real estate in a place with estate tax could hurt you, too. Typically that would require a nonresident estate tax return to be filed (for a way around this, see page 150). Some states have a domicile questionnaire that must be attached, aimed at ferreting out proof that you were, in fact, a resident. Depending on the state, it may ask about everything from dates of club memberships to whether you were in a nursing home, rented a safe deposit box or were buried in the state. If you haven't kept good records, the family member or personal representative who completes the form may not have the necessary information.

It is therefore important to understand how state law can affect the bottom line and plan any moves carefully. These are some issues that may be affected.

Asset protection. State law has a huge impact on the extent to which various assets are protected from creditors – a category that may include everyone from disgruntled spouses and ex-spouses to people who win law-suits against you. Deadbeats, scam artists and people running from their debts have given asset protection a bad name. Even so, this subject has moved into the mainstream of estate planning – and rightfully so (asset pro-tection is discussed in depth in Chapter 18). Various state-law exemptions are the first line of defense against creditors who try to reach your money and property.

State estate tax. Although very few states have gift tax (Colorado and North Carolina are two exceptions), a growing number of states have im-posed a separate estate tax, and the exemptions they allow may be less than the $3.5 million permitted under federal law. (Chapter 4 discussed strategies that spouses can use to plan around the differences.)

> ## Did You Know?
>
> Some states have an estate tax. In these, the exemption is less than the $3.5 million federal one: Connecticut, Kansas, Maine, Maryland, Massachu-setts, Minnesota, Nebraska, New Jer-sey, New York, Ohio, Oregon, Rhode Island, Washington, Wisconsin and the District of Columbia.

When real estate is con-cerned, keep in mind that state estate taxes affect not only taxpayers who live in those states but also those who are resident elsewhere but own property in a state that taxes out-of-state resi-dents. For example, if you live in Arizona, California, Florida or Texas, which do not have an estate tax, but own a summer home in Nantucket, you need to be aware that it can be subject to state estate tax in Massachusetts. The tax is based on the ratio of the real estate to the total estate, and with costly property it can quickly add up.

One strategy to address this potential tax trap is to convert real property to intangible personal property by putting the real estate into a limited li-ability company or family limited partnership. Unlike real property, which is taxed by the state in which it is situated, intangible personal property is taxed in the state where the owner resides. So far, most states have not taken a position about whether this strategy should be permitted. But pres-sures to generate revenues could cause some to clamp down on this tech-nique in the future.

Community property. As discussed in Chapter 4, the rules on property ownership and inheritance in the nine states that have community property law are unique. The big advantage, from an estate planning perspective, is that both spouses' shares get a step-up in basis when the first spouse dies, minimizing or eliminating the capital gains tax if the property is sold soon after. The major downside is that community ownership complicates the division of property in a divorce.

It's important to think about these issues when you relocate. If you move to a community property state from a noncommunity property state, you and your spouse have a choice about whether to keep property acquired before the move as separate property, or whether to treat it as community property – what you own when you move to the state does not automatically become community property. You specify your wishes in a contract called a community property agreement. Likewise, if you move to a noncommunity property state, you can enter into a similar type of agreement either to keep existing property as community, or convert it to separate property.

Income tax on trusts. If you are the trustee, beneficiary or grantor of a trust, your residence can affect the taxation of the trust. Conceivably a trust could be taxable in more than one state, and it's not always possible to get a credit for the other state's tax.

The precise rules on taxing trusts vary widely. More important than knowing which state does what is alerting advisers to any outstanding trusts before you move, so they can suggest a strategy appropriate for your situation. For example, California is one of the more difficult states regarding trusts, taxing them if their trustees or beneficiaries are residents. If the trust is revocable, the solution may be as easy as having someone who moves to California resign as trustee.

Your will. All states will honor a will that's valid in the state where it was signed, but specific terms drafted for when you were living in the old state could be problematic in the new one. For example, in Florida, someone who is not a resident of the state can't serve as executor – the person who carries out your wishes under a will. Some states permit people disposing of personal property to leave a memo that's binding on the executor. Others have rules that such a memo, listing particular items to go to certain people, is just advisory, and that the executor doesn't have to follow it (as noted in Chapter 2).

You won't necessarily have to redo your will if you move, but you should have a local lawyer review it, along with any other estate planning documents. Since you will be subject to a new set of state laws, you should be sure your documents are appropriate for the state you are moving to. If you move to a community property law state, have new wills drafted by a local lawyer.

Power of attorney. As discussed in Chapter 1, this important estate-planning document authorizes a person whom you trust to act as your agent in a variety of financial and legal matters. State laws vary as to both what powers you can convey and the requirements for the document to be valid. Therefore, when you move, you should have any existing powers of attorney reviewed by a local lawyer. For example, in Florida, there must be two witnesses when you sign the document, and it must be notarized if you want your agent to be able to sell real estate on your behalf. If you move from a state with different requirements, the document may be ineffective for your needs. And if you became mentally incompetent before you sign a new power of attorney, it might be necessary to get a court-appointed guardian to handle certain tasks instead.

To-Do List

Beware the Ties That Bind

Changing your domicile or home state for tax purposes can be complicated. It's important both to establish a residence in the new state and to sever enough ties in the previous one that tax authorities will have no claim against you. Spending more than six months a year in a state is the best way to prove you live there. Evidence that you intend to remain is also helpful. These are some steps to take:

❧ Get a state driver's license and register your car

❧ Register to vote and cast your ballot

❧ Change your address for all important mail and documents, including your federal income tax return and your passport

❧ Join community groups, local clubs and, if you're religious, a house of worship

❧ File a declaration of domicile, if the state has a procedure for doing that

❧ Apply for special tax breaks, if any, that are available to residents of your new state

❧ Move your safe deposit box

❧ Set up a family burial site in the new state

❧ Make donations to local charities

❧ Establish relationships with local professionals, such as doctors, lawyers and accountants

❧ If you redo your estate plan, sign the documents in the new state and be sure they indicate that it is your residence

Chapter 11

Hidden Traps When Crossing Borders

*Read this chapter if you or a family member
is a citizen of another country,
lives abroad or has foreign investments.*

With families increasingly spread among different countries and shifting assets across borders, it is important to be aware of how various links to foreign countries can affect your estate plan. This is true whether or not you are a U.S. citizen.

The United States is one of the few countries that impose taxes during life and at death on property anywhere in the world. These far-reaching tax rules apply to U.S. citizens, resident aliens and domiciliaries – a legal term for people who expect to live in a place indefinitely. They may be subject to income tax on money earned anywhere in the world, estate tax on worldwide assets totaling more than $3.5 million and generation-skipping transfer tax on worldwide assets worth more than $3.5 million going to grandchildren and more remote generations. In some cases a tax credit may be available for taxes paid to foreign countries.

In This Chapter...

- ✤ *Foreign Assets Owned by U.S. Citizens and Domiciliaries*
- ✤ *Gifts and Inheritances From Foreigners*
- ✤ *Gifts and Bequests to Non-Citizen Spouses*
- ✤ *The Long Arm That Reaches Foreign Trusts*
- ✤ *Expatriate Tax Rules*

Although U.S. residents who are not domiciliaries must pay income tax on worldwide income, they are subject to gift and estate tax only on transfers of U.S. assets (such as stocks or real estate). A resident for income tax purposes is someone who has a green card or is in the U.S. more than 183 days in any one year or more than 120 days a year in three consecutive years.

Foreigners who do not live in the U.S. (non-resident aliens) may be surprised to find that without some precautionary steps, U.S. assets that they acquire may be subject to tax when those assets are transferred during life or at death.

Foreign Assets Owned by
U.S. Citizens and Domiciliaries

Suppose you have kept a foreign bank account that you set up during an overseas posting, or you are thinking of buying a ski chalet in the Alps. Since U.S. estate tax applies to your worldwide assets, both could be taxed if you leave behind total assets worth more than $3.5 million. If you transfer those foreign assets during life to anyone other than a spouse who is a U.S. citizen, you will have to pay gift tax if the total value of your gifts exceeds the $1 million lifetime gift tax exemption.

There's also the possibility of double tax on your overseas assets – inheritance tax in the country where they are situated, as well as U.S. estate tax. Only 16 countries have estate or gift-tax treaties with the U.S. that may prevent or minimize double taxation: Australia, Austria, Canada, Denmark, Finland, France, Germany, Greece, Ireland, Italy, Japan, the Netherlands, Norway, South Africa, Switzerland and the United Kingdom.

Forced heirship rules in some countries are another issue that may arise. These rules, which are designed to avoid disinheritance of a spouse or child, give that person a preset share of what you leave behind. Where forced heirship rules exist, they can frustrate estate-planning strategies that are popular in the U.S. For example, if you have children, you may not be able to leave foreign real estate entirely to your spouse – something you would typically do in order to take advantage of the unlimited marital deduction that U.S. law affords (as discussed in Chapter 3).

If instead you must leave part of the property to your children and their portion is worth more than the $3.5 million federal exemption (or the state exemption if you live in a state with a separate estate tax), the foreign property could be subject to estate tax in the U.S. Were it not for the forced heirship law, you would be able to avoid that tax when the first of you dies by leaving the entire property to the surviving U.S. citizen spouse.

Likewise, an estate planning tool used to avoid inheritance tax in certain foreign countries – retaining the right to live in a house while you are alive and giving your children a remainder interest in the property after that – would be ineffective for U.S. estate tax purposes. In fact, this arrangement would cause the entire value of the property to be included in your estate and potentially be subject to tax.

Owning real estate abroad therefore requires coordination between your estate planning lawyer in the U.S. and a knowledgeable adviser in the country where the property is situated. It may be possible to avoid both foreign tax and inheritance laws by putting the foreign property into a foreign corporation. That way the assets are owned by the corporate entity you create, rather than by you directly. However, local taxes may be imposed on such transfers.

Another question that arises is whether you need a separate will just to cover valuable property in a foreign country, prepared in that country in accordance with its laws. This greatly complicates and adds to the cost of your estate planning and should be avoided if possible. Some countries have entered into multinational treaties requiring certain formalities in preparing and signing a will and recognizing the validity of wills done in participating countries. (The U.S. is a signatory to one such treaty, known as the Washington Convention.) You might need a separate will if your assets are in a country that has not signed the treaty or in other special situations, such as when a country's succession rules are inconsistent with your estate planning goals. Trusts, for example, are rarely or never used in many countries. Another reason to write a separate will is if you are expecting an inheritance battle; the will can include provisions, based on local law, that can minimize or avoid the kinds of problems that you anticipate.

> ## Did You Know?
>
> If you plan to spend time overseas and buy or sell real estate, transact business or open a bank account, you need a durable power of attorney that's valid in that country. This document appoints an agent to act on your behalf in case of physical or mental disability.

Foreign bank accounts or brokerage accounts, as well as other foreign investments, raise additional issues. Concern about money-laundering since the Sept. 11th terrorist attacks has led to reporting requirements for these accounts. Whether you inherited such an account or opened it with your own funds, you must disclose it on your annual tax return. If the total of all these accounts is more than $10,000 at any point during the year, you must also submit a Foreign Bank Account Report, known as the FBAR (pronounced eff-bar) to the Treasury Department by June 30 of the following year. Not filing the report or not answering all the questions, or supplying false or fraudulent information, can result in substantial penalties and, in certain cases, criminal charges. If you have questions about the FBAR, you can submit them to FBARquestions@irs.gov or call 800-800-2877.

Gifts and Inheritances From Foreigners

Certain assets, including U.S. equities, real estate and tangible personal property in the U.S., will be subject to U.S. gift tax, federal estate tax (and possibly state estate tax) and generation-skipping transfer tax when they are transferred, even if both the owner and the gift recipients are non-resident aliens. Many people are not aware of this. For example, if an Indian citizen who is a resident of Mumbai dies owning a condominium in New York, his children cannot inherit that property, regardless of their nationality, until they have paid both federal and state estate tax.

Unlike U.S. citizens and domiciliaries, foreigners are not eligible for the $1 million lifetime gift tax exemption or the $3.5 million estate tax exemption. When they transfer interests in U.S. property during life, they must pay gift tax if the value of a gift is more than the $13,000 annual exclusion. Gifts in excess of that amount are taxed, based on their aggregate value during the foreigner's lifetime, at a rate of up to 45 percent. An exception applies when the gifts are made to a spouse who is a U.S. citizen; in that case, the unlimited gift-tax marital deduction applies (as noted in Chapter 3).

Transfers through an estate plan get a credit of $13,000 (in effect an exemption of $60,000 because of the graduated estate tax rates that apply in this context). For amounts above that, an estate tax of 18 to 45 percent applies. Here, too, there's an unlimited marital deduction for assets inherited by a spouse who is a U.S. citizen.

But these taxes can be easily avoided if a foreigner acquires and holds the assets through a corporation situated in a jurisdiction that does not have estate or income tax (such as Bermuda or the Cayman Islands), rather than owning them directly. That converts what would otherwise be considered U.S. assets into offshore assets, which aren't subject to U.S. estate tax. Another advantage is privacy, because the shareholder of record is the corporation, not an individual.

Often shares in the corporation are owned, in turn, not by individuals, but by an offshore trust that is also situated in a tax-friendly jurisdiction. The trust can shield the assets from creditors (see Chapter 18) and provide for distributions under its terms, both during life and afterward. This can avoid tax on the assets by either the U.S. or the foreigner's home country. It also can avoid forced heirship in countries that have such rules.

Different rules apply when the transfers do not involve U.S. property. These assets are generally not subject to gift or estate tax. So, for example, a U.S. person could receive a gift or inheritance of any amount from her Canadian father and not have to pay any U.S. tax (though there may be foreign tax implications).

However, money coming into the U.S. is tightly regulated, and it may be necessary to report the gift or inheritance even if there is no tax on it. Consider the U.S. person with a Canadian father: If the amount she receives in a given year from him and any other nonresident aliens and foreign estates totals more than $100,000, she must report each gift of more than $5,000 to the Internal Revenue Service on Form 3520. Why? The IRS is on the lookout for income masquerading as gifts and wants to decide for itself, based on the information you supply, whether what you received is taxable income rather than a nontaxable gift. Assuming the transfer is indeed a gift, no tax will be due, but you must still file the form – there is a penalty of up to 25 percent of the amount of the gift if you are required to file the return and don't. The reporting requirement does not include direct payments of tuition or medical expenses, which are discussed in Chapters 9 and 13.

A much smaller threshold – $14,139 in 2009, indexed for inflation – applies to gifts received from foreign partnerships, foreign trusts or foreign corporations. The rule covers funds you receive directly, as well as money doled out on your behalf, such as the payment of credit card bills.

Gifts and Bequests to Non-Citizen Spouses

If your spouse is not a U.S. citizen, you will not be able to rely on the unlimited gift tax and estate tax marital deduction. Annual gifts to your spouse of more than $133,000 (indexed for inflation) count against the $1 million lifetime exemption.

Assume Lucy, an American, marries Ricky, a Cuban who has a green card, and they live in Miami. If Lucy dies first and leaves Ricky more than $3.5 million, anything above that limit is immediately subject to a 45 percent tax unless it goes into a special kind of trust, called a qualified domestic trust, or QDOT. If this trust distributes principal, it must withhold estate tax – at the rate that was in effect when Lucy died. (When Ricky receives distributions of income, they are subject to income tax but not estate tax.) The QDOT was discussed extensively in Chapter 3.

In contrast, if Ricky gives or leaves property to Lucy, these transfers are entitled to the unlimited marital gift-tax or estate-tax deduction. Therefore, a QDOT to benefit Lucy is not necessary.

Complications arise when you own property jointly with rights of survivorship or in tenancy by the entirety, two forms of title discussed in Chapters 3, 4 and 18. Although typically when spouses own property this way only half its value is included in the estate of the first to die, a different rule applies when one of them is not a U.S. citizen.

For real estate, the tax treatment in this situation depends on when the couple acquired the property. If it was after July 14, 1988, the

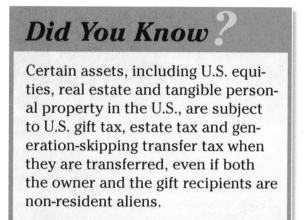

Did You Know?

Certain assets, including U.S. equities, real estate and tangible personal property in the U.S., are subject to U.S. gift tax, estate tax and generation-skipping transfer tax when they are transferred, even if both the owner and the gift recipients are non-resident aliens.

whole property is included in the estate of the first to die unless the survivor can show how much he contributed to the purchase price. In that case, what is counted as part of the estate would be reduced to reflect the portion that he paid. For real estate bought before 1988, state law determines how each spouse's interest is calculated.

Likewise, if the property is sold or the couple ends the joint ownership arrangement by putting title in just one of their names, any proceeds or share in excess of what the recipient contributed is considered a gift. The non-citizen spouse can make this transfer to the citizen spouse without paying gift tax (just like Ricky's gifts to Lucy). But if annual gifts from the citizen spouse to the non-citizen spouse exceed $133,000 (indexed for inflation), it counts against the $1 million lifetime gift tax exemption.

Similar issues arise with joint bank accounts or brokerage accounts that give each spouse the right to make withdrawals freely. If either spouse takes

Connectin

Ties to a foreign country can affect the tax on transfers during life and throug who owns the assets, where they are situated and who is receiving them.

Whom does the tax cover?	What assets does the tax cover?
U.S citizens/domiciliaries	Worldwide
Foreigners (non-resident aliens or resident aliens who are not domiciliaries)	U.S. equities, real estate and tangible personal property
Expatriates who gave up U.S. citizenship after June 17, 2008	Worldwide

*Unlimited marital gift tax deduction or estate tax deduction applies to transfers to a spouse who is U.S. citize

e Dots

ur estate plan. The tax that applies in a given situation may depend on

hen does e tax apply?	How much is exempt?	Tax rate (once exemptions exceeded)
Lifetime gifts	• $13,000 annual exclusion • $133,000 annual exclusion gift to non-citizen spouse • $1 million lifetime exemption*	Up to 45%
Bequests	• $3.5 million*	45%
Lifetime gifts	• $13,000 annual exclusion*	Up to 45%
Bequests	• $13,000 credit*	Up to 45%
Lifetime gifts to U.S. persons	• $13,000 annual exclusion*	Highest rate in effect
Bequests to U.S. persons	• $13,000	Highest rate in effect

out more than the portion he or she put in, it's considered a gift. And when one spouse dies, his contribution and share of the appreciation is considered part of his estate. These rules make it very difficult for spouses to hold valuable property as joint owners when one is a citizen and the other is not.

❧

The Long Arm That Reaches Foreign Trusts

From a tax perspective, U.S. persons – U.S. citizens and resident aliens who hold a green card – are better off being beneficiaries of domestic trusts than foreign ones, but under federal rules a trust could easily be characterized as a foreign one instead.

Unless the trust is a grantor trust – one in which the person creating the trust retains certain rights or powers – it typically pays the income tax on its earnings but takes a deduction for net income (income minus expenses) distributed to beneficiaries. With non-grantor foreign trusts, however, the trust pays tax only on income that comes from a U.S. source, such as dividends from corporations, rents from real estate or capital gains from the sale of real estate or stocks. In contrast, U.S. beneficiaries of these trusts are taxed on all distributions of income, including income from capital gains, whether it comes from a U.S. source or a foreign one.

Under Treasury Department regulations, a trust is treated as a domestic trust only if it meets both these criteria: a U.S. court can exercise primary supervision over the administration of the trust (the "court test") and one or more U.S. persons have the power to control all substantial decisions of the trust (the "control test"). Under the regulations, "substantial decisions" include whether and when to distribute income or principal; the amount of any distribution; whether to remove, add or replace a trustee, and the power to make investment decisions. A trust can have a foreign investment adviser without being considered a foreign trust if the adviser can be dismissed by the U.S. trustee.

If a trust flunks either test, it is considered a foreign trust. The fact that the trust says the laws of a particular state apply to it or that it was created under a will that was probated in a U.S. state doesn't change the result.

How might you inadvertently turn a domestic trust into a foreign one? Having a foreigner serve as a trustee with the power to make substantial decisions is one way, for example, when non-resident aliens set up trusts to provide for

164

U.S. beneficiaries (as discussed in Chapter 5). Their inclination might be to name a family member from the home country as trustee. That could make the trust a foreign trust.

The IRS is on the lookout for foreign trusts. On the annual federal income tax return, you must indicate whether you have received distributions from foreign trusts during the past year or whether you set up or transferred any funds into one of these trusts. If so, you must report that on Form 3520, filed with the return. The penalty for not filing is 35 percent of the distribution. Other penalties apply if the trust distributes accumulated income from previous years.

Expatriate Tax Rules

Tax law discourages people from expatriating just to avoid taxes. Two provisions of the tax code, added in 2008 through the Heroes Earnings Assistance and Relief Tax Act of 2008 (the so-called HEART legislation), could have a significant impact on expatriates or U.S. persons who receive gifts or inheritances from them.

Who's covered? These provisions apply to someone who expatriates on or after June 17, 2008, by giving up his citizenship, or in the case of long-term residents (those who have spent at least 8 of the 15 years before expatriating living in the U.S.) by giving up his green card, if in either case they fit at least one of these descriptions:

❧ Their average annual income tax for the previous five years was more than $139,000 (indexed for inflation)
❧ Their net worth is $2 million or more (including interests in trusts)
❧ They fail to certify, under penalty of perjury, that they have complied with the tax law during the previous five years.

There are exceptions for certain minors and for those who have been dual citizens since birth who remain a citizen of another country at the time of expatriation and have not been U.S. residents for more than 10 of the last 15 years before expatriating.

What's the tax pain? When you expatriate, the law imposes an exit tax on your worldwide property (not just your U.S. assets), including property in a trust if you are the grantor – the person who created it. Whether or not you sell that property when you expatriate, it is treated as if you had on the day before you expatriated, and there is capital gains tax due on any appreciation of more than $600,000 (adjusted for inflation). If you want to defer that tax until the asset is actually sold or you die, you must make a deal with the IRS – for example, by posting a bond.

Certain interests in deferred compensation plans and trusts that you did not set up are not subject to the exit tax. Instead, there is a 30 percent withholding tax on payments from these plans or trusts as you receive them.

Perhaps more importantly, once you expatriate there's a steep tax when you benefit U.S. citizens or residents through lifetime gifts, distributions from trusts that you have set up or bequests under your estate plan. (Note that, in this context, the income and net-worth thresholds are applied as of the date of a gift or immediately before death, not at the time of expatriation.) Anything they receive that exceeds the $13,000 annual exclusion amount (indexed for inflation) is subject to gift tax or estate tax at the highest rate in effect at the time. Recipients, whether they are individuals or U.S. trusts, are liable for the tax unless you have filed a gift tax return or your estate has filed an estate tax return. Payments that would qualify for the unlimited marital deduction are not subject to this requirement (again, special rules apply if your spouse is not a U.S. citizen).

There is no $1 million gift tax exemption or $3.5 million estate tax exemption in this context. If you are planning to expatriate you should consider using your $1 million gift tax exclusion to make gifts to friends or family before you do. Otherwise, that exemption will be lost when you expatriate.

To-Do List

Get the Right Advisers on Your Team

International estate planning is a highly specialized field. Although most competent trust and estate lawyers could handle the basic issues involving a U.S. citizen who is married to someone who isn't, for anything more complex, it pays to consult a sub-specialist (for general advice on finding a lawyer, see Chapter 19). You may also need whomever you choose to coordinate with advisers in the country where you live, own assets or have family. You should seek an international estate-planning expert if you are:

❧ A U.S. citizen or green card holder and expect a significant gift or inheritance from someone who is a resident of a foreign country

❧ A U.S. citizen or green card holder and the beneficiary of a foreign trust

❧ A U.S. citizen or green card holder and the grantor of a trust that names a foreigner as trustee

❧ A U.S. citizen or green card holder and own or are about to buy property, such as real estate or business interests, in a foreign country

❧ Planning to live abroad – for example, to work or retire – but still consider the U.S. your home country

❧ Thinking of giving up your U.S. citizenship or green card

❧ An expatriate and plan to make a significant gift or bequest to a U.S. person

❧ A citizen and resident of another country and own or are about to buy U.S. equities, real estate or tangible personal property

❧ A citizen and resident of another country and want to benefit a family member who is coming to the U.S. to work or study or who is a U.S. citizen or green card holder.

Chapter 12

The Family Business: a Legacy Or a Headache?

*Read this chapter if you have
your own business or a share
in a family-held enterprise.*

W hether you are an entrepreneur or own a share of a family business, thinking about what will happen next can raise emotionally charged issues. Many business owners are so consumed with day-to-day operations they don't have time to consider estate planning – and don't want to. (It's awful to contemplate a time when you won't be at the helm.) Family members who don't work in the enterprise may not share the owners' devotion to the company and could have mixed feelings about the value of sustaining it. For various reasons, most such businesses do not continue to the third generation. The death of a company founder can cause revenues to slip. The product or business model may be hopelessly out of date. The 45 percent federal estate tax, which applies to estates worth more than $3.5 million, could leave your heirs cash strapped.

In This Chapter...

- What Is Your Succession Plan?
- Do You Have a Buy-Sell Agreement?
- Should You Transfer Shares?
- How Will Your Family Pay Estate Taxes?

Planning while you are hearty is the best way to improve the odds that your company will thrive after you are gone, but you must be realistic. Find out whether any of your children want to continue in the business. If none do, your estate plan can reflect the expectation that the company will be sold. If one or more children want to keep the company going, you can even out the inheritances of children who will not be involved; the most common way is with life insurance (see Chapter 8). To the extent that you can afford it, shift assets to younger family members while you are alive. And whatever else you do, leave a source of cash to cover the tax bill.

What Is Your Succession Plan?

Whatever the long-term goals and the assumptions about the economic viability of the company, every family-owned business should have a succession plan. These are some issues to cover:

How much is the company worth? Answering this question is a prerequisite for various forms of succession planning, from transferring shares to children to selling the company. In the life of a business, the value can fluctuate – for example, as a result of market conditions or because a sale or initial public offering is on the horizon.

Whether the value of the business has increased or fallen, that information can help you chart a course. If things have taken a turn for the worse, advisers who work with companies in financial distress may be able to help put the business back on track or find a buyer. If your company is on the verge of increasing its worth, your estate planning should take that into account.

How long should you stay involved? Company founders often think of the business as an extension of themselves, and that makes it tough to let go, even if they have been grooming another family member or key employee for years. Sometimes a founder who is psychologically ready to step down can't do without the salary, health and retirement benefits she has been receiving from the business. In these cases, it may be possible for the founder to continue, at least temporarily, to receive an income stream as a consultant or part-time employee, rather than giving up everything, as the business makes a transition to family management or new ownership. The company might also adopt a deferred compensation plan to provide income to the founder after she reaches a particular age, whether or not she continues working. Another possibility is to structure a transaction, either with family members or a trust, that involves an installment sale or a loan that will continue to generate revenue for the original owner (see below and Chapter 13).

Who is the likely successor? This is a potential lightning rod for many families, especially when the candidates include both family members and such outsiders as key employees or in-laws, or when some children are involved in the company and others are not. In the most successful transitions, owners have taken steps to minimize future conflicts – for example, by having children begin their careers and earn their spurs elsewhere before assuming a role in the family enterprise, and by equalizing inheritances.

Do You Have a Buy-Sell Agreement?

Think of this as a business prenup or a postnup, depending on when owners draw it up. In a buy-sell, partners (the process is the same for corporations and limited liability companies) decide what will happen to their interest in the company if events like disability, death, divorce or personal bankruptcy occur.

By requiring a sale under certain circumstances known as trigger events and by specifying the terms beforehand, a buy-sell can prevent such evils as becoming an unwilling partner with an owner's heirs or leaving a surviving spouse illiquid because the remaining owners refuse to buy the survivor's inherited shares.

The best time to arrange the details is before you begin a venture, but generally there is no harm in waiting six months or so until you're sure the business is workable. For older companies, it's better late than never. Either way, some issues must be sorted out.

What events should you include? Some events – leaving the company, starting a competing business, offering shares to an outsider – may seem obvious; others could require considerable soul-searching. If a founding partner retires, for example, the remaining owners may feel torn between a desire to reward his past work and not wanting him to get a free ride while they keep pouring themselves into the company.

Who can – or must – buy the business interest when one party wants out? In what's called a cross-purchase agreement, the option or obligation belongs to the remaining owners. Alternatively, there's a redemption agreement, which designates the company as the buyer. A hybrid approach typically gives an owner the right of first refusal, with the company next in line if the owner doesn't exercise it.

When owners' interests are divided unequally – say, one is a majority shareholder – you may also want to incorporate what's known as a tag-along provision. Then, if a 90 percent owner sells to Microsoft, for example, the deal must give the 10 percent shareholder the option of selling under the same terms.

Sometimes agreements include a drag-along provision, in which the 10 percent owner is required to sell if the 90 percent owner does.

How can you value the interests being sold? There are many ways to approach this. If you name a set amount, you'll need to update it annually to reflect changes in the company, the industry or the economy. A more practical solution is to describe a process for determining the value, whether through an appraisal of the company's fair market value, or by using a formula. Note, however, that a formula can create problems if the Internal Revenue Service finds it does not reflect the fair market value of the company when the owner died. It can also lead to various complications in estates worth more than $3.5 million.

What are the payment terms and financing? A lump-sum payout provides all the cash at once, and that cash often comes from life insurance. You'll need fewer policies if the company buys a policy for every owner, rather than if each owner insures the others individually. However, company-owned policies might not be as tax-efficient as policies owned by the co-owners in a cross-purchase agreement. For that reason, the owners might want to form a separate entity, such as a limited liability company, to hold the life insurance that will fund a cross-purchase.

The alternative to a lump-sum deal is an installment sale, with payments plus interest over a defined period. These arrangements are common in buyouts where the owners don't anticipate a ready source of cash, which could happen if one owner gets divorced or wants to quit the business. The legal bill to prepare a buy-sell agreement may be $2,500 to $25,000, depending on complexity. If your budget is tight, you can rely on the free buy-sell agreement that many life insurance companies offer policy buyers, but it will probably cover only an owner's death, not other trigger events, and it doesn't replace the advice of a lawyer who understands these issues.

Should You Transfer Shares?

The best time to shift business assets to family is before your company hits a home run, such as a sale or initial public offering or the announcement of a revolutionary product. Once the enterprise soars in value, all the appreciation would be stuck in your estate. If you can afford to transfer some holdings before that happens, it is possible to shelter the increased value from estate tax.

The challenge is to avoid or minimize the gift tax associated with such life-time transfers. Currently, you can make gifts of up to $13,000 in cash or other assets each year ($26,000 if you are married) to as many recipients as you would like without incurring gift tax. In addition to this annual exclusion, you can give away $1 million during your life ($2 million for married couples) be-fore a gift tax of up to 45 percent applies. Various estate planning techniques, designed to minimize or steer clear of the gift tax altogether, can pack even more value into both the annual exclusion and the lifetime exemption amount. These techniques are covered briefly later in this chapter and discussed exten-sively in Chapters 15 and 16.

Which transfer methods work best depends on a variety of business and personal factors. Among the most important are the maturity and current value of your business, your expectations for its future and whether and how soon you anticipate the company might be sold or go public. You should also evaluate your cash flow needs, decide whom you want to benefit and weigh your tolerance for complexity.

At the outset, many business owners divide the company into voting and non-voting shares, recapitalizing if necessary. This serves two purposes. By retaining the voting shares, owners can maintain control over business decisions, which may be important to them as they approach a critical juncture. The strategy may also allow the value of the nonvoting shares intended for transfer during life to be further discounted, because they carry no control rights.

Once you have done that, here are some possible situations to consider:

The value of the business is still relatively low. The best wealth transfer technique may be the simplest: transfer shares to family members using your annual exclusion.

You can make these gifts to individuals directly, or to an irrevocable trust that can benefit multiple people and protect the assets from creditors (see Chapter 18). You and your spouse can each put in $13,000 worth of stock each year for every trust beneficiary. Those annual exclusion gifts offer a lot of bang for your buck, especially if the company stock isn't worth very much right now. If it increases in value – for example, because of a sale or initial public offering – the trust would receive its share of the proceeds.

Your company could be a boom or a bust. A grantor retained annuity trust, or GRAT, lets you bet on the upside potential without any downside risk. Here's how it works: the person setting up the trust, known as the grantor, puts company shares into a short-term irrevocable trust and retains the right to receive an annual income stream, known as an annuity, for a preset time (for this type of asset, it is typically 5 to 15 years). If the grantor survives that period – a condition for this tool to work – any property left in the trust when the annual payments end passes to family members or to a trust for their benefit (they are the remainder beneficiaries).

The annuity should be approximately equal to the value of the assets transferred, plus an assumed interest rate that the government imposes, known as the Section 7520 rate. If the assets in the GRAT appreciate by more than that rate, all the excess passes to the grantor's heirs with little or no gift tax. On the other hand, if the appreciation never occurs, the grantor is no worse off, except for the fees paid to set up the trust, because the annuity would be paid by returning some shares to the grantor.

GRATs are appropriate for young enterprises, as well as mature ones. They offer enormous flexibility for parents who may be concerned that a business bonanza might make their children too rich. For example, you could provide in the trust document that if the remainder interest grows to more than a certain amount, the excess will come back to you, rather than going to your children. At that point you could choose to donate the funds to charity or spend them for another purpose.

With assets that are difficult to value, as may be the case with closely held stock or real estate, a GRAT offers an additional benefit. By expressing the annuity as a percentage of the initial value of the GRAT, you permit the trust to simply pay a larger annuity if the IRS determines the property is worth more than you initially figured. This minimizes the additional gift tax the IRS might try to impose if it audits the value of the gift.

But GRATs are not ideal for transfers to grandchildren and more remote descendants. The $3.5 million exemption from generation-skipping transfer tax can't be applied until the trust term ends, by which time you hope asset values will be higher.

Your company is growing slowly but steadily. A popular alternative – or complement – to a GRAT is what's called an installment sale to an irrevocable grantor trust. With this technique, senior family members sell assets to a trust that will benefit younger relatives and, in exchange, take back an interest-bearing promissory note. Assuming a sale at fair market value and interest at the applicable federal rate – which is lower than the Section

7520 rate – there is no gift and therefore no gift tax.

Your hope is that the value of the business interests will increase by more than the interest rate by the time the loan term ends. If it does – for example, if a sale occurs – you will have shifted all that excess to family members without having to pay gift tax.

This strategy requires that the trust have other assets, ideally worth at least 10 percent of the trust's total assets once the property is transferred. Often the grantor supplies this seed money using the $1 million lifetime gift tax exemption.

Like a GRAT, this transaction involves what's called a grantor trust – so named because the grantor retains certain rights or powers (see Chapter 15). As a result, the grantor, rather than the trust or its beneficiaries, must pay income tax on the trust earnings. The benefits can be enormous. For example, if a company is sold, the trust will receive a cash infusion that triggers capital gains tax. If the grantor, rather than the trust, pays this tax, all the proceeds of the sale can remain in the trust, rather than being partially depleted by taxes. But you do need to consider whether you can afford the tax payments (see Chapter 15).

You want to support charity, as well as family. As noted earlier, when giving shares to family, you are likely to achieve maximum estate planning benefits if you transfer assets before there is any appreciation, because the value of the business will probably be lower. In contrast, when charity is the intended beneficiary, you are usually better off making the donation when asset values are higher because you can maximize the potential income tax deduction for your donation.

The main advantage of donating company stock, assuming the charity is open to this gift, is that it avoids capital gains tax. A nonprofit, which is tax exempt, does not have to pay tax on the proceeds of a sale or initial public offering.

With a charitable remainder trust, which can benefit you or family members as well as a charity, individuals must pay their share of the tax. But this tax is deferred and applied proportionately to each trust distribution the person receives (see Chapter 17). Note that if your company is organized as an S corporation – a company structure that avoids double tax on company earnings (first at the corporate level, and then on the individual's tax return as dividends are distributed) – putting the stock in a charitable remainder trust will cause the company to lose its S designation, which could have unfavorable income tax consequences.

There are also drawbacks to donating closely held stock to a private foundation. The primary one for donors is that you can only deduct the basis or initial cost of the shares – not the fair market value. Another potential tax trap is unrelated business taxable income, or UBTI, which falls outside the tax-exempt status charities usually enjoy. A charity must pay tax on income financed by debt or generated by business activities unrelated to its tax-exempt purpose, both of which are characterized as UBTI. Without careful planning, some donors have been unpleasantly surprised to learn that their gifts of privately held company stock to a private foundation gave rise to taxable income, defeating one purpose of making the gift in the first place.

When making charitable donations, you must also be mindful of certain restrictions imposed by law or IRS rules. If a donor has a binding obligation to sell the company before giving the stock to charity, some courts have found that the donor must pay tax on the gain. To avoid running afoul of this prearranged sale rule, there must still be a chance that the deal could be called off. Another caveat: penalties might apply when a private foundation or a charitable trust enters into a transaction that involves its contributor or certain of her relatives.

Some children are involved in the company and others are not. In this situation, parents sometimes ask children who work in the business to pay for at least part of the shares they are receiving rather than treating the whole thing as a gift. These arrangements are most common in situations when the parent does not have other, comparable assets to give any children not working in the company.

Whether you choose just one of these strategies or use them in combination, it is best to start with the least complicated approach that will achieve your goals. Lawyers' fees for these transactions can range from less than $10,000 to many multiples of that sum, depending on the details. And any time you give away shares of a business, you should get an appraisal, which can easily cost $5,000 or more.

How Will Your Family Pay Estate Taxes?

Estate taxes often present difficulties for family business owners, particularly when the business is illiquid. Normally heirs must pay estate tax within nine months of the death of the senior family member. A substantial estate tax bill could force heirs to sell off key assets or even lose the company. Loans for this purpose, which might have been available in the past, may be much harder to get in a tight credit market.

The simplest alternative is to buy life insurance that would cover the tax bill. You should start by setting up an irrevocable life insurance trust, which can buy the policy and, when you die, hold the proceeds for whomever you have named as beneficiary. If instead you are the owner of the policy, it would be considered part of your estate and the proceeds could be taxed.

Next, you need to funnel money into the trust so it can pay the premiums. There is no gift tax on your contributions as long as you stay within the annual exclusion, with no limit on the number of recipients. Each trust beneficiary counts as one person. (Other techniques for financing premiums were discussed in Chapter 8.)

Depending on the circumstances, your family may also be able to elect to pay the estate tax in installments. Although the rules are complex, Section 6166 of the Internal Revenue Code extends the deadline for payment of tax attributable to a closely held business that makes up more than 35 percent of an estate. Normally heirs must pay estate tax within nine months of the death of the senior family member. An estate that makes a Section 6166 election on its tax return can stretch payments over as many as 15 years. During the first four years, it can make interest-only payments. After that, the tax and any interest due can be paid in up to 10 equal installments. Although the interest is not deductible, special rates make this an attractive option.

Unfortunately the definition of closely held business contained in Section 6166 is very narrow: a closely held business is one with no more than 45 shareholders. But under the American Jobs Creation Act of 2004, a company with up to 100 shareholders can qualify as an S corporation. That means many S corporations can't take advantage of Section 6166.

An alternative test to qualify for Section 6166, based on ownership, is also problematic. For partnerships, the estate must own 20 percent of the company's capital to qualify. For corporations, the estate must hold 20 percent of the value of the voting stock.

Finally, the IRS can require a bond ensuring payment of the deferred estate tax or impose a tax lien. Both options could be costly. While the bond would be a direct expense, a tax lien could pose other financial harm because lenders and customers might take it as a sign that the company is in trouble.

Although families make a Section 6166 election when the business owner dies, you need to plan ahead to make sure the option is available. If an estate is relatively illiquid, for example, make sure the value of the business represents more than 35 percent of the estate. That might mean giving away other assets through lifetime gifts.

To-Do List

Give Your Family Business a Stress Test

One way to determine whether your estate plan adequately accounts for your business is to run through a series of "what ifs." If something happened to you, what would be the answer to each of these questions:

❧ Would your company be able to meet payroll, fund retirement benefits and pay other operating expenses?

❧ Is there a family member or trusted employee whom you have groomed to take over?

❧ Would the company be likely to lose clients or customers?

❧ Do you have enough insurance to cover the estate tax bill?

❧ Would your heirs need to sell the business at fire sale prices in order to pay estate taxes?

❧ Would your estate qualify for an extension of the time to pay these taxes?

Chapter 13

Subsidize Friends Or Family

Read this chapter if you would like to offer financial help to adult children, grandchildren, parents, siblings or others.

M any people don't realize that subsidizing family and friends is regulated by the tax law. This kind of assistance is considered a lifetime gift unless it's for someone, such as a child, whom you are legally obligated to support.

As far the government is concerned, noble motives don't matter; you must follow the same rules that would apply to any other lifetime transfers, including those intended mainly to pare down your estate and leave less for the government to tax.

This issue, often a source of confusion, suddenly became more relevant to many people in the wake of the economic meltdown of 2008. Prosperous baby boomers who expected to inherit from their parents found themselves supporting the older generation instead. In other cases, grandparents financed adult children who were

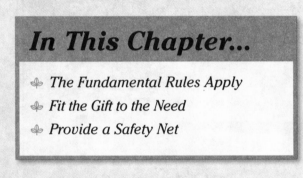

In This Chapter...

- ⚜ *The Fundamental Rules Apply*
- ⚜ *Fit the Gift to the Need*
- ⚜ *Provide a Safety Net*

overwhelmed by the high costs of raising their own offspring.

The bottom line? Gifts of cash or other assets can subject you to gift tax of up to 45 percent if you have used up your $1 million lifetime gift tax exemption. While generosity with family members often occurs under the radar, the law is clear: if the gift exceeds a certain value and the Internal Revenue Service catches it, you could be forced to pay the tax as well as interest, and, in some cases, penalties.

The Fundamental Rules Apply

The simplest and most tax-efficient way to subsidize others is by using the annual exclusion, which allows you to give $13,000 in cash or other assets each year to each of as many individuals as you want without having to worry about gift tax or generation-skipping transfer tax. Spouses can combine their annual exclusions to give $26,000 to any person tax-free. For example, a married couple with a child who is married and has two children could make a joint cash gift of $26,000 to the adult child, the child's spouse and each grandchild – four people – providing the family with $104,000 a year. Gifts that exceed this amount count against the $1 million ($2 million for married couples) lifetime exemption. After you have given away more than that, gift tax of up to 45 percent applies.

Although simply writing a check is the easiest approach, you can use a variety of other strategies to help people, with or without using the annual exclusion. Some are available only to family members; others can be used for unrelated people.

Fit the Gift to the Need

Here are strategies for subsidizing relatives and, in some cases, friends without having to pay gift tax.

Pay directly for medical, dental and tuition expenses. Without using your annual exclusion, you can pay for tuition, dental and medical expenses of anyone you want. These payments are exempt from both gift tax and generation-skipping transfer tax no matter how much you spend. Note that you must make the payments directly to the providers of those services – you can't just reimburse the person whom you want to benefit.

This chance to pay for medical and dental expenses, often overlooked, can be enormously useful. For example, you can apply this tax break to pay for dental implants for a cash-strapped friend. Or if someone you know is temporarily out of work and loses health insurance coverage, you could pay the premium for that person, or that person's family. You can cover anything that the person would be allowed to deduct on a tax return as an unreimbursed expense, including therapy for special needs children, fertility treatments and orthodontia.

This is a great way to help elderly parents with medically necessary home improvements, home-care attendants or nursing-home bills. You can also pay part of another person's long-term-care insurance – up to $3,080 for someone 61 to 70 years old, and up to $3,850 if the person is over 70. The medical care exclusion does have some restrictions: it doesn't include cosmetic surgery and massages, for instance.

As discussed in Chapter 9, you can pay someone's tuition (not room and board or other expenses) at any stage of education, from preschool to graduate school, as long as you write the check to the institution. Tuition may be paid annually or prepaid for multiple years. The risk of prepaying, of course, is that the money could be forfeited if the child winds up not going to that school or completing his or her education there.

Fund college savings plans. One way to apply a person's portion of the annual exclusion is to put money in Section 529 education savings plans (this was discussed extensively in Chapter 9). Establishing these plans for relatives could relieve siblings or children of the need to save for college at a time when they are overwhelmed with current expenses. You can set up a separate account for each family member whom you wish to benefit. Although your contributions to a 529 account are considered gifts, there are two unusual benefits: money in these account grows tax-free and can be withdrawn tax-free, provided it is used to pay for college, a graduate, vocational or another accredited school, or for related expenses, as well.

Offer rent-free living. You can let someone live in your house or buy a house and let them occupy it rent-free, so long as the fair market value of the rent comes within the annual exclusion. Remember, spouses can combine their annual exclusion amounts, if necessary, to make the gift fit.

Employ friends and family members. Whether they provide child care, manage real estate or keep the books, the compensation you provide must be reasonable – not more than you would pay a stranger for the same work. Paying a higher salary than you would pay outsiders exposes you to a potential double-whammy: Not only could you be personally liable for gift tax on the excess, but your company won't be able to deduct the full salary as a business expense. If you do hire friends and family members, you can also deduct at least part of the cost of health insurance and long-term-care insurance that they receive as a fringe benefit.

Lend and borrow money. Credit between family members requires the formalities of a bank loan, but the rate can be more favorable.

If you lend money to family members, you must charge a minimum rate of interest set each month by the Treasury, called the applicable federal rate to avoid potential gift tax and income tax consequences. If interest rates go down while the loan is in effect, you can refinance. The difference between the government-approved rate and what the borrowers would pay on a loan from a financial institution amounts to a tax-free gift. But if you are more generous than the government allows, the difference between the interest payments you are receiving and what you should be getting is considered a gift.

Family members can use money you lend them for any purpose.

Alternatively, you can benefit relatives by borrowing money from them and paying higher interest than they could get from money markets or bank CDs. There's no maximum government-set rate, but you can mimic the market by paying what a bank in your area would charge for a comparable personal loan.

Make a family member your dependent. To do that, you must pay at least 50 percent of the person's support. The law defines dependents very broadly – it can include most of your relatives and their spouses, for example.

Note, though, that you may not claim someone as a dependent if his or her annual gross income is more than $3,400. Social Security payments do not count, but required withdrawals from retirement plans, like IRAs and 401(k)s, do.

Those who claim a relative as a dependent can reap a huge tax benefit by adding the dependent's unreimbursed medical expenses to their own and deducting however much exceeds 7.5 percent of their adjusted gross income.

Give of yourself. If you have a talent that can relieve others of the need to pay for certain services, you may be able to give the greatest intangible gift. Whether you're a physician, architect, investment adviser, plumber, technology whiz or loving babysitter, there's no gift tax due when you lend a hand.

Gift Rap

People who give generously to family and friends often don't realize that they may be required to report the gift on Form 709, the gift tax return that is due on April 15 of the year after you make your gifts. If the IRS finds out you exceeded your $1 million lifetime gift tax exemption and didn't pay gift tax, it can assess back taxes, interest and penalties. This true-false test can help you gauge your gift tax acumen and avoid potentially costly oversights.

1. **You're required to pay income tax on gifts you receive from family and friends.**
   False. Contrary to common belief, the transfer is considered a gift, not income, and the donor is responsible for paying any gift tax due – not the recipient.

2. **You don't have to file a gift tax return unless you owe gift tax.**
   False. Anything above the $13,000 annual exclusion (adjusted for inflation) is considered a taxable gift, and you need to report it. Whether you will owe any tax depends on whether you have used up your $1 million lifetime gift tax exemption. One reason you must file a gift tax return is to show the IRS how much of the exemption amount you have used so far.

3. **Gifts worth less than $13,000 never have to be reported.**
   False. To come within the annual exclusion, a gift must be a present interest, meaning that the recipient can use it immediately. This becomes an issue with gifts to certain trusts whose beneficiaries don't have any rights until sometime in the future (as discussed in Chapter 6). Whenever you make a gift that isn't a present interest, it must be reported, no matter how small the amount.

4. **Married couples don't have to file a return as long as their combined gifts to each person come to $26,000 or less.**
   False. Spouses can pool their annual exclusions to give a combined gift of up to $26,000 per recipient tax-free. This practice, known as gift-splitting, generally requires each spouse to file a gift tax return and to consent, on the other's return, to gift-split. When making cash gifts, the easiest way to avoid having to file a return just for this purpose is for each spouse to make out a separate check for the $13,000 annual exclusion amount, rather than writing one check for the entire $26,000.

5. **If you didn't file gift tax returns for past tax years, it's too late to correct the situation.**
   False. Generally speaking, you have until the IRS catches the problem. When you're not liable for gift tax, there's no penalty for late filing.

6. **Filing a gift tax return increases your risk of an audit.**
   True. However, gift tax audits are far less common than estate tax audits. In any case, you can't always choose whether to file a return. When you make a transfer that's clearly a taxable gift, the law requires you to report it.

7. **You don't need to keep gift tax returns longer than three years.**
   False. Since your exemption amount and any gift tax you pay are cumulative, you must keep the returns indefinitely. Your executor needs them to calculate your estate tax. An estate tax audit is the most likely time for the IRS to flag unreported gifts or to question the value of the gifts you made. You do your heirs a favor by leaving them all the documentation they need.

Provide a Safety Net

When a friend or family member is relying on your largess, make sure you provide a fallback in case something happens to you. One possibility is to leave the individual an outright inheritance. But it's much better to create an irrevocable trust that can be funded through lifetime gifts, a bequest or a combination of the two. As discussed in Chapter 6, it's possible to set up trusts to benefit multiple people and provide as much flexibility or control as you want over how the funds will be distributed. Trusts have the additional advantage of protecting assets from the beneficiaries' creditors (see Chapter 18).

You can fund the trust with the proceeds of a life insurance policy (as discussed in Chapter 7) or income-producing assets, like bonds or shares in a closely held company. Better yet, if you are able to use rapidly appreciating assets, such as stock, real estate or interests in a business start-up, both the gift and any subsequent increase in value will be out of your estate.

Using your annual exclusion, you can add $13,000 a year ($26,000 if you're married) worth of cash or other assets for each trust beneficiary, so the more beneficiaries the more you can give away without paying tax. One issue you will face, assuming the trust is not expected to pay out immediately, is that to qualify for the annual exclusion, your gift must be a present interest. The most common way to meet this requirement is to give each beneficiary Crummey powers – the right for a limited time, usually 30 or 60 days, to withdraw from the trust the yearly gift attributable to that beneficiary (Crummey powers were discussed more fully in Chapter 6).

If you are using the annual exclusion to help the trust beneficiaries with current expenses, you may need to apply your $1 million lifetime exemption ($2 million for a married couple) to the assets you put into the trust. Depending on the type of trust you create, it may also be necessary to allocate or apply your $2 million generation-skipping transfer tax exemption as you contribute assets to the trusts (see Chapter 14).

To-Do List

Manage Future Risks

The stock market decline of 2008 and 2009 underscored the need to provide for maximum flexibility when structuring new trusts that family members may depend on to meet current expenses. These are some ways to do that:

❧ Establish your trust in a tax-friendly state, and give the trustee the authority to move the trust if changes in the law make a shift advantageous.

❧ Permit the trustee to substitute high-performing assets for underperforming ones.

❧ Choose a trustee who can actively manage the trust investments with an eye toward market fluctuations.

❧ Allow the trustee to decant the trust – to pay out funds from one trust to another.

Chapter 14

What You Can Do For Grandchildren

*Read this chapter if you would like
to provide a financial cushion for your
descendants in the years ahead.*

There are many ways to make gifts to grandchildren. The possibilities range from cash gifts to various ways of financing tuition and medical expenses to complex trusts that can offer grandchildren and subsequent generations a financial cushion for the rest of their lives. These techniques give you a chance to give away money gradually, as grandchildren's needs change and as you feel comfortable parting with the funds. Wealthy people can also take advantage of some devices to move significant sums downstream tax-free.

As you know from earlier chapters, when you make lifetime gifts, you need to be concerned about gift tax. When you transfer assets at death, estate tax may be an issue. Any time you give assets directly to grandchildren, or set up or add assets to trusts that benefit this generation or future ones, you need to plan for the 45 percent generation-skipping transfer or GST tax. This tax applies on top of the other two taxes.

In This Chapter...

- ⚜ *Gifts That Don't Count*
- ⚜ *A Trust for One Skip Person*
- ⚜ *When – and How – to Apply The GST Exemption*
- ⚜ *Pitfalls in Existing Plans*

GST tax is relevant whenever you make transfers, during life or at death, to what are called skip persons. Within a family, this means anyone other than your spouse who is two or more generations younger than you. Outside of the family, it covers anyone who is more than 37.5 years younger than you. A skip may be direct, meaning that the assets immediately go down at least two generations (for example, a grandmother gives her diamond ring to her granddaughter), or indirect, so that an earlier generation gets a share first – as would happen with a trust that provides payouts first to children and then to grandchildren.

GST tax can be imposed at one of two junctures. Perhaps the easiest to identify is when transfers are made to a skip person. These transfers can take various forms. They can involve a direct skip – such as when you make an outright gift to an individual or put money into a trust that exclusively benefits skip persons. Or, there may be a taxable distribution: for example, when a trust that benefits both skip persons and older family members makes a payout to a skip person. Generally, with a direct skip, you or your estate pay any GST tax; with a taxable distribution the recipient pays it.

The other type of event that could generate GST tax is what's known as a taxable termination. This is when the interests of all non-skip persons in a trust have ended, and skip persons are the remaining beneficiaries. For example, in a trust set up to pay income to your child for life and then give principal to the grandchildren, there could be a taxable termination when your child dies, because only grandchildren are eligible for trust payments. When there's a taxable termination, the GST tax is paid by the trustee using funds in the trust.

Generation-skipping transfer tax does not generally apply to you if a grandchild's parent (your own child) dies before you make a gift or create a trust. Under this exception to the usual rule, the child's share is treated as if it drops directly to the grandchild, rather than skipping a generation.

There are several ways to avoid or minimize GST tax, which was given its current form in 1986. Certain types of gifts don't count as generation-skipping transfers at all, so no GST tax is associated with them. There is also a special type of trust that you can fund without paying GST tax, so long as you make your contributions using the gift tax annual exclusion, discussed on page 195. (Under these conditions money distributed from the trust is not subject to the tax, either.) And for anything that doesn't fit within these categories, each of us has a $3.5 million GST tax exemption ($7 million for married couples) that we can use before the tax even kicks in.

If you don't expect to give your grandchildren more than a tiny fraction of the GST exemption amount, you might get the impression that you don't even need to think about this subject. That would be a mistake – just the kind of mistake that causes people to have to pay the GST tax unexpectedly. A common blunder is setting up a trust that could benefit members of an older generation and grandchildren while not allocating or applying at least part of your exemption to the trust at that time. What could happen? If the value of the trust assets increases dramatically, you might not have enough exemption left to cover that amount along with any other gifts you have made. This would cause a GST tax as grandchildren receive distributions or there's a taxable termination.

GST planning can help you avoid such mishaps and take advantage of the many opportunities to benefit grandchildren without having to pay the tax.

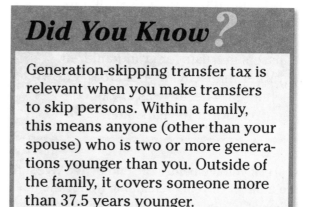

Gifts That Don't Count

Certain types of gifts commonly made to grandchildren are exempt from GST tax. They include:

Cash gifts that come within the annual exclusion. You are allowed to give $13,000 in cash or other assets each year to as many individuals as you want without having to worry about gift or GST tax. Married couples can combine this annual exclusion to jointly give $26,000 to any number of people tax-free – a practice known as gift-splitting. There are three ways to gift-split: each give $13,000 from an individual account; give $26,000 from a joint account, or give $26,000 from one of your accounts (the rules on filing gift-tax returns are discussed in Chapter 15).

Did You Know?

Generation-skipping transfer tax is relevant when you make transfers to skip persons. Within a family, this means anyone (other than your spouse) who is two or more generations younger than you. Outside of the family, it covers someone more than 37.5 years younger.

Any gift to a grandchild that's more than the annual exclusion counts against both the GST exemption and the lifetime gift tax exemption – the amount that each individual can give away during life without having to pay gift tax. Once you have passed the limit, which is $1 million ($2 million for married couples), gift tax of up to 45 percent applies.

If the grandchildren are minors, their portion of a cash gift would often go into a custodial account that designates an adult to oversee the money until the child is able to withdraw the assets under state law (usually at age 18 or 21). You should not name yourself as the custodian, because the money plus any appreciation could be considered part of your estate. You can name the child's parent, who can use the fund to pay for what might otherwise be unaffordable extras, such as dance lessons, summer camp and after-school programs. If you are concerned that the assets may fall into a child's hands too soon, the gift can be made in a specially designed trust. (How to deal with custodial accounts that have grown too large was discussed in Chapter 9.)

Contributions to college savings plans. Another way to apply the grandchildren's portion of the annual exclusion is to put money in Section 529 education savings plans (discussed extensively in Chapter 9). You can set up a separate account for each family member whom you wish to benefit. Money in a 529 account is federal-tax exempt provided it is withdrawn to pay for college, graduate, vocational or other accredited school and for related expenses.

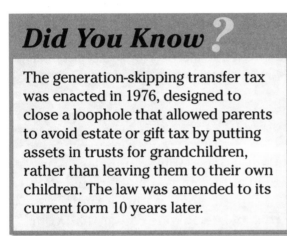

Did You Know ?

The generation-skipping transfer tax was enacted in 1976, designed to close a loophole that allowed parents to avoid estate or gift tax by putting assets in trusts for grandchildren, rather than leaving them to their own children. The law was amended to its current form 10 years later.

The law permits lump-sum deposits into Section 529 plans of as much as $65,000 per person at once ($130,000 for married couples), but you must file a gift tax return electing to treat the gift as if it had been spread over five years. If you die before the end of five years, the portion of the gift reflecting the number of years remaining will be included in your estate. During this five-year period, you cannot make additional annual exclusion gifts to the person you are benefiting with the 529 plan.

Direct payments for medical, dental and tuition expenses. Without using your annual exclusion or $1 million lifetime exemption from gift tax, you can pay for tuition and unreimbursed dental and medical expenses of anyone you want. These payments are exempt from both gift tax and GST tax no matter how much you spend. But you must make the payments directly to the accredited providers of those services (as discussed in Chapter 13).

You can make tuition payments at any stage, from preschool to graduate school, as long as you write the check directly to the institution. Tuition may be paid annually or prepaid for multiple years. The risk of prepaying is that the payments must be nonrefundable, according to the Internal Revenue Service, and could be forfeited if the child winds up not going to that school or not completing his or her education there.

A Trust for One Skip Person

By far the most popular way of making gifts to grandchildren is to put assets in a trust, because a trust generally provides the greatest flexibility and control over how the funds will be distributed. Unfortunately, this is also the most difficult terrain to negotiate.

The first strategic decision is whether you can accomplish your goals with a special kind of trust that will not cause GST tax, so you can save the GST exemption for other gifts. Section 2642(c) of the Internal Revenue Code describes the requirements for a trust that generally does not give rise to GST tax. The trust must be irrevocable and can only benefit one skip person – for example, a grandchild. If the grandchild dies before the funds have been fully distributed, the trust must say that the remaining funds become part of the grandchild's estate (making them tax vested – potentially subject to estate tax at that point).

Most estate planners meet this last requirement by giving the grandchild what's called a general power of appointment: the right to name the next person to receive the trust property, including, for example, the child's estate. Unless the child is married and wants to be sure the interest will go to his spouse, that power doesn't usually get exercised, but having it in the trust agreement makes the trust qualify under Section 2642(c). Anticipating that the power probably won't be exercised, the trust usually has a general provision directing how the assets should be distributed if the beneficiary dies before the funds are completely paid out. Typically, the assets will go to other grandchildren.

But setting up the perfect Section 2642(c) trust is not enough. As noted above, adding more money to the trust than is covered by the gift-tax annual exclusion is a direct skip, requiring you to pay GST tax for the transfer to the trust (though not for distributions from the trust to the skip person) if you don't have enough GST exemption to cover it. But you can avoid the need to pay the GST tax or use your GST exemption if the gift itself is exempt from GST tax. Gifts that use the gift-tax annual exclusion accomplish this goal. When you fund a Section 2642(c) trust using these gifts, the gift to the trust does not use your GST exemption or give rise to a GST tax.

As discussed in Chapter 9, to come within the annual exclusion, a gift must be a present interest, rather than a future interest. There are two ways for gifts to trusts to meet this requirement. By far the most popular is to give beneficiaries Crummey powers: the right for a limited time, usually 30 or 60 days, to withdraw from the trust the yearly gift attributable to that beneficiary. Each year, the trustees notify the beneficiaries (or the parents, if the beneficiaries are minors) in what is called a Crummey notice that they have the right to withdraw their portion of the annual gift to the trust. Any trust that includes this power is called a Crummey trust, although the trust may be named for its other distinguishing features (for example, "a Section 2642(c) trust with Crummey powers").

You can also meet the present interest requirement through a Section 2503(c) trust discussed in Chapter 9. Like a Section 2642(c) trust, these trusts must have only one beneficiary and must be subject to estate tax when he dies. The main difference between the two is that the beneficiary of a Section 2503(c) trust must have the right at age 21 to withdraw all the assets (although there are ways to persuade the child to leave the assets in the trust), and there must be no restriction on the right of the trustee to make distributions of principal and interest before that.

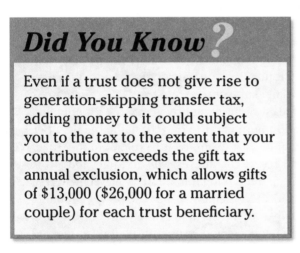

Did You Know?

Even if a trust does not give rise to generation-skipping transfer tax, adding money to it could subject you to the tax to the extent that your contribution exceeds the gift tax annual exclusion, which allows gifts of $13,000 ($26,000 for a married couple) for each trust beneficiary.

A common way of leveraging the annual exclusion amount in trusts to benefit grandchildren is to fund the trust with the proceeds of a life insurance policy. In this case, the 2642(c) trust would also be an irrevocable life insurance trust, or ILIT, described in Chapter 8. The trust buys life insurance on behalf of an older family member and holds the proceeds, when that person dies, for the beneficiaries. The named insured can be the grandparent or even the child's parent. The annual exclusion gift is only the money you put into the trust to finance the premium, not the full policy proceeds.

When there are multiple grandchildren, a trust for each of their benefits can buy a separate policy on the same person's life – say it's Grandpa's. Alternatively, a number of trusts can, in effect, function as partners, sharing the premiums and proceeds from a single policy.

However you choose to fund Section 2642(c) trusts, they are not appropriate for every situation. For example, because these trusts can only benefit grandchildren, you can't use them when you want the child's parents to receive benefits under the trust before the funds get distributed to grandchildren. Nor are they appropriate when you want the flexibility of being able to shift assets among your grandchildren, as the need arises – for example, to help pay for education or a first home. To accomplish these goals and many other purposes that trusts can serve (discussed in Chapter 6), you will need to consider the more complicated structure of a non-exempt trust – a trust that would trigger tax if you did not allocate your exemption to it, or if you had already used up the exemption.

When – and How – To Apply the GST Exemption

The GST exemption can be applied to an outright transfer or to a non-exempt trust. This might be a trust that has older family members (like your spouse or children) as the primary beneficiaries but that could benefit grandchildren afterward. Or, it might be a dynasty trust, which can go on in perpetuity in the states, including Alaska, Delaware, South Dakota and Wisconsin, that permit them. You do not need to be a resident of one of these states to choose that state as the situs or location of a trust. This is done in the trust document, which should choose the same state's law to govern the trust. However, in most cases, you need some connection with the state, such as having a trustee there, in order to be sure that its law will apply. Like certain other trusts discussed in this book, dynasty trusts can be structured so that while the property is in the trust it should not be subject to estate tax either.

Although tax law provides for automatic allocation for lifetime transfers to trusts that fit its definition of GST trusts, it's not always clear whether a particular trust fits. To be on the safe side and have a record of what you wanted to do, you should make the allocation when first transferring funds to a trust you want to be a GST exempt trust. After that, you can elect to have it treated as a GST trust and have the exemption automatically allocated to all future transfers to that trust. Conversely, if for some reason you don't want a trust to be treated as a GST trust even though it may fall within the law's definition, you can make a one-time election not to treat it as one. The place to make the allocation – or opt out of it – is on Form 709, the federal gift tax return that is

A Variety of Choices for Tax

Certain gifts can be used in combination, if you don't exceed the annual exclusion

	When does grandchild have direct access to the funds?	Does gift qualify for the annual exclusion?
Outright gift	Immediately	Yes
Gift to custodial account for a minor	Age 18 or 21, depending on the state	Yes
Direct payment of medical or tuition expenses	Never; payments must go directly to the provider or the institution	Gift doesn't count against annual exclusion or $1 million lifetime gift tax exemption
Gift to Section 529 plan	Never; withdrawals must go directly to college, vocational or graduate school	Yes
Gift to 2642(c) trust	Controlled by terms of the trust	Only if trust is also a Section 2503(c) trust or includes Crummey powers

ree Gifts to Grandchildren

f $13,000 ($26,000 for married couples)

Can gift exceed the annual exclusion amount?	Is gift exempt from GST tax?
Yes, but counts against $1 million lifetime gift tax exemption	Yes, up to annual exclusion amount and above that by allocation of GST exemption to the gift
Yes, but counts against $1 million lifetime gift tax exemption	Yes, up to annual exclusion amount and above that by allocation of GST exemption to the gift
Yes, without counting against $1 million lifetime gift tax exemption	Yes
Yes; up to $65,000 per recipient ($130,000 for spouses), but must elect on gift tax return to treat it as spread evenly over five years	Yes, up to annual exclusion amount (including lump-sum spread over five years)
Yes, but counts against $1 million lifetime gift tax exemption	Yes, up to the annual exclusion amount, and above that by allocation of the GST exemption to the gift

due on April 15 of the year after you make your gifts.

What if you already funded a trust and forgot to make the allocation? If the assets haven't appreciated in value (or have declined), you might be fine making a late allocation. Otherwise, you would typically need to get a ruling from the IRS – a costly procedure – granting you an extension of time to make your allocation. If you succeed, your allocation would be considered timely and could reflect the value of the assets when you put them into the trust.

A classic GST pitfall that the law only partially addresses involves the problems that surround the premature death of a trust beneficiary. Say you set up a trust to pay income to your son until age 35, at which time the son gets the principal. You wouldn't normally allocate the GST exemption to such a trust because you would expect the son to survive to 35, and you might want to use your GST exemption elsewhere. But if the son dies before then and has children, the trust assets would go to your grandchildren, creating a taxable termination.

Did You Know?

Generation-skipping transfer tax does not generally apply to you if a grandchild's parent (your own child) dies before you make a gift or create a trust. Under this exception to the rule, the child's share is treated as if it drops directly to the grandchild rather than skipping a generation.

Since such a trust doesn't fit the definition of a GST trust, there wouldn't have been automatic allocation to it. But if you still have GST exemption left, you can elect to allocate it retroactively to the trust. You would do this on a gift tax return filed on time for the year in which the child died.

Another issue you need to consider when setting up GST trusts is the inclusion ratio – generally the portion of assets in a given trust that are GST exempt. Over time, exempt and non-exempt assets can get mixed in the same trust. This can happen when gifts to the trust exceed your GST exemption, for instance. The result is a blended inclusion ratio. In lay terms, the effect is the same as if any distribution to a skip person was partially exempt and partially subject to GST tax.

Estate planners try to design trusts covered by the GST exemption to have what's called a zero inclusion ratio, meaning that it's completely GST exempt. That way, there isn't any tax on either a taxable distribution or a taxable termination. Other trusts would have an inclusion ratio of one, meaning that they would be entirely subject to GST tax. However, there would be no GST tax when those trusts make distributions for tuition and health care expenses directly to the providers of those services, even to benefit skip persons. These trusts can be extremely useful for that purpose.

Ideally you would use non-exempt trusts to benefit only non-skip persons, but there is a remedy when trusts have become blended: In many cases you can now split the trust into totally exempt and non-exempt trusts going forward. You don't need to go to court to do this, assuming the terms of the trust or state law allows such a severance. This rule is helpful in planning for new trusts and trying to correct problems in old ones.

Pitfalls in Existing Plans

With even the slightest oversight, generous gifts to grandchildren could be reduced by the onerous GST tax. These other common GST pitfalls may be lurking within your current estate plan:

IRA skips. Leaving individual retirement accounts to grandchildren is a great income tax strategy (discussed in Chapter 7). The main advantage is that the young person can stretch payouts out over his or her life expectancy and thereby defer income tax on the withdrawals.

Just remember that IRAs left to grandchildren may be subject to GST tax in addition to estate tax and income tax. (Beneficiaries are entitled to an income tax deduction for the portion of the estate tax and in some cases for GST tax attributable to an inherited IRA.) As with any other asset, an IRA left to the owner's child could be hit with GST tax if the child disclaims or turns down the inheritance, passing it to a grandchild.

If you don't have more effective ways to use your GST exemption, you might choose to generation-skip an IRA. This might appeal to people who are not extremely wealthy but happen to have sizeable IRAs, whose children don't need the money and who are not in a position to make large lifetime gifts.

Formula clauses. If you have not reviewed your estate planning documents lately, you should consider whether there is more money destined for GST trusts than you would like. This could happen if your will includes formula clauses to fund these trusts. Terms like "that portion," "that fraction" or "that amount" (without saying what it is) are signs of lawyers trying to take maximum advantage of the exemption, which kept changing. Instead of naming a specific sum that will go into a trust, many wills refer to an amount up to the exemption or express the sum as a percentage of whatever the limit happens to be when the person dies.

This is good standard practice, but remember that the GST exemption, which went up gradually starting in 2001, took a big jump to $3.5 million in 2009, from $2 million the previous year. Wills written long before that might not reflect your intentions anymore: Too much may now be going to benefit grandchildren and too little to older family members. If so, you will want to change your plan.

Future gifts. When adding funds to trusts in the future, keep another potential trap in mind: just because a particular transfer to a trust uses the gift tax annual exclusion does not mean it is always exempt from GST tax. Unless the trust is a 2642(c) trust, GST exemption needs to be allocated when you add assets to a trust that benefits skip persons. Otherwise, even if there is no GST tax when you make the gift, there could be tax later.

To-Do List

Set Your Priorities

When setting up trusts for grandchildren, discuss these questions with your advisers:

❧ What purposes can the trust funds be used for?

❧ How long should the trust last?

❧ If you have multiple grandchildren, should you have a separate trust for each one?

❧ When should the grandchildren have direct access to the money?

❧ Do you want the trust to benefit children as well as grandchildren?

❧ Who should be the trustee?

❧ What assets are available to fund the trust?

❧ Should you supplement these assets by having the trust buy a life insurance policy on your life?

❧ Should an independent trustee have the power to amend some or all of the trust provisions to anticipate changing family circumstances?

❧ Will you be responsible for income taxes on trust assets while you are alive?

Chapter 15

Give Now,
Save Tax Later

*Read this chapter if saving taxes
is a high priority.*

Most chapters of this book include at least some information that will resonate with almost everyone. This chapter and the next one are different. They focus on tools that are generally useful only to people who already have at least $10 million – or expect to in the near future.

In This Chapter...

- ⚜ *Capitalize on the Annual Exclusion*
- ⚜ *Harness Your Lifetime Exemption*
- ⚜ *Use Trusts That Offer Income Tax Benefits*
- ⚜ *Weigh the Pros and Cons of Paying Gift Tax*

If you find it hard to imagine that you may ever have that much money, consider this: Many people who build their own fortunes, rather than inheriting them, miss out on substantial opportunities to save estate taxes because they don't think about the subject until they have already become rich. So, even if you decide to skip this chapter, please remember that it's here, and come back to it should the need arise. Or read it now to see what the possibilities are.

What makes $10 million the magic number? The first $3.5 million you leave behind is exempt from federal estate tax. With planning, a married couple can avoid this 45 percent tax until their combined assets are more than $7 million and would face estate tax only on $3 million of their assets. By taking advantage of the unlimited marital deduction, they can postpone that tax until the second of them dies. (State taxes, discussed in Chapter 4, also need to be considered.) To avoid tax altogether, this couple would need to give away $3 million while they are alive.

Capitalize on the Annual Exclusion

One of the best ways to reduce estate taxes is to give away assets while you are alive. A threshold question for anyone contemplating this strategy is: Can I afford it?

First, you should be sure you are leaving yourself enough – and, to be on the safe side, assume that you will live to an advanced age. "How much will I need?" has always been a difficult question with a very personal answer, influenced by both economics and psychology. The subject heated up when the economic meltdown of 2008 left many people feeling financially shaken.

If you are not comfortable giving away large chunks of assets at one time, you can make smaller, affordable gifts. Currently, you can give up to $13,000 ($26,000 for a married couple) each year to each of as many recipients as you would like without incurring gift tax. This annual exclusion, which is indexed for inflation, is a "use it or lose it" tax break. In other words, if you do not make gifts in a given year, you cannot carry over the exclusion and give more to each person the following year.

To wealthy people who want to cut estate taxes dramatically, gifts of $13,000 per recipient every year may seem like peanuts, but in time the tax savings can add up. Let's say Sally has a total of 10 children and grandchildren and makes annual exclusion gifts to each of them over 20 years. The yearly gift will be $130,000 ($13,000 per person times 10). If that money is invested to earn 5 percent, at the end of 20 years she will have effectively moved about $4.51 million[1] downstream to subsequent generations, tax-free.

Without these gifts, if Sally dies at the end of 20 years, the family would be left with much less. Assuming her $3.5 million estate tax exemption is applied to other assets and that the federal estate tax rate is 45 percent, her heirs would need to pay about $2.03 million in estate taxes on the assets (45 percent of $4.51 million). Not counting the generation-skipping transfer tax that may also diminish sums going to grandchildren (see Chapter 14), the inheritance would be reduced to about $2.48 million.

Which gifts work best will depend on your finances, the nature of your assets and the needs of the recipients. It's possible to give away tangible personal property like art, jewelry or automobiles, but cash is by far the most frequent gift – to help a child who wants to buy a car, pay off a loan or start a business, for example.

[1] *Calculation by Lawrence P. Katzenstein*

With minors, cash gifts can be made to a custodian for the child's benefit under the Uniform Transfers to Minors Act, though you may not want to let custodial accounts grow too large, since under state law the child will have access to the money at a certain age – typically 21 (as noted in Chapter 9). These annual exclusion gifts don't count against the generation-skipping transfer (GST) tax exemption (see Chapter 14).

Many people also use annual exclusion gifts to fund trusts. One example is life insurance trusts, a time-tested technique for avoiding estate tax on the proceeds of a life insurance policy (as discussed in Chapter 8) as well as for protecting the funds from creditors (see Chapter 18). These trusts are commonly funded with annual exclusion gifts that the trust uses to pay the life insurance premium. This technique automatically achieves leverage because the gift is only the premium, not the full policy proceeds.

Did You Know ?

When making gifts of tangible personal property, you should hand over the items as soon as possible. You can't write a child's name on a painting and keep it on your wall, for example. If you do and you die, it will be considered part of your estate.

One condition for the annual exclusion is that the gift must be a present interest, meaning something the recipient can use right away, rather than a future one. This is an issue when funding trusts, since they are usually not expected to pay out immediately. One way to meet the present interest requirement is to give each beneficiary a Crummey power – the right for a limited time, usually 30 or 60 days, to withdraw from the trust the yearly gift attributable to that beneficiary (as discussed more fully in Chapter 6).

If you are not using your annual exclusion for other purposes, you can apply it to funding qualified state tuition programs, known as Section 529 plans. These plans, available in all 50 states and the District of Columbia, allow you to set up a tax-advantaged separate account, earmarked for higher education, for each child or grandchild (or any other individual). The funds, which are typically overseen by a private money manager, are exempt from federal income tax, provided they are withdrawn to pay for certain educational expenses (as noted in Chapter 9).

The most tax-efficient use of the annual exclusion is to make gifts of appreciating assets, such as stock that has declined in value but is expected to recover, real estate or interests in a business start-up that has growth potential. The gift is valued at the time of the transfer. If the asset later increases in value, that appreciation benefits your family member and will not be subject to estate or gift tax.

Annual exclusion gifts must be complete (received and, in the case of a check, either deposited or cashed) by December 31 of the year in which you make them. When starting an annual giving program, some people make gifts in December and again in January, effectively doubling what they can give away in a short stretch of time. Going forward, it's best to make gifts early in the year, rather than waiting for the December holiday season. That gets one more year of appreciation out of your estate. And if you die during the year ahead, the property will have already been transferred.

As with all gifts, you should put yourself in the shoes of the recipients. If your children must promptly sell the assets to raise cash, there's no point giving them appreciating – or appreciated – property. For income tax purposes, their cost basis in the property is the same as yours would be. And the capital gains tax they would have to pay could erode the value of the gift.

Harness Your Lifetime Exemption

One thing that makes annual exclusion gifts so appealing is that they pass outside of the transfer tax system and don't count against the lifetime exemption – what you can give away during life without triggering gift tax. Once you have passed the limit, which is $1 million, a gift tax of up to 45 percent applies. On the estate tax return, your $3.5 million estate tax exemption is reduced by the amount of the $1 million gift tax exemption you used. If you exceeded the limit, heirs can take a credit for the gift tax you paid for making lifetime gifts.

Plenty of people can accomplish their estate planning goals without ever using this exemption. For example (as discussed in Chapter 3), with minimal planning spouses can avoid estate tax until their combined assets total more than $7 million. They might not want to shed $1 million until their net worth is significantly more than that, especially given the unlimited marital deduction that permits them to postpone estate tax until the second of them dies.

Unmarried couples, however, do not have the benefit of the marital deduction and might be inclined to use their lifetime exemption sooner (see Chapter 4). So might surviving spouses who hold much more in the marital share than will be covered by their own $3.5 million exemption.

If you need the exemption to accomplish your tax goals, don't hoard it like a precious stash. The sooner you use it, the more future income and potential appreciation you can shift out of your estate. The lower the value of the assets – for example, because markets are depressed or because you are transferring shares of a start-up enterprise – the less exemption amount your gift will consume. A variety of techniques can get even more bang from each buck of the exemption (see Chapter 16).

Be aware, though, that the cost basis for assets transferred during life is different from that of inherited assets. Those that are inherited get a basis adjustment to the fair market value on the date of the owner's death. The advantage of this fresh start is that it limits the capital gains tax inheritors must pay if they sell the property. In contrast, if you transfer assets during life and they go up in value, as you would hope, there will be more gain to tax than if those same assets were inherited.

Still, the long-term capital gains tax rates of 15 percent for assets held more than a year is much more attractive than the 45 percent gift and estate tax rate. The presumption is that family members will still be better off with a lifetime gift because you will have prepaid the transfer tax when asset values are low. If asset values decline, on the other hand, you will have wasted part of your gift tax exemption, by paying more than you would have if you had waited to make your gift.

Use Trusts That Offer Income Tax Benefits

Sometimes an income tax strategy offers enormous estate planning benefits. Converting a traditional IRA to a Roth (discussed in Chapter 7), is a great example of that. Grantor trusts are another.

A grantor trust is not a single variety of trust, but a set of characteristics that can be incorporated into various types of popular trusts. The term refers to the fact that the person who creates the trust, known as the grantor, retains certain rights or powers. As a result, the trust is not treated as a separate entity for income tax purposes and the grantor, rather than the trust or its beneficiaries, must pay tax on trust earnings.

A 2004 Revenue Ruling made it clear that paying the tax is not considered a gift to the trust beneficiaries. Yet this tax, on income that the grantor probably never receives, shrinks his estate. At the same time, assets can appreciate inside the trust without being depleted by ordinary income taxes or capital gains taxes.

For example, let's say a couple set up a trust to benefit their five grandchildren and fund it with annual exclusion gifts of $130,000 per year ($26,000 apiece times five grandchildren). Consider the benefit of grantor trust status if this trust successfully invests a single year's contributions – perhaps by purchasing stock in a new business that one of the grandchildren has started. Let's say that five years later the company goes public and the stock originally bought for $130,000 is

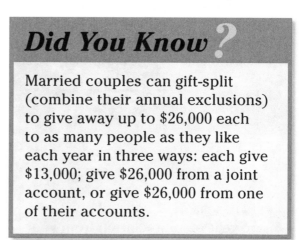

Did You Know?

Married couples can gift-split (combine their annual exclusions) to give away up to $26,000 each to as many people as they like each year in three ways: each give $13,000; give $26,000 from a joint account, or give $26,000 from one of their accounts.

worth $2 million. If the trust sells this stock, the grandparents, rather than the trust, would pay the capital gains tax on the $1.87 million in appreciation. At today's 15 percent rate for long-term capital gains, that tax would be $280,500 (15 percent of $1.87 million). By paying this tax, the grandparents effectively make an additional tax-free gift to the trust.

Another attractive feature of these irrevocable trusts is that assets placed in the trust are removed from the senior family member's estate. From an estate and gift tax perspective, the transfer is treated as a completed gift. The value of the assets is frozen at the time of the transfer, so that future appreciation is not subject to estate or gift tax. These trusts can be useful for a broad range of people, from young entrepreneurs with mushrooming assets to elderly couples with securities portfolios.

Creating a grantor trust. A variety of powers, contained in the trust document, will have the effect of conferring it with grantor trust status. Examples include the right of the grantor or the grantor's spouse to receive loans from the trust without collateral, and the option to reacquire certain trust assets and substitute others of equivalent value. Whether such powers are actually exercised – and often they are not – putting them into the instrument makes it a grantor trust.

Types of trusts that can be grantor trusts. Grantor trust powers can be included in trusts established for many different purposes, which are discussed elsewhere in this book. For instance, they work well in trusts designed to receive gifts under the annual exclusion. They are also extremely helpful in an irrevocable life insurance trust or ILIT (as discussed in Chapter 8). The more quickly funds accumulate inside the trust, the sooner it will be able to pay the premiums without further gifts from the grantor. When an ILIT is a grantor trust, both the grantor and the trustee will also have more flexibility to adapt the insurance and other trust assets to changing circumstances. For example, the IRS has ruled in several cases that insurance policies can be transferred between two grantor trusts without triggering taxable gain.

> ## *Did You Know* ?
>
> You should make gifts to individuals or to trusts early in the year, rather than waiting for the December holiday season. That removes one more year of appreciation from your estate. And if you die during the year ahead, the property will have already been transferred.

Another type of trust that becomes more attractive if it has grantor trust status is the bypass- or credit-shelter trust (discussed in Chapter 3). This trust, which is crucial for spouses' estate planning, preserves the $3.5 million federal estate tax exemption for both of them.

To review how this trust typically works: You arrange to fund the trust up to $3.5 million when you die. The trust distributes income and principal to your spouse and other family members while the surviving spouse is alive, and then passes on whatever is left to family. Since funds in the bypass trust are covered by the exemption amount, they will not be taxed when you die. Nor are they considered part of your spouse's estate, so they are not subject to tax when she dies either.

But there is one major obstacle to making a credit-shelter trust a grantor trust: If you wait until death to fund it, the person you would like to be the grantor will be dead, and a dead person can't be the grantor of a trust. Three lawyers have developed a two-step work-around that enables the surviving spouse to be the grantor.[2]

The first step is for each spouse to create a lifetime qualified terminable interest property, or QTIP, trust for the benefit of the other, and fund it up to the $1 million lifetime exemption amount. As with any QTIP trust, the trustee must pay all income to the beneficiary spouse for life (the trustee can also make distributions of principal), and the trust can't make distributions to anyone other than the spouse while he or she is alive. By design, this trust is a grantor trust with respect to the spouse who created it.

Next, when the QTIP beneficiary dies, the assets pass into a credit-shelter trust using the beneficiary's estate tax exemption. In effect, the QTIP basically turns into a credit-shelter trust but, under the grantor trust rules, the spouse who created the QTIP remains the grantor. Since the surviving spouse pays tax on the trust income, the credit-shelter trust has all the advantages of any other grantor trust. This arrangement can greatly expand the pot available for the couple's descendants.

One potential complication: under the law of most states, if the grantor is the beneficiary of a trust, the grantor's creditors can reach the trust assets. The way to address this problem by making the situs or home of the trust in a state that has a different rule (see Chapter 18).

Making your spouse the beneficiary of a grantor trust. Even outside the context of a credit-shelter trust, there may be times when you will want to make your spouse a beneficiary of the grantor trust. This strategy has several advantages.

One is that the benefits of grantor trust status can last longer that way. As noted earlier, typically grantor-trust status ends when you die, and the trust becomes responsible for paying its own income taxes. However, if you die first and your spouse is a beneficiary, your powers as grantor are attributed to your spouse. Your spouse can continue paying the trust income taxes.

Another advantage if your spouse is the beneficiary is that you can reduce the size of a trust that has grown too large. Perhaps your own financial circumstances have changed, and you need extra funds to maintain your lifestyle. Or maybe you are afraid of spoiling your descendants. In such cases, you can funnel some money out of the trust by making distributions to your

---

[2] *"Supercharged Credit Shelter Trust," by Mitchell M. Gans, Jonathan G. Blattmachr and Diana S.C. Zeydel, 21 Probate & Property 4, July/August 2007.*

The Power of a Grantor Trust

Tax-free compounding within a grantor trust can translate into significant sums. Let's say a trust is funded with $1 million of assets, invested for growth to produce a total return of 7 percent per year before tax, or 5 percent per year after tax.

Compare what the value of the assets would be in 20 years if the grantor pays this tax, so the assets can grow tax-free, with the value if the trust pays the tax.

Year	Grantor pays the tax (Assets grow tax-free)	Trust pays the tax
5	$1,402,552	$1,276,282
10	$1,967,151	$1,628,895
15	$2,759,032	$2,078,928
20	$3,869,684	$2,653,298

Source: Lawrence P. Katzenstein

spouse. Depending on the situation, your spouse can either keep those funds or donate them to charity, which would generate a charitable income tax deduction (see Chapter 17).

Naming a spouse as beneficiary also offers a means to finance the trust income taxes, which can become a major concern. If, for any reason, the income tax burden becomes unmanageable, the trustee can make distributions to your spouse, who can then use the funds to pay the tax for which you would be liable on a joint return.

Note: one downside of having your spouse as a beneficiary is that in funding the trust, you will not be able to exercise the option, available only to married couples, of combining your lifetime exemption amounts. Instead, you will be limited to an exemption of $1 million apiece.

Escape hatches. With all estate planning techniques, you must be able to part with the property you are transferring, but grantor trusts pose an additional risk: You must also retain enough money to pay the tax bills if the trust assets hugely appreciate. For example, if the trust owns a large position in low-basis stock that is about to soar suddenly in value – say, because the company is being sold – the tax liability could be more than you are prepared to pay.

As noted above, naming your spouse as a beneficiary provides a vehicle for channeling money to you as a couple that can be used to pay the taxes.

Another option when you expect the tax bill to be unaffordable is to terminate or turn off grantor-trust status. How you toggle off the trust will depend on the provisions that made the instrument a grantor trust in the first place. For example, you could renounce the power to reacquire certain trust assets and substitute others of equivalent value. Some lawyers rely on grantors to relinquish any relevant powers and give the trustee authority to turn off the rest. Others set things up so that an independent party, known as a trust protector (as noted in Chapter 6), can terminate all the appropriate provisions. While it is possible to draft a trust so that someone can also restart grantor trust powers, it is not a good idea to structure things this way because it starts to look as though the grantor is retaining enough control of the trust that it might be subject to inclusion in his estate.

Weigh the Pros and Cons of Paying Gift Tax

Let's say you have made the most of the legal limits on lifetime gifts, using both the annual exclusion and the lifetime gift tax exemption, but your heirs would still face a huge estate tax bill. Should you go beyond the amount that is exempt from gift tax and make taxable transfers to family members?

First of all, if you're asking this question, congratulations: you are in a lucky minority. Most people who get to this point are either so well off that they will never need to worry about money or so opposed to paying taxes that they will take all legal steps to avoid it. Sometimes both factors are at play.

When deciding whether to make a gift that will require you to pay gift tax, consider that with all lifetime gifts, post-gift compounding augments the benefits of the transfer. Especially when assets are appreciating, there can be opportunity costs to postponing a gift. Given enough time, the tax you save on post-gift appreciation can easily surpass what you spend on the front end.

These are two other key factors to consider:

Gift tax is cheaper than estate tax. Although the rates are similar – 45 percent estate tax, and up to 45 percent gift tax – the taxes are calculated differently. Family members may wind up getting more through a lifetime gift than they would through an inheritance.

Assume Jack has used up his lifetime gift tax exemption and is in the top gift tax bracket. He makes a $3 million gift of cash to his daughter, Jane. In effect Jack's gift costs him $4.35 million: $3 million goes to Jane and Jack pays another $1.35 million in gift tax (45 percent of $3 million). But there is tax only on the sum he gives away – not on the money he uses to pay the tax. This is called a tax exclusive system.

In contrast, estate tax is tax inclusive, meaning that the tax applies not only to an inheritance but also to the money used to pay the tax on that bequest. So if Jack takes the same $4.35 million and leaves it to Jane in his will, assuming that entire sum was subject to tax, the tax bill would be $1.9575 million and she would receive only $2.3925 million. Thus, for the same $4.35 million cost to Jack (or his estate) Jane gets $607,500 more with a lifetime gift than she would from an inheritance.

Lifetime gifts have a dual benefit. They reduce the size of your taxable estate. And, if an asset increases in value after you have made a gift, the appreciation passes tax-free.

Back to Jack and his $3 million gift. Assume that instead of cash, he gives Jane a piece of land today valued at $3 million. Assume, too, that the land will be worth $6 million when Jack dies three years from now. The estate tax at that time is 45 percent, but because the appreciation occurred after Jane took title, there is no transfer tax on the increase in its value.

But if Jack had kept the land and left it to Jane in his will, there would be estate tax on the entire value of the parcel when he died – a $2.7 million levy (45 percent of $6 million). That's twice what Jack would have paid in gift tax if he gave Jane the land three years earlier. And if the estate didn't have enough other assets, it might be necessary to sell some of the land to raise cash to pay the tax.

If, based on these factors, you decide that it makes sense to pay gift tax now to save estate tax later, your goal will be to structure your lifetime gift so that it will incur as little tax as possible. Tools for doing this are discussed in Chapter 16.

To-Do List

Follow Gift Protocols

Take the following steps to avoid some common gift mistakes:

❧ Spouses who combine their annual exclusions to give away up to $26,000 per recipient tax free – a practice known as gift-splitting – usually must each file a gift tax return and consent, on the other's return, to gift-split. When making cash gifts the easiest way to avoid filing a gift tax return just for this purpose is for each spouse to write a separate check for the $13,000 annual exclusion amount.

❧ Report annual exclusion gifts on the gift tax return any time there's room for debate about what the interest is worth. Under the tax law and Internal Revenue Service regulations, to start the statute of limitations running on your gift tax return, you must make "adequate disclosure" of the gift. The only way to do that is to file a gift tax return reporting the gift.

❧ To document your decision to transfer tangible property, send a letter to the recipient saying something like: "Dear nephew, I've decided to give you my piano. I'm going to give half to you on December 31 and the other half to you on January 1. Please arrange to pick it up." If you pass away before actually transferring the item, the property will be out of your estate.

❧ Send annual notices each year letting trust beneficiaries know about their right to withdraw their portion of your annual exclusion gift to their trust (see Chapter 6) made during the year. Keep copies with your important papers. It's not unusual for the IRS to ask for these Crummey letters during an estate tax audit, particularly when there is an irrevocable life insurance trust in place at the time of death. If no one can produce them, the IRS can argue that since the beneficiaries were not aware of the withdrawal rights, there were no present interest gifts under the annual exclusion. All gifts to the trust would then be treated as taxable gifts that do not qualify for the annual exclusion. Those gifts would be applied against your $1 million lifetime gift tax exemption or, if it has already been used up, could result in back gift taxes being due.

Chapter 16

Make Lifetime Gifts Go Further

*Read this chapter if you have
the resources to transfer large
sums of money while you are alive.*

This chapter, like Chapter 15, is designed for people whose heirs will be saddled with an enormous estate tax bill if they did not do careful planning. Most methods of addressing this problem involve reducing your net worth through irrevocable transfers made while you are alive. These transfers leave less for the government to tax, and if the assets increase in value after you have passed them along, the appreciation is tax-free.

But even people in a position to do this quickly run up against the lifetime exemption: you can give away only $1 million ($2 million for married couples) before a gift tax of up to 45 percent applies. This chapter continues the discussion in Chapter 15 and looks at several advanced techniques designed to pack as much value as possible into both the lifetime exemption and the annual exclusion, which allows you each year to give up to $13,000 ($26,000 for married couples) to as many recipients as you like.

In This Chapter...

- Create GRATs
- Use Family Entities to Achieve Discounts
- Sell Assets Instead of Giving Them Away

Which tools you use depends on various factors: the type of assets, when and how much you expect them to appreciate, your cash flow needs and your tolerance for risk and complexity. Unlike many simpler tools, these techniques may require participation by financial advisers, and their fees may be substantial. You should be sure the potential tax saving justifies the expenditure.

If this approach still sounds appealing, start by identifying those assets with the lowest current value and the greatest likelihood of growth. As always, it is best to choose the simplest and most effective method to accomplish your goals.

Create GRATs

With a grantor retained annuity trust, or GRAT, you put appreciating assets into an irrevocable trust and retain the right to receive an annual payment for the entire trust term. This annuity is based on a rate set each month by the U.S. Treasury called the Section 7520 rate (named after a section of the Internal Revenue Code). The latest Section 7520 rates are available at www.tigertables.com.

If the value of the trust assets increases by more than this rate, your GRAT will be economically successful. In that case, the excess appreciation will go to family members (the remainder beneficiaries) or to trusts for their benefit when the GRAT term ends. But if the appreciation never occurs, you are no worse off; the trust would simply satisfy its payout obligations by returning some assets to you. At that point it's possible to "re-GRAT" the assets – to create another GRAT – in the hope that they will do better in the future.

It is currently possible to set up a GRAT that results in no taxable gift – or at least a nominal one. Under these circumstances, there's no lifetime gift tax exemption wasted if the asset does not perform as you hoped.

Within this basic structure, many variations are possible, and you can engineer both the GRAT term and the annuity for maximum financial benefit. Since you must live until the end of the trust term for a GRAT to work, many people choose short-term GRATs – two years is the minimum. (If you die before the GRAT term ends, all or a portion of the trust will be included in your estate.)

A short-term GRAT is also the better approach if you're dealing with a volatile asset, anticipate significant appreciation soon and want to capture it before the value dips. You can even hedge the mortality and investment risks by forming a series of short-term GRATs created over a certain time span – say 10 GRATS, each with a two-year term.

With longer-term investments – for example, shares in a family business passing to children through a GRAT – those who are hearty and optimistic might opt for longer trust terms. This locks in the Section 7520 rate, which would be desirable if interest rates are low when you set up the GRAT. Whether you go short-term or long-term, you can use the annuity stream to fund additional trusts, creating a series of cascading GRATs.

Likewise, you can structure the payout to reflect your expectations about investment performance. Often, GRAT annuities are designed to be lower in the first year and increase by a preset percentage of up to 20 percent annually in successive ones, as the trust asset appreciates. But if the GRAT asset is very volatile – as it would be for a call-spread option, a put-spread option or a currency trade, for example – or if you expect a big capital gain in Year 1, you can provide for a higher initial payment to reflect that.

With assets that are difficult to value, such as closely held stock or real estate, a GRAT offers an additional benefit. By expressing the annuity as a percentage of the initial value of the GRAT, you permit the trust to simply pay a larger annuity (with no gift tax consequences) if the Internal Revenue Service determines the property is worth more than you initially calculated.

Note that GRATs are not appropriate for transfers to grandchildren and more remote descendants. The $3.5 million exemption from generation-skipping transfer tax can't be applied until the trust term ends, by which time you hope asset values will be higher. (The generation-skipping transfer tax was discussed in Chapter 14.)

Once you have created a GRAT, you or your financial advisers need to monitor the performance of the assets you put into it. Although you can't add any assets to a GRAT, it is possible to reacquire trust assets and substitute others of equivalent value. There are two occasions when you might want to do that. One is when asset values have declined, making the GRAT unsuccessful. The other is when assets have increased in value but you think they may go down before the GRAT term ends.

In both of these cases, there might be a benefit to getting the volatile assets out of the GRAT and putting them into a new one at the lower rate, essentially giving you a fresh start. You can do this by exchanging the property either for cash or for another asset of equal value. Alternatively, you can buy the assets from the GRAT using a promissory note.

Since a GRAT is a grantor trust – one in which the person creating the entity retains certain rights or powers – it is possible for that person to do all of these transactions with the trust and not have to pay income tax. (Grantor trusts were discussed in Chapter 15.)

❧

Use Family Entities to Achieve Discounts

Some people use closely held enterprises, such as family limited partnerships, or FLPs, and limited liability companies, or LLCs, to maximize investment opportunities and for asset protection (see Chapter 18). They can also be used to discount assets before transferring them to family members or trusts for their benefit.

GRAT Results

Sally is 50 and puts $1 million worth of property into a two-year GRAT. If the Section 7520 rate is 4 percent and the GRAT is designed so there is no taxable gift, Sally would receive a yearly annuity of $530,194.*

If the assets increase at the rate shown below, the GRAT will have the following results:

Rate of annual trust earnings	Gift-tax free transfer to children when GRAT ends
7 percent	$47,398
10 percent	$96,592
15 percent	$182,583

This example assumes that the payments are equal, although many GRATs are designed so the second payment is 20 percent more than the first one.

Source: Lawrence P. Katzenstein, Tiger Tables Actuarial Software

Here is how these family-controlled entities work: A senior family member puts assets, such as marketable securities, real estate or shares of an operating business, into the entity, which is most often an FLP but may be a LLC (some lawyers are more familiar with that structure). Then the individual sells or gives away shares in the entity that holds the assets – not the assets themselves. Since the interests can't readily be sold outside the family, their value is discounted for both lack of marketability and lack of control (typically a total discount of 20 to 30 percent).

By reducing the value of partnership units or membership shares for gift tax purposes, discounts enable you to minimize the tax cost of transferring assets. That can make your gift fit within the annual exclusion or lifetime exemption amount or, for gifts that exceed these amounts, reduce how much gift tax you will have to pay.

Note, though, that using family-controlled entities for estate planning purposes is an invitation to an estate tax audit, in which the IRS disputes the amount of the discount you took when selling or transferring the shares. Good records are essential to settling the audits favorably. For starters, you need to get a professional appraisal at the time you set up the entity and make the first transfers, with follow-up appraisals if the value of the entity has changed when you make subsequent transfers. Those appraisals, which should be attached to the gift tax return due on April 15 of the year after you make the gift, can cost $10,000 to $15,000.

Avoiding or defending a tax audit goes far beyond that. The IRS has brought numerous cases challenging these arrangements, winning some and losing others. Although the decisions are sometimes hard to reconcile, certain facts have tipped the scale in the government's favor (with a strong case, taxpayers have been able to settle with the IRS for 25 to 30 percent of the disputed amount). Family-controlled entities seem especially vulnerable to attack when:

- the senior family member who sets up the entity and primarily funds it retains control over critical decisions or the right to income or use of partnership property
- one partner withdraws funds from the partnership without making corresponding distributions to the other partners
- the entities are formed by people who are terminally ill or extremely old.

Not surprisingly, taxpayers also tend to lose these cases when they transfer most of their assets into the entity, use it to pay personal expenses, commingle personal assets with partnership ones or put a home into the entity and continue to live in it rent-free. In fact, the biggest problem with these entities is not the legal documents but the way people run them after they leave the lawyer's office. The IRS has been successful in demonstrating that people did not respect the formalities of the FLP as a business.

So far, the best defense against an IRS challenge has been to assert that there was a non-tax reason for using a partnership. Examples include:

- *Protecting property from creditors.* As a rule, creditors of a limited partner cannot take partnership assets or force a liquidation, although they can reach distributions the entity makes to the partner.
- *Streamlining or facilitating wealth transfer.* Instead of struggling to divide certain assets like real estate or stock portfolios, which may be difficult to apportion, it's possible to transfer the assets to an entity and give various people shares in the enterprise.
- *Avoiding probate on real estate you own in other states.* By putting the

land or building into a family partnership, you convert real property, which must be probated in the state where it is situated (as discussed in Chapter 2), to intangible personal property that is probated in the state where the owner lived.

❧ *Reducing investment management costs by consolidating the assets of various family members in one portfolio.* Many financial institutions offer reduced fee schedules for large accounts.

Another issue to think about is your tolerance for the sort of administrative details that will help the arrangement withstand an audit. Basically, you must operate the entity like a business. That means only making distributions in proportion to each person's partnership interest. You should also hold regular partnership meetings, keep minutes of those meetings and make sure they reflect some of the non-tax purposes the entity is serving.

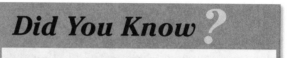

Did You Know

The financial crisis that began in 2008 created opportunities. Low asset values and the decline in interest rates used in some wealth-transfer tools drastically cut the tax cost of lifetime transfers. Heirs would benefit from any appreciation with no additional tax due.

Finally, you need to consider these entities in the context of your own family dynamics. Since family members will be yoked together in the enterprise, it's preferable that they get along well.

Sell Assets Instead of Giving Them Away

Although you can make gifts of any assets, including partnership interests, using the annual exclusion and lifetime exemption amounts, you can avoid gift tax altogether by selling the assets to the people whom you want to benefit instead of giving them away. Here, too, both the property sold and any future appreciation are removed from the your estate. Since you will need to set a fair sale price, it is preferable to use assets that are not difficult to value.

Typically the sale is done in exchange for a promissory note with interest. You must charge interest at the applicable federal rate, set each month by the Treasury. Otherwise the "missing interest" could be treated as a taxable gift. In some cases, the IRS can also attribute interest income to you and tax you on the amount you should have earned.

If you, like many people, worry that lifetime transfers will leave you short of money, you may feel more comfortable with a technique like this one that creates an income stream. (A GRAT has the same virtue.) The drawback is that cash received as interest and principal payments on the note bring assets back into your estate, even as you strive to trim what will ultimately be taxed.

While you can sell the assets directly to family members, there is a distinct advantage to using a grantor trust in these installment sales. Here's why: Since the trust is not treated as a separate entity for income tax purposes, the grantor, rather than the trust or its beneficiaries, must pay tax on trust earnings. Therefore, there is no capital gains tax on the sale to the trust and no tax on interest payments you receive. And by paying the taxes on income generated by the trust, you in effect make an additional tax-free gift to the trust beneficiaries. (Grantor trusts were discussed in Chapter 15.)

This tool requires that the trust have other assets – as a rule of thumb, at least 10 percent of the value of the assets being transferred through the installment sale. Often the grantor supplies this seed money, using the $1 million lifetime gift tax exemption.

The installment sale to an irrevocable grantor trust is a popular alternative to a GRAT because it addresses the two key drawbacks of the GRAT: the risk of dying during the trust term and the inability to use the generation-skipping transfer tax exemption until the GRAT ends. However, installment sales have their own set of potential pitfalls. One is that there are only scattered court cases – but no federal law – to support them.

Other risks relate to the vicissitudes of the market. If asset values plummet, as they did in 2008 and the first quarter of 2009, the note could easily be worth more than the trust property. In that case, the trust might need to use some of its initial funding to make interest payments. The grantor, who would be getting back assets he put into the trust, will have wasted any lifetime gift tax exemption or gift tax used to fund the trust.

On the other hand, if the trust assets wildly appreciate, a grantor who has not set aside enough money to pay the tax bills could be wiped out. Although there are ways to avoid this problem if you and your advisers anticipate it, the situation can be more difficult to address after the fact.

To-Do List

Weigh the Pros and Cons

In choosing between a transfer to a grantor retained annuity trust, or GRAT, and an installment sale to a grantor trust, consider these differences.

	GRAT	Installment Sale
Interest rate hurdle	Higher hurdle: Section 7520 rate (set monthly by Treasury)	Lower hurdle: applicable federal rate (set monthly by Treasury)*
Compelling reasons to choose this tool	• Potentially volatile asset • Increase in value likely to occur suddenly, and within GRAT term (short-term focus) • Asset is difficult to value	• Predictable, growth-oriented asset, with minimal volatility • Timeline for appreciation is uncertain (long-term focus) • You want to benefit grandchildren • You are old or in poor health
Effect of decline in property values	Annuity is paid back "in kind" using contributed assets, and remainder beneficiaries may get nothing	The note might be worth more than the trust property
Must grantor survive until end of term for technique to be effective?	Yes	No
Legal support	Strong case law; federal regulations	Scattered case law; no statutes or regulations

The rate for a short-term (three years or less) or mid-term (more than three years and up to nine years) loan is lower than the Section 7520 rate.

Chapter 17

Your Charitable Legacy

*Read this chapter if there are causes
you care deeply about and would like
to benefit now or later.*

P hilanthropy is ingrained in our culture, and most of the money comes from individuals rather than from corporations or foundations. Studies have found that Americans, on average, are significantly more generous than people in other nations, and while the wealthiest Americans give the most (the top 10 percent accounts for 25 percent of giving), low-income Americans generously give the highest portion of their income.

Whether you give to charity during your life or through your estate plan, philanthropy can create a meaningful legacy while reducing your tax burden.

In This Chapter...

- *Benefiting Family (or Yourself), As Well as Charity*
- *Creating a Continuing Fund, Rather Than a One-Shot Gift*
- *Choosing the Best Assets to Donate*
- *Strategies That Postpone Tough Choices*

As noted previously, gifts made during life, if you can afford them, give you a chance to see your money put to good use. They can also be much more tax efficient. With lifetime gifts, you can take an income tax deduction for the year in which you make the gift, and reduce the size of your estate, leaving less to be taxed. In contrast, if you make a gift in your will, your estate can take a charitable deduction only against the estate tax – there is no income tax deduction.

Some people are reluctant to make large lifetime donations because they depend on income from their investments or want to make a priority of taking care of family first. But there's a middle ground: split-interest gifts made during life or through an estate plan that provide an income stream for you or a person you designate, as well as a payout to charity.

Minimally, every estate plan should include what's sometimes called a bomb clause, naming the charity that would receive your assets if you and your closest heirs are wiped out simultaneously, as in an accident, and you prefer to benefit charity rather than some distant relative. Those who go further carve out a portion of their estate or a specific dollar amount for charity (see Chapter 2).

Whichever approach you choose, thinking about innovative ways your money could be used adds a lively note to a difficult topic. You can benefit causes that you supported during life or embark in new directions. For many people the choices are influenced by schools they attended, cultural pursuits that gave them pleasure, ties to their community or diseases that have afflicted family members.

The simplest way to make a bequest is to designate one or more charities in your will or living trust, or on the beneficiary designation form of your retirement account (see Chapter 7). This may be any charity to which you could make a gift and then take a corresponding charitable deduction from your taxable income. Or, you can launch a program of lifetime giving that allows you to teach your children about philanthropy, and with further funding through your estate plan, sets aside money for them to carry on that charitable legacy after you are gone.

Which tools you choose will depend on your interests and priorities, current need for funds, concern about taxes and family values. You may even want to use multiple vehicles in conjunction with each other.

Benefiting Family (or Yourself), as Well as Charity

E ven very wealthy donors who previously might have made an outright gift to charity have become more cautious after the financial crisis that began in 2008. "Will I have enough to retire comfortably?" and "Could a charitable bequest shortchange my family?" are reasonable questions that might dissuade people from philanthropy and make charity a second-choice beneficiary.

If you share these concerns but also want to include charity in your estate plan, there is another option: gifts that provide funds for you or your family and also benefit charity. These are the possibilities:

Charitable gift annuity. This is a contract in which the donor contributes assets – typically cash or marketable securities – and the charity agrees to pay a fixed amount of money annually to that person and perhaps the surviving spouse. The size of an annuity payment is based on the age at which it begins. Most charities use suggested maximum rates from the American Council on Gift Annuities (available at www.acga-web.org). Gift annuities factor in an assumption that when the donor dies the charity will get about 50 percent of the initial value of the amount transferred. Therefore the rates are lower than those of annuities from commercial insurance carriers.

A gift annuity is backed by the assets of the charity, even if it must dip into other funds to make the payment. But these contracts are not a certainty. If the endowment dries up or the organization shuts, the payments will stop. In a bankruptcy case, the annuity holder becomes an unsecured creditor.

At the time of your donation, you can take an income tax deduction. It is based on actuarial tables that take into account the rate the charity is offering, the age of and number of annuitants (one or two) and federal interest rates at the time you enter into the arrangement. A portion of each annuity payment is considered return of principal and not taxed. The rest is taxed as ordinary income if you contributed cash. If you contributed appreciated property held for more than a year, part will also be taxed as a long-term capital gain.

Charitable trusts. Two major types of trusts can be set up during life or through an estate plan and used to benefit both individuals and charity: the charitable remainder trust and the charitable lead trust. Both are split-inter-

The Legendary Lead Trust
That Never Materialized

When Jacqueline Kennedy Onassis died in 1994, the nation got an up-close look at a sophisticated estate-planning tool that has since become part of the Jackie O legend. In her will, the former First Lady described a trust that would pay an annuity to charity for 24 years. After that, whatever was left would go to her grandchildren or their descendants. Onassis called this charitable lead trust the C&J Foundation, using the initials of the first names of her two children, Caroline Kennedy Schlossberg and John F. Kennedy Jr.

In theory, the trust was an effective way to combine philanthropy with smart tax planning. It could be structured to avoid estate tax on money going into the trust, as well as generation-skipping transfer tax on funds eventually paid out to grandchildren. Anything that exceeded the required payout to charity would go to the family tax-free.

When the will first became public, the provision for this trust received widespread publicity, as various commentators speculated that the Onassis estate was worth $100 million or more. Under that scenario, by some estimates, as much as $192 million would be distributed to charity through the trust and the grandchildren might receive $98 million when it ended in 2018.

Funding for the trust was to come from the residuary estate – what remained after family, friends, lawyers and taxes had received their share. In the will, Onassis gave her children the option of disclaiming, or turning down, a portion of their inheritance. In that case, certain items would go to the Kennedy library, and the rest would go into the residuary estate and be available to fund the charitable lead trust.

As things worked out though, the trust was never created. That's because the children did not disclaim, except for property going to the Kennedy library. When the dust settled, the family's lawyers said the residuary estate was valued at $18 million but owed $23 million in estate taxes, which would need to come out of the children's inheritances.

Still, this trust-that-never-was lives on in estate planning lore.

Doing the Math

One powerful incentive to use charitable remainder trusts is the present income tax deduction available to the donor or the estate when this irrevocable trust is funded.

The deduction equals the value of the charity's remainder interest – the right to receive the trust assets at some point in the future. To calculate it requires the use of what is known as the Section 7520 rate (named after the section of the Internal Revenue Code that applies), set each month by the Internal Revenue Service.

With an annuity trust, the higher this discount rate, the bigger the deduction (for a unitrust, the interest rate doesn't affect the deduction). You're allowed to use the most favorable rate during a three-month period of the month when you set up the trust and the two previous months. Other factors that will influence the value of the remainder are the term of the trust (for those that last only a preset number of years) and the number and age of the beneficiaries.

To illustrate, let's say Jack, who is 68, sets up a $1 million charitable remainder annuity trust that will pay him 5 percent, or $50,000, each year for the rest of his life. Using a 3.8 percent discount rate, the present value of the annuity is $554,780, so the value of the remainder interest is $445,220 (the two must total the initial trust value of $1 million). When setting up the trust, Jack would get a deduction for $445,220. If instead the discount rate was 5.6 percent, the annuity would be worth $483,250 and the remainder would be worth $$516,750, so Jack would get a higher deduction.*

Two requirements for charitable remainder annuity trusts can be difficult to satisfy when interest rates are low. One is that the present value of charity's interest must be at least 10 percent of the initial trust funding. The other is that there must be no more than a 5 percent probability, based on Internal Revenue Service actuarial tables, that the trust funds will run out before the charity's remainder interest vests. If these rules prevent you from creating an annuity trust, you might want to consider a unitrust instead. Although the same 10 percent requirement applies, it is not as sensitive to interest rate fluctuations.

*Assumes payments will be made quarterly at the end of each quarter.
Lawrence P. Katzenstein, Tiger Tables Actuarial Software.

est arrangements, meaning that charitable and noncharitable beneficiaries each get a share of the trust assets, but at different times. In a charitable remainder trust, individual beneficiaries receive income for whatever period of time you specify – their lifetimes or a term of up to 20 years. When this interest ends, the charity receives what is left, known as the remainder interest. The charitable lead trust is the same idea in reverse. The charity receives its payout up front for the period you select. When this payout ends, the noncharitable beneficiaries, usually family members, get what is left.

Each of these vehicles, which are irrevocable, carries significant tax advantages. With a charitable remainder trust, you or your estate receives an income tax deduction upon transfer of assets into the entity (see "Doing the Math," page 236). A charitable lead trust, on the other hand, can produce gift and estate tax savings and in some cases income tax savings. If the trust earnings are sufficient, the money gets added to the principal. Down the line, this appreciation not only goes to family members – but most important – goes to them tax-free.

Did You Know ?

One way to save money when creating a charitable trust is to leave the paperwork up to the charity that will benefit. Many organizations will handle the formalities and be trustee, if state laws permit, without charge when they have more than half the charitable interest.

The charitable lead trust is for people who can afford to give the income to charity and whose families can do without the principal for a long time. Depending on how investments perform, it's possible that the charitable lead trust will be depleted by the end of the term, in which case the family would get nothing. Since these features don't appeal to many people, the charitable remainder trust is the more popular of the two.

The payout can be structured as either an annuity or a unitrust interest. In a charitable remainder annuity trust, the noncharitable beneficiary receives a fixed dollar amount at least annually – the minimum is 5 percent of the initial trust value. With a charitable remainder unitrust, the income interest is expressed as a percentage of the fair market value of the trust revalued each year (again the minimum is 5 percent). While the amount of the annuity interest stays constant, the payout in a unitrust will change from year to year.

A popular variation is the net income with make-up charitable remainder unitrust, which expresses the payout as the lesser of net income or a fixed percentage of the trust assets valued annually. There's also the appropriately named flip charitable remainder unitrust, used for trusts funded with assets that produce little or no income, such as real estate or closely held stock. With this trust there's no payout requirement until the assets are sold. At that point it is converted into a standard unitrust, with payments according to the predetermined rate.

Charitable remainder trusts can be established during life or at death, and the benefit need not be limited to a single charity. A key attraction of lifetime charitable remainder trusts funded with highly appreciated property is that no capital gains tax need be paid when the assets are put into the trust. Nor is there any tax due as the assets appreciate or are sold inside this vehicle, since the charitable remainder trust is tax-exempt. As individual beneficiaries receive yearly payouts, they pay tax according to a four-tier system. Under this method, to the extent the trust has ordinary income from the current year or accumulated income from a previous year it is distributed first and taxed at ordinary income rates. Next comes capital gain, then other income and finally trust principal.

It's possible for the remainder interest to go to multiple charities or to a donor-advised fund (see "Creating a Continuing Fund, Rather Than a One-Shot Gift," below). You can retain the right to change the remainder beneficiary to a different charity or postpone the choice of charity altogether and leave it up to the trustee.

If there is a special needs child in your family, you might want to make a special needs trust the income beneficiary of a charitable remainder trust (see Chapter 5). In this case the remainder beneficiary might be a charity concerned with the child's particular disability.

Creating a Continuing Fund, Rather Than a One-Shot Gift

For people who want to benefit multiple charities over a period of time, the typical choice is between a donor-advised fund and a private foundation, both of which can be set up either during life or as part of an estate plan.

Private foundation. Starting a private foundation involves forming a separate legal entity and applying for tax-exempt status from the Internal Revenue Service.

Complex tax code provisions regulate these entities, covering everything from the types of investments and grants a private foundation can make to transactions with officers, directors, trustees and substantial contributors (most are off-limits). To justify the expense of establishing and running a private foundation, most advisers recommend an initial endowment of $5 million to $10 million.

People who set up private foundations often assume that there will be extensive family involvement. Yet a variety of factors conspire against that. Sometimes adult children simply aren't interested. Even when they are, if they are scattered geographically, it can be difficult to build consensus for grant proposals and other relevant matters without assistance. Siblings who don't get along may be unwilling to work together toward a charitable goal. Sometimes no succession plan is in place, or asset values have declined to the point where the expense of running the operation is disproportionate to the endowment. A common solution is to dissolve the foundation and distribute its assets to a public charity.

Another possibility for avoiding family friction is to design a foundation with a limited life span, rather than thinking of it as something that will last forever. This approach might include a sunset provision providing that the entity will terminate when a specific event occurs, such as when the last of the founders dies. For example, the Bill & Melinda Gates Foundation is scheduled to close within 50 years after its current trustees have died. Among other things, this avoids the threat that grants will stray from the donor's intent with each succeeding generation.

> ## *Did You Know* ?
>
> You can't take a charitable deduction for what you contribute when your house of worship passes the basket. Federal law requires you to back up cash deductions with a canceled check, or a receipt with the charity's name, the date and the amount of the contribution.

Donor-advised fund. These funds have become a popular alternative to a private foundation because they offer many of the same virtues without the expense and paperwork. Contributors make irrevocable contributions to a nonprofit organization that administers the fund in conjunction with funds set up by other donors. You can make these contributions while you are alive, through your estate plan or a combination of the two. At any time in

Weighing the Possibilities for a

The advantages and disadvantages of using a private foundation or a dono

	Assets that can be contributed	Deduction limits	Donor's role in investment
Private Foundation	• Cash	30% of adjusted gross income (AGI)	Able to exercise investment
	• Marketable securities	20% of AGI Deductible at fair market value (FMV)	management within certain rules
	• Shares of closely held stock • Real estate • Tangible personal property	20% of AGI Limited to cost basis	
Donor-Advised Fund	• Cash	50% of AGI	Fewer investment choices
	• Marketable securities • Shares of closely held stock • Real estate	30% of AGI Deductible at FMV	

Any deduction that cannot be taken in the year of the donation – for instance, if the donor's contribution exceeds the limit on charitable deductions – can be carried forward up to five years. Tax deductions mentioned here refer specifically to federal taxes. Rules and regulations regarding tax deductions for charitable giving vary at the state level.

the future, you or your heirs (or any other people you designate) can recommend which nonprofit organizations should receive grants from the account.

Organizations sponsoring donor-advised funds include religious entities, universities and community foundations. Some large financial institutions have started donor-advised funds that are public charities. To set up a

ontinuing Fund for Charitable Gifts

vised fund

Donor's role in rant making	Required distributions	Role of donor's family	Privacy
omplete ontrol	At least 5% of value of non-charitable assets each year	Donor can: • appoint relatives to board • give them responsibility over the day-to-day activities • pay them salary, within limitations	None: yearly tax filing, Form 990-PF, is a public record of assets, contributors and grants
an recommend rants to any RS-qualified ublic charity	None unless fund rules require it (proposals to change this are circulating)	Donor can appoint successor advisers to recommend grants	Donor can request anonymity

donor-advised fund account during life, you make a donation to the charity offering the program and claim a federal income tax deduction for your irrevocable contribution. It is also possible to fund a donor-advised account through your estate plan, by making it a beneficiary of a charitable trust, a revocable trust (see Chapters 1 and 2) or simply naming it under your will.

Depending on how you want the funds disbursed after you are gone, you can appoint friends or family members as advisers to recommend future grants, or have the money go into the charity's central fund, in which case the organization would decide how it was spent.

Which works best? For people with sufficient funds for either a private foundation or a donor-advised fund, the deal-maker or -breaker is often how much control they want over both investment management and grant-making. With a private foundation, donors have total investment oversight, and they can manage the assets themselves while adhering to specific rules, or they can hire an investment manager. With donor-advised funds, donors can recommend that grants be made to IRS-qualified public charities, but legally you have given up the money and your grant recommendations are not binding. Fund trustees have the ultimate say over whether recommendations are followed.

Still, there are certain kinds of grants you can't make with a donor-advised fund. Donors generally can't recommend grants to individuals or create scholarships. Many donor-advised funds won't allow you to support charities organized under the laws of other countries. On the other hand, a private foundation willing to deal with the paperwork burden can do all these things. So it's only with a private foundation that you retain ultimate control over grant-making.

Choosing the Best Assets to Donate

To satisfy charitable bequests, the trustee of your living trust or your executor, the person you designate to carry out your wishes under a will, is likely to liquidate your estate and donate the cash. If you plan to make lifetime gifts that will reduce your taxable estate – for example, by funding a charitable trust, gift annuity, private foundation or donor-advised fund – you have strategic choices about the best assets to donate.

For gifts to a public charity, donors are entitled to an income tax deduction for up to 50 percent of adjusted gross income (AGI) for cash contributions and up to 30 percent for donations of other appreciated assets held more than 12 months. Any deduction that cannot be taken in the year of the donation can be carried forward up to five years.

There are significant benefits to giving away appreciated property. With marketable securities, for example, your deduction, which is subject to the AGI limitations, is based on the full market value of the securities. Since you are not selling the property – merely donating it – you do not have to pay capital gains taxes. Therefore, by donating these assets, rather than selling them

Raising the Ceiling on Charitable Deductions

Generally deductions for gifts to a public charity are limited to 50 percent of adjusted gross income (AGI) for cash and to 30 percent for assets held longer than a year, with the possibility of applying a five-year carryover in both cases. But you can elect to deduct up to 50 percent of AGI for certain gifts that would ordinarily only qualify for a 30 percent deduction.

The election is available for gifts to a public charity of appreciated property held longer than one year and applies to securities, real estate and tangible personal property related to the charity's exempt purpose. The tradeoff is that instead of being able to deduct the full fair market value of the property, you are limited to cost basis. But if the property being donated hasn't appreciated much, there is less benefit to valuing the donation at fair market value.

Who should consider making this election? Someone who, for one reason or another, is not likely to be able to deduct the full fair market value of a 30 percent gift even using the five-year carryover. That could be true if the value of the donated property is very high, or the person is elderly or in poor health and might die before the end of the carryover period. This election is also used when preparing the final income tax return for someone who has died (the carryover will be lost after that).

You can make the election on a year-by-year basis, so in each case you will want to run the numbers before making a decision. Remember, too, that if you choose to make this election for a particular gift, you must also make the election for all other long-term property donated during the same tax year. While the election doesn't change any deduction that you took in earlier years, it does reduce any carryover from those years because the initial donation is treated as a gift valued at cost basis, rather than at fair market value.

and donating the after-tax proceeds you can, in effect, make the dollars earmarked for charity go much further. And if you still want your portfolio to include that stock because you think it will increase further in value, you can simply buy additional shares at the higher price. In the process, you acquire a new, higher cost basis than you had on the donated shares, which could be beneficial if the assets go up further and you decide to sell them.

On the other hand, if the asset has declined in value, you are better off selling it, using the loss to offset investment gains, and donating the proceeds.

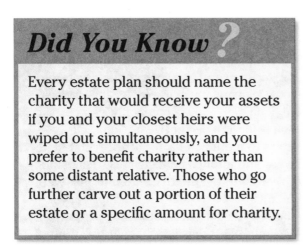

Did You Know?

Every estate plan should name the charity that would receive your assets if you and your closest heirs were wiped out simultaneously, and you prefer to benefit charity rather than some distant relative. Those who go further carve out a portion of their estate or a specific amount for charity.

Innovative donors and open-minded charities are moving beyond traditional gifts of cash and marketable securities and benefiting from donations of noncash assets. One potential tax trap to consider: When a donor has a binding obligation to sell any noncash asset, including real estate, before giving it to charity, the prearranged-sale rule forces the donor to pay tax on the gain.

For all gifts other than cash and marketable securities, it is necessary to get a qualified appraisal before taking a deduction for more than $5,000 – more than $10,000 for gifts of stock in a closely held company. Under federal regulations, the appraisal cannot be made more than 60 days before the donation and must be complete by the time the income tax return is due. And don't expect appraisers to grossly overvalue things on your behalf. Those who do risk stiff penalties.

Within these parameters, here are some noncash assets you could donate.

Real estate. Although real estate remains the most popular type of noncash gift, these donations carry certain complications. Most charities prefer that the property not be mortgaged because, depending on the nature of the real estate, the term of the note and the charitable vehicle used, the gift can run afoul of various tax law restrictions. In addition, just as if it were purchasing the property, the nonprofit must check for liens and be sure there are no environmental hazards that would carry cleanup obligations under federal law. And since the property will generally be sold, the value must be high enough that the charity is willing to devote the effort and resources to marketing it.

Assuming the charity would like to receive the real estate, there are a variety of ways to contribute it in addition to an outright donation. If you are holding appreciated property that you are prepared to sell – perhaps you invested in land that has since been developed – donating the property to a charitable remainder trust offers a way to avoid capital gains tax and diversify.

If you want to continue using the property, such as your home, you can donate a remainder interest in the personal residence. With this arrangement, you and your spouse can reserve the right to use the property for your own lifetimes and have it pass to charity when you die. Meanwhile, you get an income tax deduction for the actuarial value of charity's remainder interest, based on the ages of the life beneficiaries (the older you are, the larger the deduction), the value of the property and the Section 7520 rate.

Another possibility, typically used when the charity plans to keep the property, is to enter into a bargain sale: sell the asset to charity for less than the fair market value and take a charitable income tax deduction for the difference.

Tangible personal property. In addition to real estate, charities are receptive to a wide range of other donations, including collectibles and art. In one sense, gifts of art and collectibles are especially beneficial. While the capital gains rate is 15 percent for sales of appreciated stocks, bonds and real estate, the rate for tangible personal property is 28 percent. By donating valuable assets like art, you can avoid paying this tax and can take a charitable income tax deduction. Note that an artist who donates his own work can only take a deduction for his basis (for example, paint and canvas), not the fair market value. The same rule extends to someone who received a piece of art as a gift from the artist during life.

When considering a gift of tangible personal property, you need to keep in mind a limitation that applies to these types of gifts: In order for your donation to qualify for a full fair market value deduction, the charity must use the asset in a manner related to its exempt purpose. If the item donated does not satisfy this related use rule, your income tax deduction is limited to your basis in the asset or its fair market value, whichever is less. For example, a donor who gives violins to a symphony orchestra can deduct the fair market value (assuming the orchestra will use them, rather than sell them) but giving the same instruments to an animal rights group would limit the deduction to cost basis.

There's a harsh mechanism for enforcing this rule when deductions of more

Timing Is Everything

If you want favorable tax treatment for your charitable donations, they must be complete in the eyes of the Internal Revenue Service by Dec. 31 of year for which you want to take a deduction. Here are the rules to keep in mind.

Form of gift	Complete to charity
By check	On the postmark date if sent by U.S. mail (provided the check is honored) On the arrival date if sent by private courier (provided the check is honored)
By credit card	Date charge is posted, even if you have not yet paid your credit card bill
Stock *If you hold certificate*	On the postmark date if you have sent an endorsed certificate by U.S. mail On the arrival date if you have sent an endorsed certificate by private courier
If held by the broker	When you have relinquished control over the asset and the broker has transferred control to the charity

than $5,000 are involved. If the charity sells the asset within three years, part of the deduction is recaptured. If the sale was in the year of your donation, your deduction will be reduced to cost basis. For sales in subsequent years, you must include as income the difference, if any, between your cost basis and the fair market value deduction you took. Various penalties apply, including a $10,000 fine for someone who identifies property as having a related use knowing that it is not intended for it.

Stock in a closely held company. During the booming 1990s, Internet entrepreneurs donated pre-initial public offering stock to charity, anticipating that their businesses would go public. Ten years later the whole idea seemed quaint, and charities had become much less enthusiastic about these donations. But when the economy recovers, they may fly again.

The main impediment for donors is to find a charity willing to accept the gift and to get the shares appraised before you donate them. These appraisals can be expensive – they could easily cost $25,000. The appraiser would have to look at the company's financial statements as well as those of comparable businesses.

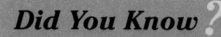

Did You Know?

Your tax deduction for gifts of tangible personal property depends on whether a nonprofit uses an item for its charitable purpose: If an orchestra uses the violin you donate, you can deduct the full fair market value. If it sells the violin, your deduction will be your cost basis.

IRA assets. As noted in Chapter 7, charities, unlike individual beneficiaries, do not need to pay income tax on withdrawals from these accounts. If your estate is subject to estate tax, the amount left to charity is deductible.

Since money in a retirement account usually passes outside of a person's will or living trust, it's necessary to spell out your wishes to leave it to a specific charity on the beneficiary designation form that you give to the IRA custodian (see Chapter 7). The options include making the charity a 100 percent beneficiary of the IRA or indicating that the charity is a beneficiary of a certain percentage of the IRA, and that the rest should go to individual beneficiaries.

Life insurance. Life insurance offers a way to benefit charity without reducing your family's inheritance. As noted in Chapter 8, sometimes donors use life insurance to back up a large pledge – for instance, one that would be recognized in the naming of a building, an endowment or a school within a university. That way, if the donor dies before the pledge is fulfilled, the life insurance proceeds can be used to carry out the donor's intentions. Although state insurable interest laws generally prohibit investors from owning insurance on the lives of strangers, most states make an exception for charities so they can insure key donors and continue their endowments.

As with most other charitable donations, this entitles you to an income tax deduction. How you calculate that deduction will depend on whether the policy is new or older, and whether it is paid up, meaning no further premiums remain to be paid. For tax reasons, if a policy still requires premium payments, it's best to donate funds to the charity and let it pay the premiums.

Strategies That Postpone Tough Choices

Let's say you care deeply about charity but find so many uncertainties at the moment that you aren't prepared to make significant charitable bequests through your estate plan. Perhaps you're not sure if your heirs will need the money. Or maybe you can't decide which charities you would like to benefit.

In that case, there are a couple of steps you can take now to maximize flexibility later.

One is to pave the way for your heirs to shift assets to charity by disclaiming within nine months of your death, as noted previously (see Chapter 2). This means turning down an inheritance and having it go to whoever is next in line – typically a person. If you want at least part of the disclaimed assets to go to charity, your estate planning documents must name the specific charity or charities or a charitable trust that will receive whatever is disclaimed – the choice is not up to the people who would otherwise inherit the assets. Be aware, though, that although many wills include disclaimers, in real life even very rich heirs rarely invoke them when charity is next in line (see "The Legendary Lead Trust That Never Materialized," page 235).

Another way to keep your options open is to make your charitable beneficiary a private foundation or (more likely for most people) a donor-advised fund. This postpones the need to select recipient charities when you write your will. By naming family members to recommend future grants, you can use either of these entities to support your charitable legacy or encourage your heirs to develop charitable interests of their own. Knowing they will have a pool of funds set aside to support their philanthropy might even give children an incentive to disclaim to charity, if your estate plan includes that possibility.

To-Do List

Back to Basics

Providing for charity in your estate plan doesn't necessarily mean giving like Andrew Carnegie. But it does require you to think ahead and update your plan periodically. Whether you want to allocate a lot or a little to charity, here are some basic steps to take.

❧ Identify any charities that you would like to benefit, either through a specific bequest or as alternate beneficiaries if family members disclaim the funds or none of them survive you.

❧ Check that your estate planning documents, including your will, trusts and IRA beneficiary designation forms include charity as either a primary or an alternate beneficiary.

❧ Ask your children or grandchildren if they would like you to create a fund that they can use for their own charitable giving and whether they are prepared to devote a great deal of time to administering it.

❧ If your net worth recently increased or decreased and you have included a specific bequest to charity in an earlier version of your estate plan, make sure the balance between how much would go to family and to charity still reflects your wishes.

❧ If your estate plan includes a substantial gift to charity, notify the nonprofit of your intentions and discuss any preferences you have about how the money will be used.

❧ If you are concerned that a charitable bequest will short-change your family, give heirs the option, though your will or beneficiary designation form (for IRA assets), to disclaim, or turn down, the inheritance and have it go to the charity you have named on the relevant document.

249

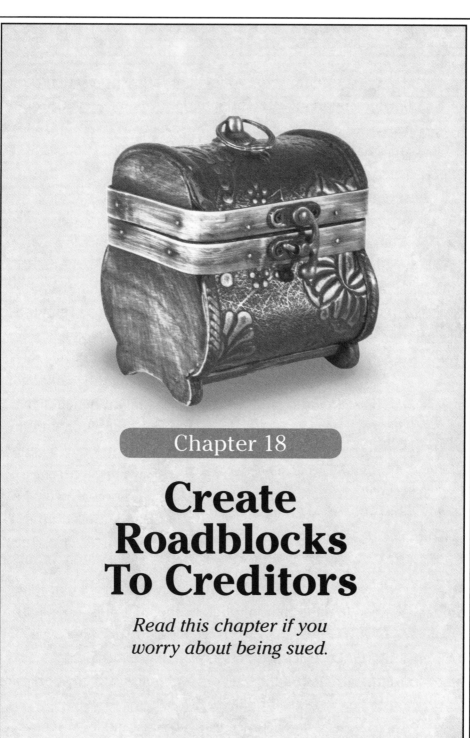

Chapter 18

Create
Roadblocks
To Creditors

*Read this chapter if you
worry about being sued.*

P reserving resources for yourself or future generations goes beyond sound investment and money management. You also need to guard against losing assets to creditors, a category that may include everyone from disgruntled spouses and ex-spouses to people who win lawsuits against you.

The best defense is to erect a variety of roadblocks that make it difficult, if not impossible, for creditors to reach your money and property. These asset protection strategies can range from relying on state-law exemptions to creating multiple barriers through the use of trusts and family limited partnerships or limited liability companies. The strategies vary by state.

In This Chapter...

⚜ *Specific State-Law Exemptions And Traps*

⚜ *Special Protection for Retirement Accounts*

⚜ *Trusts to Benefit Other Family Members*

⚜ *Limited Partnerships and Limited Liability Companies*

⚜ *An Irrevocable Trust to Benefit Yourself*

⚜ *Trusts in Certain Foreign Jurisdictions*

Among the many people who might benefit from asset protection are those whose work could generate lawsuits: entrepreneurs, doctors, lawyers, accountants and other professionals; construction contractors and real estate developers; executors and trustees; and directors of public companies. Keep in mind that in tough economic times, people find reasons to sue. It's prudent to ensure you are not an easy target.

A well-constructed asset-protection plan may guard against risks not covered in your malpractice, errors-and-omissions, property and casualty and other insurance policies.

Asset protection is not limitless, however. State and federal laws against fraudulent conveyance prohibit transfers with the intent to hinder, delay or defraud creditors. Unfortunately, no hard-and-fast rules spell out what these terms mean, and they are applied on a case-by-case basis. So if a court finds there has been a fraudulent conveyance, it can declare the transfer void and order the assets be made available to creditors, even if it means returning them from a foreign country.

In determining whether there has been a fraudulent conveyance, intent is an issue. So having a plan in place far in advance strengthens your argument that no fraudulent conveyance occurred.

Asset protection does not inoculate people who commit crimes. But it may insulate those who did business with a crook and can demonstrate they did not know of the crime – provided they took asset protection measures long before the crime came to light. Financial fraud has been much in the spotlight recently, with Bernard L. Madoff acknowledging that he engaged in the largest fraud in Wall Street history – a decades-long Ponzi scheme that appears to have cost investors tens of billions of dollars. He pleaded guilty in March 2009 to 11 counts of fraud, money laundering, perjury and theft.

An ideal time to address the issue of asset protection is in the course of creating or revising an estate plan. It is possible that some of your assets are already beyond the reach of creditors, and others could be, with minor adjustments.

When thinking about asset protection, consider your net worth, as well as the potential liability that surrounds your profession. Take account not only of assets you already own, but wealth that you might inherit or generate in the future – for example, if an existing or startup venture is sold or goes public. Depending on your situation, it may be possible to rely on a variety of strategies, either separately or in combination with each other.

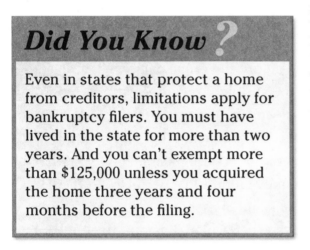

Specific State-Law Exemptions and Traps

The simplest and sometimes the best way to protect your assets is to take advantage of any state-law exemptions that apply. These vary. Some states, for example, offer creditor protection for annuities, life insurance (either for the cash value, the death benefit or both), and individual retirement accounts. Others do not. You must be a resident of the state to take advantage of its exemptions.

People living in Florida, a debtor-friendly state, can take advantage of its unlimited exemption for the equity in a personal residence, subject to certain restrictions that apply if you file for bankruptcy. Other states with such generous homestead laws, as they are called, include Iowa, Kansas, Oklahoma, South Dakota and Texas. Elsewhere, the homestead exemption may be limited to a certain dollar amount. Depending on state rules, paying off a mortgage could make both that sum and your existing equity in the property secure from creditors.

Did You Know ?

Even in states that protect a home from creditors, limitations apply for bankruptcy filers. You must have lived in the state for more than two years. And you can't exempt more than $125,000 unless you acquired the home three years and four months before the filing.

Another asset protection strategy that varies by state is the option for spouses to hold property in tenancy by the entirety. When assets are owned this way, only the couple's joint creditors have access to them; creditors of just one spouse cannot collect on a lien unless there is a divorce or until one spouse dies. Even then, the creditor only can reach the property if it is the debtor who survives.

About 30 states permit tenancy by the entirety, some of them only for real estate – not for stocks, bank accounts and other assets. A few states allow it for all such investments. In these states, a married couple that held its brokerage account in tenancy by the entirety could ensure that only the couple's joint creditors would have access to the brokerage account, so it could not be used to satisfy a judgment against one of them alone.

But beware another form of joint ownership, and the most common one, at that – joint tenants with rights of survivorship. This form of joint ownership (it appears on some joint bank or brokerage statements abbreviated "JTWROS") is available to both people who are married and those who are not.

The advantage of joint tenancy is its convenience. Both owners have access to the assets during life, and when one dies, the survivor immediately becomes the sole owner of the whole property, regardless of what the will says, or even if there is no will. These features make this type of ownership universally appealing – to aging parents and their adult children, siblings, spouses and domestic partners.

The drawback, from an asset protection perspective, is that joint tenancy exposes each owner to the other's potential liabilities. For example, if you are a joint tenant on your mother's brokerage account and someone wins a lawsuit against you, half the assets in your joint account could be wiped out.

Perhaps a better choice for people who are not married or who can't own assets as tenants by the entirety is a type of ownership called tenancy in common. With this form of title, you own just part of the property, known as an undivided interest. Typically your share would equal whatever you contributed, though if someone gave you the asset – say an interest in land – as a gift or bequest, it would equal whatever percentage of ownership you received. Legally, you cannot do anything with the property unless your co-owner consents. When one owner dies, just that person's share gets included in his or her estate. As a rule, creditors have access only to the portion owned by the person who owes them money, rather than to the whole thing. This form of title can work well for unmarried partners (see Chapter 4).

Special Protection for Retirement Accounts

Even in states where the law is unfavorable to debtors, federal law provides an important exemption for retirement plans covered by the Employee Retirement Income Security Act (ERISA), making such plans one of the most solid asset protection tools. Remember, though, that ERISA plans are subject to federal (but not state) tax liens.

IRAs, however, are not covered by ERISA. If the account holder has filed for bankruptcy, bankruptcy law protects up to $1 million in the account unless the account is an IRA that has been rolled over from a company plan (see Chapter 7), in which case the entire account balance is protected in bankruptcy. In other situations, state laws determine whether IRAs (including Roth IRAs) are shielded from creditors' claims. Most states exempt 100 percent of the assets while they are in the account. But state laws vary widely on whether withdrawals are covered, protections extend to inheritors as well as the initial owner and former spouses can reach the funds.

If you recently retired or changed jobs, you have the option of rolling over assets from a qualified plan, such as a 401(k), into an individual retirement account. From an estate planning perspective, this strategy has various benefits (see Chapter 7). However, if you have a large retirement account and live in a state where IRAs are not protected from creditors, you may prefer to leave the assets in the company plan if your former employer allows it. You should consult a lawyer familiar with the rules of the state where you live.

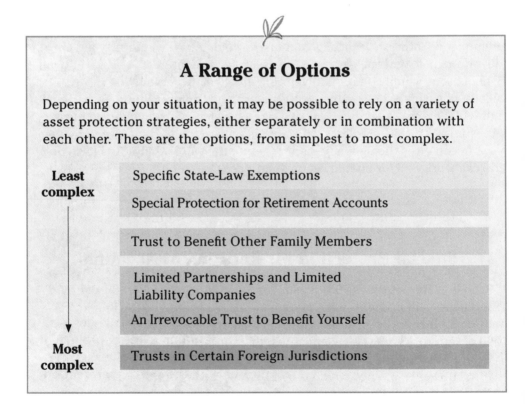

A Range of Options

Depending on your situation, it may be possible to rely on a variety of asset protection strategies, either separately or in combination with each other. These are the options, from simplest to most complex.

Least complex

Specific State-Law Exemptions

Special Protection for Retirement Accounts

Trust to Benefit Other Family Members

Limited Partnerships and Limited Liability Companies

An Irrevocable Trust to Benefit Yourself

Most complex

Trusts in Certain Foreign Jurisdictions

Trusts to Benefit Other Family Members

Many people are concerned about keeping family money in the family, especially as children grow, get married and embark on lives of their own. Trusts are an efficient way to do that (see Chapter 6). They are also an excellent means of sheltering assets from creditors. For many people this is the main reason to set up trusts and to leave assets permanently in this legal wrapper.

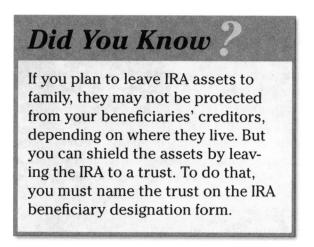

Did You Know ?

If you plan to leave IRA assets to family, they may not be protected from your beneficiaries' creditors, depending on where they live. But you can shield the assets by leaving the IRA to a trust. To do that, you must name the trust on the IRA beneficiary designation form.

Even if you do not think of trusts as a long-term arrangement, you might want to rely on one until children or grandchildren reach a certain age, are able to handle the funds or are in stable marriages. You can choose arbitrary ages at which the trust should make payouts of income or principal, or leave the choice up to the trustees. Another option is a hybrid approach, in which the trust specifies payouts at specific ages but the trustee can postpone distributions if the beneficiary is a spendthrift or has creditor problems.

The more flexibility you build into the trust, the better it can provide protection from creditors. For example, you can give trustees the power to move the situs, or location, of the trust in response to new state laws that achieve better creditor protection. In some states, trustees can decant the trust – pay out funds from one trust to another, which could help them continue creditor protection.

What you should *not* do is make your beneficiaries the co-trustees of their own trusts, with the power to make distributions to themselves. While it is generally fine for them to participate in investment decisions, giving them discretion over payouts could interfere with the creditor protection that the trust affords.

Limited Partnerships
And Limited Liability Companies

Some people are already using family limited partnerships (FLPs) and limited liability companies (LLCs) for estate-planning purposes or to maximize investment opportunities (see Chapter 16). These entities can achieve the additional benefit of asset protection.

Here is how they work: A senior family member puts assets into the entity, which is most often an FLP but may be a LLC in states where the LLC law is the more favorable for valuation purposes. Then the individual gives or sells shares in the entity that holds the assets to family members or to a trust for the family members' benefit.

From an asset protection perspective, the chief attraction of FLPs and LLCs is that in many states creditors cannot take all the assets in the entity or force a liquidation, no matter how much they are owed. In these states, the only thing they can get is what is known as a charging order – a court order giving them the right to the debtor's distributions up to the amount of the debt plus interest.

For even better asset protection, it may be possible to use a FLP or LLC in conjunction with a trust – for example, by selling or transferring an interest in the entity to a trust that benefits other family members. This popular estate planning strategy also helps with asset protection by creating two layers of insulation.

An Irrevocable Trust to Benefit Yourself

Known as a domestic asset protection trust or self-settled spendthrift trust, this type of trust is a relatively new option available in certain states – but not permitted in most states.

Domestic asset protection trusts are designed to give you access to the income and principal of the trust while protecting the assets from the claims of future creditors. These trusts typically include a spendthrift clause that prevents beneficiaries from assigning their interests and creditors from reaching the trust assets.

In most states, the general rule is that whatever trust assets the grantor (the person who set up the trust) can reach are also available to creditors. At least 10 states – Alaska, Delaware, Missouri, Nevada, New Hampshire, Rhode Island, South Dakota, Tennessee, Utah and Wyoming – have changed their laws to permit self-settled trusts to be outside the reach of creditors. These states require that the trust be irrevocable and be administered in the state, that there be at least one local trustee and that at least some trust assets be held in the state. Whether or not you live in one of these states, it is possible to set up an asset protection trust there by designating the state as the situs for the trust.

So what happens if someone gets a judgment against you in a state that does not permit asset protection trusts, like Texas, and you have set up a trust in a state that allows them – for example, Alaska? The full faith and credit clause of the Constitution says a judgment in one state must be honored in another. But, so far, there is little, if any, track record of how courts will apply the clause to these trusts.

Nor can all assets just as easily be put in self-settled trusts. Marketable securities are the best candidates because the certificates can be readily transferred to an account in the state where the trust has its situs. Real estate, on the other hand, can be problematic, because it is generally subject to the jurisdiction of the state where it is situated (for a way around this, see Chapter 10). Operating businesses are troublesome for the same reason.

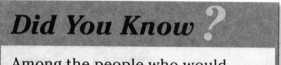

Did You Know?

Among the people who would benefit from asset protection are those most likely to be sued: doctors, lawyers, contractors, real estate developers, executors and trustees. An asset-protection plan may guard against risks not covered by insurance.

If you are interested in a domestic asset protection trust, discuss it with your financial advisers. They can help you determine whether this strategy makes sense for you and your family, as well as the best strategy for creating this type of trust. Be aware, however, that anytime you use a technique like this one that is based on an area of the law that is unsettled, you may wind up incurring significant legal costs defending the strategy against attack – which in this case could be based on federal law, state law or both.

Trusts in Certain Foreign Jurisdictions

Offshore trusts can provide significant tactical advantages, because theoretically they are beyond the reach of the United States courts. Therefore, a creditor faces the inconvenience of having to litigate in the country where the trust is formed. Generally, a U.S. judgment would not be enforceable in this location.

Popular locations for offshore trusts include the Bahamas, Belize, the Cook Islands, Liechtenstein and Nevis. Their fraudulent conveyance rules may be more lenient than U.S. laws, affording asset protection even when a trust is set up shortly before a lawsuit is filed.

Offshore trusts have several drawbacks, however. The U.S. courts have not looked favorably on them, and in one notorious case that has become part of asset protection lore, a couple who used a Cook Islands trust to stash the cash from their fraudulent investment scheme were jailed for contempt because they refused to bring the assets back. The trusts can be expensive and complicated to create and maintain. In addition, some individuals may be more comfortable keeping their assets on U.S. soil. Keep in mind, also, that even if assets are offshore, they are still subject to U.S. income tax.

Whether you are considering a domestic asset protection trust or an offshore trust, it is best not to fund it with everything you own. You will also want to make sure the value of the assets used to fund the trust is large enough to justify the associated costs. And be sure any lawyer you retain to help you set up and monitor the trust has done dozens of them before (see Chapter 19). You don't want to turn into a test case.

To-Do List

Follow the Asset Protection Continuum

The best approach to asset protection is to start with the least complicated strategy necessary to achieve your goals. It is possible that some of your assets are already beyond the reach of creditors. Others could be, with minor adjustments. Here are some issues to explore with your financial advisers.

❦ *Does your state have a homestead exemption?*
If so, find out whether paying off a mortgage would make both that sum plus your existing equity in the property secure from creditors.

❦ *Does your state allow spouses to hold property as tenants by the entirety? (Those that do typically cover only real estate, but some permit it for other assets like stocks and bank accounts.)*
If so, and you are married, determine whether, for asset protection reasons, any property should be transferred from one spouse to the other or out of joint ownership into the name of one spouse individually in order to protect the assets from creditors. Note that special tax rules apply to transfers to non-citizen spouses (see Chapter 3).

❦ *Did you recently retire or change jobs, or do you expect to soon?*
If so, consider the pros and cons of rolling over assets from a qualified plan, such as a 401(k), into an individual retirement account.

❦ *Does your family have any trusts?*
If not, discuss the possibility of creating trusts for this purpose.
If so, ask advisers whether they need to be adapted, or whether you should create additional trusts to address your family's need for creditor protection.

❦ *Does your estate plan include the use of a family entity, such as a limited liability company or family limited partnership?*
If not, determine whether there are reasons to set one up, including the possibility of protecting your assets (see Chapter 16).

From Planning To Action

*Read this chapter even if you
already have lawyers and financial
advisers whom you trust.*

I t always feels painful to spend money on estate planning, because you don't live to reap the benefits, even if you know your heirs will. But by now you should be convinced of how important it is to move forward. Estate planning starts with a fundamental goal: Once you have provided for your own needs, take care of those you love. That's true whether you have a lot of money or a little.

Your estate plan does not have to be complex, especially now that the amount that is exempt from taxes has reached $3.5 million ($7 million for married couples) in 2009. If you haven't revised your estate plan in 5 or 10 years, the current tax-free amount may be much higher than it was when you last met with your lawyer: in 2004 the exemption was $1.5 million; in 1999, it was $650,000. With very little effort you may now be able to structure your plan so that taxes will not be an issue.

In This Chapter...

- ⚜ *When to Update Your Plan*
- ⚜ *How to Find Good Legal Advice*
- ⚜ *The Seasons of Estate Planning*

You can accomplish a great deal just by having the basic documents prepared, and keeping enough assets in your own name that you can take full advantage of the estate tax exemption. That, plus avoiding some key estate planning mistakes covered throughout this book, might be all you need to do right now.

As your finances and personal concerns change, you may have to update or completely revise earlier arrangements. A guiding principle mentioned again and again in this book is that when various means to an end are available, you should generally choose the simplest tool that achieves your goals.

When to Update Your Plan

Vast sums of money have been lost through missed estate planning oppor-tunities and family battles over documents that had not been updated. Estate plans should be reviewed at least every five years, more often if your personal circumstances change – for example, if you get married or divorced, become a parent or a grandparent or lose your spouse. These are some other important developments that may require action on your part:

Changes in the law. The year 2009 was a watershed because the amount of an estate that is exempt from federal estate tax and from generation-skipping transfer tax in each case took a big jump to $3.5 million, from $2 million in 2008. That, coupled with the financial crisis that lowered many people's net worth, makes a review urgent.

Near term, check to see if your will includes formula clauses, which are recognizable because they include phrases like "that portion," "that fraction" or "that amount" (without saying what it is). These are signs of lawyers trying to take maximum advantage of the exemption, which kept changing.

Instead of naming a specific sum that will go into a trust, such as a bypass or credit-shelter trust (see Chapter 3) or a generation-skipping trust (Chapter 14), many wills refer to an amount up to the exemption or express the sum as a per-centage of whatever the limit happens to be when the person dies. This is good standard practice, but with the exemption at $3.5 million, make certain the will re-flects your intent. For example, it's possible that under your current arrangement, the designated fraction or percentage means less money would go to your spouse than you would like (Chapter 4) or that too much would go to your grandchildren.

State estate tax is another issue to consider, if you live in or own real estate in a state that has such a levy (about half do). Often the state exemption is smaller than the federal one, and this poses a dilemma for spouses (as dis-cussed in Chapter 4).

To stay current about laws that may affect your estate plan, visit the Web site for this book, www.estateplanningsmarts.com. You can also register at the site to receive e-mail notifications of updates.

Impending good fortune. Whether you have made a promising investment or own a business and are expecting a huge success (such as a sale or initial pub-lic offering or the introduction of a revolutionary product), think about shifting some of the upside potential to family. Once the appreciation occurs, making transfers will consume more of your $1 million lifetime gift tax exemption or require you to pay gift tax on a larger amount. If you can afford to transfer some holdings before they increase in value, that appreciation will be sheltered from both gift tax and estate tax. Various methods for making these transfers while minimizing or eliminating gift tax were discussed in Chapters 15 and 16.

Economic decline. The financial maelstrom that began in 2008 created extraordinary estate-planning opportunities. A combination of low asset values and the decline in interest rates used in structuring various wealth-transfer tools drastically reduced the tax cost of making lifetime transfers, whether through gifts or intra-family transactions.

Unfortunately the same economic forces also made people extremely anxious about their own financial security and less inclined to reduce their net worth through lifetime transfers – even of beaten-down assets. Still, the potential to turn lemons into lemonade is something to remember as you go forward. Strategies such as the grantor retained annuity trust, or GRAT, and installment sales to family members or to trusts for their benefit (covered in Chapter 16) create an income stream for the person making the transfer. This may be an attractive feature if you worry that reducing your net worth in order to save estate taxes later will leave you short of money.

Bad health. With any luck you will never need the information under this heading, but keep in mind that it's here, and come back to it if you do.

The diagnosis of a degenerative disease or terminal illness throws families into crisis. Between doctors' visits, prolonged hospital stays and seemingly endless waits for what often turn out to be unfavorable test results, each new day can challenge our coping mechanisms. These are all things we can't control.

During the rare calm moments in the eye of the storm, some people take comfort in getting their estate plans in order. This is the time to have your lawyer review any documents and bring them up to date. If estate taxes are a concern, you can use the annual exclusion that allows you to give up to $13,000 ($26,000 for married couples) each year to as many recipients as you would like without incurring gift tax. Annual exclusion gifts are the most common form of planning when a death is imminent (checks need to be cashed before the death occurs or the assets are considered part of the estate). Often a power of attorney (see Chapter 1) authorizes your agent to make these gifts if you can no longer write the checks. Since transfers under the annual exclusion are not considered taxable gifts, they are not subject to the general rule, contained in the Internal Revenue Code, that if you do not survive more than three years after making a gift, any gift tax you paid on the transfer will be counted as part of your estate.

Another relatively simple estate-planning device is available if someone who is ill survives for more than year. It involves transferring an asset (such as a house) that has appreciated in value from a healthier person to an individual (typically a spouse) who is expected to die first. Assuming the person receiving the asset is a U.S. citizen, spouses are entitled to an unlimited gift tax exemption when they make such transfers.

Why would you want to do this? When the healthy person later inherits the assets, he is entitled to a basis adjustment to their value on the date of death. If the house has appreciated, the basis step-up could reduce or eliminate the capital gains tax your heirs have to pay if the property is sold. This strategy is discussed in greater detail in Chapter 4.

There are two other, more complicated, techniques that lawyers sometimes recommend for people who are in poor health. One is the private annuity. It involves a sale of assets in exchange for an unsecured promise to pay an annuity for the rest of the seller's life. The payout is based on the seller's life expectancy under the government's actuarial tables. If the seller lives for less time, the buyer gets a bargain. Federal regulations prohibit people from using these tables if there's more than a 50 percent probability that they're going to die within a year. Someone who lives longer than 18 months is entitled to use the tables.

The greatest drawback to this transaction, typically done between parents and children (or a trust for their benefit), is that it involves an unhealthy emotional dynamic: a bet against Dad or Mom. The sooner the parent dies, the better off the buyer is financially; the longer the parent lives, the more children pay, in effect, for the property. Understandably, many people find the idea distasteful.

These arrangements also have various financial complexities. The buyer's basis, which at the time of the sale equals the value of the annuity, must be recomputed if the seller doesn't live until his life expectancy. The reason: The buyer has, in effect, paid less for the property.

To further complicate matters, under Internal Revenue Service rules, the party paying the annuity must have assets sufficient to make the payments not just for the seller's actual life expectancy, but until he reaches age 110. This exhaustion rule, as it's called, is primarily a problem for trusts. If the trust doesn't have adequate funding, it won't be permitted to value the annuity based on the seller's life expectancy, but only until the money would run out.

An alternative to the private annuity is selling assets to family members or

Now or Later?

The increase in the estate tax and generation-skipping transfer tax exemption to $3.5 million should compel some people to radically change their estate plans. Others can leave well enough alone. This self-test will help you determine which category you're in. It's not a substitute for consulting your lawyer, but will give you some idea of how soon to make that appointment.

1. How old are you?
a.	<40	4 points
b.	40-50	6 points
c.	51-60	8 points
d.	61-75	10 points
e.	>75	20 points

2. Describe your health.
a.	Good-excellent	0 points
b.	Fair	5 points
c.	Poor	10 points
d.	Terminally ill	50 points

3. Are you married?
a.	No	0 points
b.	Yes	10 points

4. What is your estate worth, including insurance and retirement plans?
a.	<$3.5 million	0 points
b.	$3.5 million-$7 million	10 points
c.	>$7 million	8 points

5. When did a lawyer last review your estate plan?
a.	Within the past year	0 points
b.	Within the past two years	4 points
c.	Within the past five years	6 points
d.	More than five years ago	8 points
e.	I have not done an estate plan.	40 points

Source: Gideon Rothschild

6. Have there been any major changes in your finances or personal circumstances?
a. No   0 points
b. Unsure if changes are considered major   6 points
c. Yes   10 points

7. Are you expecting a big increase in your net worth?
a. No   0 points
b. I don't know   3 points
c. Yes   5 points

8. How important is it for you to minimize estate taxes?
a. Unimportant   0 points
b. Somewhat important   2 points
c. Important, but not enough to change the way
I leave property to heirs   4 points
d. Important enough that I would modify my
other goals to save estate taxes   10 points

9. Does your will provide for a credit-shelter (bypass) trust or a generation-skipping trust?
a. No   0 points
b. Unsure   5 points
c. Yes   10 points

10. Do you live in a state that has an estate tax and an exemption less than the federal one?*
a. Yes   10 points
b. No   0 points

Score:
<20   You may not be significantly affected by the $3.5 million exemption.
21-50 You should consider a review within the next few years.
>51   See your estate-planning lawyer at once.

These states are: Connecticut, Kansas, Maine, Maryland, Massachusetts, Minnesota, Nebraska, New Jersey, New York, Ohio, Oregon, Rhode Island, Washington and Wisconsin, as well as the District of Columbia.

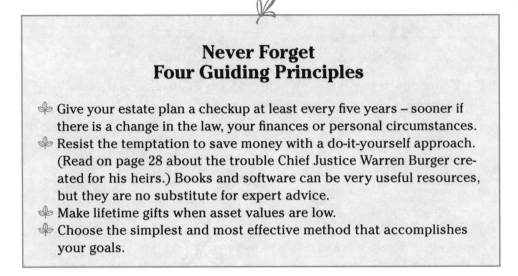

Never Forget
Four Guiding Principles

- Give your estate plan a checkup at least every five years – sooner if there is a change in the law, your finances or personal circumstances.
- Resist the temptation to save money with a do-it-yourself approach. (Read on page 28 about the trouble Chief Justice Warren Burger created for his heirs.) Books and software can be very useful resources, but they are no substitute for expert advice.
- Make lifetime gifts when asset values are low.
- Choose the simplest and most effective method that accomplishes your goals.

to a trust for their benefit in exchange for a self-canceling installment note, or SCIN. This financing technique works just like any other installment note described in Chapter 16, except that the debt is forgiven if the seller dies during the note term. The advantage of a SCIN is that family members can potentially wind up with the property without paying the full sales price. (With an ordinary note, if the seller dies while the note is outstanding, the balance is payable to the estate.)

Buyers pay a price, however, for this potential windfall: In order for the transaction to be legitimate, the SCIN must incorporate a premium for the cancellation feature. This premium is based on current interest rates and the seller's age. It can be added either to the principal or the interest portion of the note.

Another financial drawback of the SCIN is that when someone dies with one of these notes in place, all unrealized gain is taxable to the estate as income in the year of death. The estate may not have enough income tax deductions to offset it. In contrast, with a note that doesn't have the self-canceling feature, the children would continue making payments to the estate, and the gain would be deferred over the remaining years of the note. Therefore, in deciding whether to use a SCIN, it's necessary to compare the premium associated with this device and the income tax the estate would have to pay with the estate-tax savings of having the note canceled.

How to Find Good Legal Advice

Whether you are doing an estate plan for the first time or giving your existing plan a tune-up or a total overhaul, it's crucial to choose someone who not only has the necessary skills but with whom you feel comfortable. To find the best lawyer for the job and pay only for what's essential, consider these issues:

Do you need a new lawyer? If you have never done any estate planning, the answer is probably yes. This is not a job for the real estate lawyer who did your house closing, for example.

If you are updating an existing plan, the professional who created it might be able to make the changes after a brief conversation with you by phone or in person. But if your situation has changed and you need sophisticated advice about generation-skipping transfer tax (see Chapter 14), special needs trusts (Chapter 5) or protecting assets from potential future creditors (Chapter 18), make certain you are getting the expert guidance you need – and be prepared to pay for it. Don't be afraid to ask, "How many of these kinds of matters have you handled?" If the answer isn't dozens, consider finding someone else.

How do you choose the right lawyer? Start with referrals from people you know who are in similar situations or from professionals whose judgment you trust, like accountants, financial advisers or other lawyers. State and local bar associations can direct you to lawyers in your area but can't vouch for their skills. Names can also be found on martindale.com, the nationwide lawyers' directory that you can search by location and area of practice, and on www.actec.org, the Web site of the American College of Trust and Estate Counsel, a group of trust and estate lawyers.

Depending on where you live, you may have a choice between large national firms with many practice groups or estate-planning boutiques – small firms that specialize in trust and estate work. The latter tend to be less expensive because their overhead is lower.

Going to the lawyer who has done an estate plan for other family members (for example, your parents) poses confidentiality problems. That lawyer can't reveal any aspect of the others' plan to you without the consent of the individual or couple. If this poses a conflict of interest so that the professional can't handle the matter, the same issue typically applies to other lawyers at the firm. But she can probably recommend a colleague elsewhere.

Whomever you are considering, meet before you decide to work together (most professionals charge for this initial consultation only if you go forward). Pay attention to chemistry. Is the lawyer listening, or does she seem to have her own agenda? You want someone who can empathize with your concerns and put herself in your shoes. Also consider whether you would feel comfortable revealing highly personal information that bears upon your estate plan. This might include not only your finances but also the state of your marriage and relationships with other family members, and whatever concerns keep you awake at night.

Hourly rate or flat fee? While most lawyers charge an hourly rate, some offer flat fees for a package of basic estate planning documents, like a will, living trust, power of attorney, living will and health care proxy. Each billing arrangement has pros and cons. With a flat fee you know in advance what you will have to spend and you avoid surprises. But it's also possible that your lawyer is using a standard form without taking much time to adapt it to your situation. Ask the lawyer how much customization you can expect in a flat-fee arrangement. Another way to control costs – and an alternative you could propose if you don't think a flat-fee arrangement will meet your needs – is to ask your lawyer to bill by the hour, but give you an estimate of the total cost and a warning (with an explanation) if it looks as though you will incur additional charges. Either way, lawyers commonly charge for such expenses as photocopies, long-distance calls and faxes, sometimes marking them up (so clarify this in advance). You should also have a clear idea of what kind of service to expect. It's perfectly legitimate to ask questions like: "What would be the next step?" or "How long will this process take?" and "How quickly do you typically respond to telephone and e-mail messages?"

All the terms should be summarized in a contract, called an engagement letter, that your lawyer prepares. It ought to cover the scope of the work, the fee, the prices for disbursements and how disputes will be resolved. This agreement should be easy to understand. Don't hesitate to ask questions if anything isn't clear.

Should you and your spouse have separate lawyers? This adds to the cost, because two people will need to get up to speed on your situation and draft documents, rather than having one lawyer produce his-and-hers versions of the same wills and trusts. But under most state laws, when couples are jointly represented, everything you tell the lawyer, even privately, is not confidential from your spouse.

Separate representation may be desirable in second marriages when children from a previous marriage are part of the landscape. It's even more important for people in troubled marriages or when one spouse has skeletons in the closet – like a secret companion or an out-of-marriage child. Having your own lawyer may also be appropriate when one spouse is an heir to a family business and the tradition has been to exclude in-laws from ownership and management.

The Seasons of Estate Planning

As you move through life, expect your estate planning needs and priorities to evolve, though events that require you to update your estate plan may or may not coincide with specific life stages. Such stages tend to be driven not only by chronological age, but by your finances, maturity and relationships – especially those with a spouse or partner, and children or grandchildren. Consider these situations:

You are single. Be sure you have all the basic estate planning documents to provide for your own care if you can no longer handle your affairs (Chapter 1) and to leave your assets to the people (Chapter 2) or charities (Chapter 17) that you wish to benefit. You may not need life insurance, but if your employer or union provides a policy, make sure you have properly completed the beneficiary designation form (Chapter 8). Beneficiary designation forms for your retirement accounts should also be filled out and coordinated with the rest of your estate plan (Chapter 7).

You have a spouse or partner. In addition to the documents that single people need, you should title assets so that each of you can take advantage of the $3.5 million estate tax exemption (Chapter 3). Most likely, your primary goal in planning is to leave your spouse or partner well provided for financially (Chapter 4).

You have young children. People's financial situations at this stage vary hugely. Those who had business successes at a young age or had children after their careers were well established might be in a position to take advantage of some sophisticated planning techniques described in Chapters 15 and 16 to create a financial cushion for their children in the years ahead. Others have so many current expenses that they can't think much beyond that. Even if you fall in the second category, this is the ideal time to start saving for the enormous education expenses that await you (Chapter 9). And if you never thought you needed life insurance, you might want to reconsider (Chapter 7). Most importantly, be sure you name a guardian for your children and provide for them financially in case something happens to you (Chapter 5).

You have children who are young adults. Life has gotten simpler in some ways and more complicated in others. (Are you surprised to find you still lie awake at night worrying about your children?) If you accumulated $10 million or more during your peak earning years, you may be in a position to transfer some money now to save estate taxes later. This could be as simple as giving children a hand as they buy a first home or start a business (Chapter 13) or might involve complex transactions designed to shift large sums while minimizing gift tax (Chapters 15 and 16). The more money at stake, the more attractive you may find estate planning devices like long-term trusts that will protect assets from potential future creditors and others who prey on the wealthy (see Chapters 6 and 18).

You have grandchildren or great-grandchildren. They give you so much joy, and if you've done well financially, you may feel especially generous toward them. Just beware the onerous 45 percent generation-skipping transfer tax (Chapter 14) that could diminish your gifts.

Keep in mind that you're at the time in life when estate planning might become more complicated and more costly. Perhaps you're thinking about the legacy you would like to leave – for example, by providing everyone in your family with the best possible education (Chapter 9), developing a succession plan for the family business (Chapter 12), keeping a vacation home in the family (Chapter 10) or making meaningful gifts to charity (Chapter 17).

If you have amassed significant wealth and lost your spouse, steps to minimize estate tax become more important. Start by converting traditional IRAs to Roth accounts – one of the simplest, most tax-efficient estate planning tools available and one that costs nothing in legal fees and can sharply reduce income taxes (Chapter 7). Then consider various ways to transfer assets to family members during your lifetime (Chapters 15 and 16). If you're thinking of moving to another state or dividing your time between various places, factor in how it would affect your estate plan (Chapter 10).

To-Do List

Keep Advisers Current

We talk to our accountants at least once a year as we do our taxes, and we communicate with investment advisers more often. In comparison, we often leave estate-planning lawyers out of the loop. A 10-minute phone call to your lawyer can identify events that may be significant. Let your lawyer know if you:

❧ Are getting married or divorced

❧ Have lost your spouse

❧ Have a new child or grandchild

❧ Have substantially more or less money than when you last did your estate plan

❧ Have been diagnosed with a serious illness

❧ Are approaching age 70½

❧ Recently received a large inheritance or learned about one you may receive in the future

❧ Are thinking of selling your company

❧ Have started a promising business or made an investment that may pay off handsomely

❧ Want to make a significant gift to charity

❧ Have bought real estate or other costly assets

❧ Want to sell your home

❧ Plan on moving to a different state

Glossary

Alternate valuation date – a date six months after someone dies that may be used instead of the date of death to measure the fair market value of his assets to see if the estate will be subject to tax. The alternate valuation date is used when it would reduce the tax owed, but whatever date the heirs choose must apply to everything in the estate (for example, they can't use one date for the house, and another for the stock portfolio). For property sold or distributed within six months of the death, the alternate valuation date is the date of that transaction.

Annual exclusion – the amount (currently $13,000 for individuals, $26,000 for married couples) that can be given annually to each of as many recipients as the donors choose without incurring gift tax. (The amount is periodically adjusted for inflation, in $1,000 increments.)

Applicable exclusion – see *estate tax exemption*.

Applicable federal rate (AFR) – the interest rate, announced each month by the Treasury, that is used for loans and installment sales between family members. The rate depends on whether the loan is short term (three years or less), mid term (more than three years but no more than nine) or long term (more than nine).

Ascertainable standards – specific guidelines that a trustee must follow when making payouts to the beneficiaries of a trust (for example, "health care, education, maintenance and support"), in contrast to a trust that leaves distributions solely to the trustee's judgment.

Asset protection – the process of trying to make it impossible, or at least more difficult, for potential future creditors to require the liquidation of certain property or accounts to settle their claims.

Attorney in fact – one or more people appointed to act as agent under a durable power of attorney. The term is confusing because the agent need not be a lawyer. In fact, most lawyers do not want to take on this time-consuming role, which also carries the responsibility of acting as fiduciary.

Bargain sale – selling an asset, such as tangible personal property or real estate, for less than its fair market value. When the sale is to a charity, the donor can take a charitable income tax deduction for the difference. When the sale is between family members, it is considered is part sale, part gift, for tax purposes.

Basis adjustment – an increase or decrease in the cost basis of inherited assets to reflect their fair market value either on the date of death or on a date six months later. An increase in the cost basis could reduce or eliminate the capital gains tax that heirs have to pay if the property is sold.

Beneficiary – a person or charity entitled to money or other assets under an estate-planning document, such as a will or trust.

Beneficiary designation – a clause in a document that indicates who should inherit certain assets that do not pass under a will or trust. Examples: retirement accounts and the proceeds of a life insurance policy. See *designated beneficiary*.

Bequest – what a person or organization receives according to the terms of a will or trust.

Bomb clause – a provision in a will or living trust indicating how assets would be distributed if the individual creating the document and her closest heirs are wiped out simultaneously, as in an accident. The purpose is to provide for the distribution of assets among people or charities who might not otherwise receive anything.

Buy-sell agreement – an agreement among business owners covering what would happen to their interest in the company if events like disability, death, divorce or personal bankruptcy occur. By requiring a sale under certain circumstances (known as trigger events) and by specifying the terms beforehand, a buy-sell can prevent one owner from becoming an unwilling partner with another owner's heirs or leaving a surviving spouse illiquid because the remaining owners refuse to buy the survivor's inherited shares.

Bypass trust – a planning tool used to assure use of the $3.5 million estate tax exemptions of both spouses. When the first spouse dies, the trust is funded with up to $3.5 million of assets. It distributes income and principal to the survivor or other family members while the surviving spouse is alive, then passes on whatever is left to family. Funds in the bypass trust are covered by the exemption amount and are not taxed when the first spouse dies. Nor are they considered part of the survivor's estate, so they are not subject to tax when she dies.

Charging order – a term connected with the use of a family limited partnership or a limited liability company, to achieve asset protection. It refers to the fact that creditors generally cannot take all the assets in the entity or force a liquidation, no matter how much they are owed. The most they can get is a court order giving them the right to the debtor's distributions up to the amount of the debt.

Charitable gift annuity – a contract in which the donor contributes assets, typically cash or marketable securities, and the charity agrees to pay a fixed amount of money annually to that person and perhaps to the surviving spouse. The annuity can be paid immediately or deferred until the donor reaches a specific age (which might be some time during retirement).

Charitable lead trust – see *charitable remainder trust*.

Charitable remainder trust – one of two split-interest arrangements in which charitable and noncharitable beneficiaries each get a share of the trust assets, but at different times. In a charitable remainder trust, individual beneficiaries (or a trust for their benefit) receive income for whatever period of time is specified – their lifetimes or a term of up to 20 years. When this interest ends, the charity receives what is left, known as the remainder interest. The charitable lead trust reverses the priorities: The charity receives its payout up front for the period selected by the person creating the trust. When this payout ends, the noncharitable beneficiaries, usually family members, get what is left. Each of these vehicles is irrevocable and carries significant tax advantages.

Codicil – an amendment to a will, which must be signed with the same formalities as a will.

Conservator (or **guardian**) – someone appointed by a court to oversee the finances of an individual who can no longer handle her or his own affairs and has not made prior arrangements about who should play this role.

Contingent beneficiary – the alternate or secondary beneficiary (a person, charity or trust) named on a beneficiary designation form to receive assets if the primary beneficiary has died or chosen to turn them down (see *disclaim*).

Credit-shelter trust – see *bypass trust*.

Cross-purchase agreement – a form of a buy-sell agreement used by business owners in which the surviving owner has the obligation or right to buy the share held by the other's estate.

Crummey power – the right for a limited time, usually 30 or 60 days, to withdraw from the trust the yearly gift intended for each beneficiary. Each year, the trustees must send a letter, called a Crummey notice, to the beneficiaries (or the parents, guardian or representative, if the beneficiaries are minors) advising them of this right. Any trust that includes this power is a Crummey trust, although the trust may be named for other distinguishing features.

Custodial account – an account at a bank, mutual fund company or brokerage house that designates an adult to oversee the assets of a child until the child is able to withdraw them under state law (usually at age 18 or 21). See *Uniform Transfers to Minors Act*.

Custodian – the bank or financial institution that holds a retirement account or the individual or institution that holds a custodial account.

Decant – to pay out funds from one trust to another.

Decoupled – when a state has an estate tax and the state exemption amount is less than the federal one.

Designated beneficiary – a term defined in the Internal Revenue Code, with further elaboration in IRS regulations, that refers to people named to receive IRA assets when the account owner dies and to certain trusts that also qualify for a stretch-out.

Devise – an arcane and rarely used word that in the past referred to a transfer of real property at death, in contrast to a bequest, which referred to a gift of personal property, and a legacy, which covered money. A document written in plain English today might simply describe a gift or distribution instead.

Direct skip – a term that involves the application of generation-skipping transfer, or GST, tax. Refers to an outright gift to an individual or money put into a trust that exclusively benefits skip persons. In this case, the person making the transfer or her estate (rather than the recipient) generally pays any GST tax.

Disclaim – to decline an inheritance (typically with the intent of benefiting another person or a specific charity) – usually for tax reasons. People who disclaim, known as disclaimants, are generally treated as if they had died before the person from whom they are inheriting. The assets go to the person next in line as designated in the estate plan or under state law if the plan makes no such provision, or to a specific charity if that is what the estate plan specifies.

Distribution – payout from a trust, partnership or a retirement account, or according to the terms of a will.

Domestic asset protection trust (also known as self-settled spendthrift trust) – a trust designed to give the grantor access to the income and principal of the trust while protecting the assets from the claims of future creditors. These trusts are allowed in at least 10 states: Alaska, Delaware, Missouri, Nevada, New Hampshire, Rhode Island, South Dakota, Tennessee, Utah and Wyoming.

Domicile – the state someone calls home. While residency determines liability for income taxes, domicile determines whether a person's estate is subject to state estate tax. It is generally based not just on time spent in a place (the test for residency), but on additional evidence that it's the place a person is most closely connected to, as demonstrated by voting records, a safe deposit box rental and memberships in local clubs, for example.

Donor-advised fund – a popular alternative to a private foundation that can be funded during life, through an estate plan or a combination of the two. Contributors make irrevocable gifts to a nonprofit that administers the fund in conjunction with funds set up by other donors. The donor or the designated successor advisers can recommend which nonprofit organizations should receive grants from the account.

Drop-down trust – a trust that receives a personal residence or vacation home at the end of the term of a qualified personal-residence trust (see *QPRT*).

Durable power of attorney – appoints a family member, friend or adviser as an agent to act on a person's behalf in a variety of financial and legal matters and authorizes actions even after the person's disability.

Dynasty trust – a trust designed to continue in perpetuity (or for a very long time) and pass wealth through multiple generations without incurring estate, gift or generation-skipping transfer taxes. These trusts are allowed to continue in perpetuity only in states that have abolished the rule against perpetuities. These include Alaska, Delaware, South Dakota and Wisconsin. Residents of other states can choose one of these states as the situs, or location, of a trust; in most cases, some connection to the state is needed and certain conditions apply.

Elective share – a minimum portion of a spouse's estate that the surviving spouse is entitled to under state law. A spouse can waive her right to the elective share in a prenuptial agreement that specifies how assets will be distributed if the couple is married when one of them dies.

Engagement letter – a contract between a lawyer and client (typically prepared by the lawyer) that describes the terms under which they will work together. It should cover the scope of the work, the fee, the charges for expenses such as photocopies, long-distance calls and faxes (sometimes these are marked up) and how disputes will be resolved.

Estate – everything a person owns when she or he dies, including house and personal property; all investments, whether in the form of bank or brokerage accounts, retirement plans, real estate or alternative investments; and any interests in a family business or partnership.

Estate tax exemption – the amount that can be passed on to heirs tax-free before the 45 percent federal estate tax kicks in. In 2009, that amount is $3.5 million.

Executor (personal representative) – the person or institution that administers an estate and remains in charge until it is legally closed.

Exhaustion rule – an IRS rule that requires the party paying a private annuity to have assets sufficient to continue the payments not just for the seller's actual life expectancy but until he reaches age 110.

Family limited partnership (FLP) – along with a limited liability company (some lawyers are more familiar with that structure) this family-controlled entity is used to minimize the tax cost of transferring assets. A senior family member puts assets such as marketable securities, real estate or shares of an operating business into the entity, then sells or gives away shares in the entity – rather than the assets themselves. Since the interests can't readily be sold outside the family, their value is discounted for *both* lack of marketability and lack of control (typically a total discount of 20 to 30 percent).

Fiduciary – a person or institution (such as a trust company) that is legally obliged to act in the best interest of those whose assets it manages. Examples include a trustee, an agent designated under a durable power of attorney or the custodian of a custodial account.

Forced heirship – laws in some countries designed to avoid disinheritance of a spouse or child. These laws, which may apply to property U.S. persons own in that country, entitle certain family members to a preset share of assets left by a relative who has died. Forced heirship rules can frustrate estate-planning strategies that are popular in the U.S. (The state of Louisiana, which has some laws based on the Napoleonic Code, still requires forced heirship in certain cases.)

Foreign Bank Account Report (FBAR) – a form that must be filed with the Treasury Department by June 30 each year, reporting foreign investment accounts, such as bank accounts or brokerage accounts, held during the previous year.

Formula clauses – provisions in a will or trust that include phrases like "that portion," "that fraction" or "that amount" (without saying what it is) instead of naming a specific sum to be distributed – to a person, a trust or a charity. For example, these clauses might refer to an amount up to the estate tax exemption that is to go into a bypass trust or express the sum as a percentage of whatever the limit happens to be when the person dies.

Fraudulent conveyance – a term used in the context of asset protection that refers to a transfer with the intent to hinder, delay or defraud creditors, typically in anticipation of a lawsuit. State and federal laws prohibit such transfers. Unfortunately, no hard-and-fast rules spell out what these terms mean, and they are applied on a case-by-case basis. If a court finds there has been a fraudulent conveyance, it can declare the transfer void and order the assets be made available to creditors.

Future interest – something beneficiaries can't use right away, as opposed to a present interest, which they can. The distinction is important in estate planning because a future interest will not qualify for the annual exclusion. Including Crummey powers in a trust is one way to address this issue.

Generation-skipping transfer, or **GST, tax** – the tax that may apply when assets are given directly to grandchildren, or trusts are set up or added to that benefit this generation or future ones. The GST exemption is $3.5 million; a 45 percent tax applies once you have exceeded this limit. See *skip persons*.

Gift tax exemption – the amount a person can give away during life without triggering gift tax. Once a person has passed the limit, which in 2009 is $1 million, a gift tax of up to 45 percent applies. On the estate tax return, the $3.5 million estate tax exemption is reduced by the amount of the $1 million gift-tax exemption a person used. If a person exceeded the limit, heirs can take a credit for the gift tax that was paid for making lifetime gifts.

Gift-splitting – when married couples combine their annual exclusions to give away up to $26,000 to each of as many people as they choose each year. A gift-splitting couple can give $13,000 each, $26,000 from a joint account or $26,000 from one of their individual accounts.

Grantor – the person who sets up and funds a trust. See *settlor*.

Grantor retained annuity trust (GRAT) – a short-term irrevocable trust that makes an annual payment to the grantor for the entire trust term based on a rate set each month by the Treasury. Any appreciation in the trust when the annual payments end above the rate set by the Treasury passes tax-free to remainder beneficiaries.

Grantor retained income trust (GRIT) – an irrevocable trust set up by someone who retains the right to get income from the trust for a specific number of years. When that term expires, all the trust assets, including any appreciation, go tax-free to the named remainder beneficiaries.

Grantor trust – a trust in which the person who creates the trust, known as the grantor, retains certain rights or powers. The term refers not to a single variety of trust but to a set of characteristics that can be incorporated into various types of trusts. A grantor trust is not treated as a separate entity for income tax purposes and the grantor, rather than the trust or its beneficiaries, must pay tax on trust earnings. This amounts to a tax-free gift from the grantor to the beneficiaries.

Guardian – someone appointed to care for a person, her money or both. The guardian, who in many states is subject to court oversight, may be appointed by a court, as in the case of someone who is no longer able to handle her finances and has not signed a durable power of attorney (in this context the guardian is sometimes called a conservator). Parents should appoint a guardian, through their wills, to care for a child who is a minor or who has special needs. To handle the child's money, the parent would need to designate a financial guardian or, better yet, set up a trust that puts these matters in the hands of a trustee and provides more direction about how the funds should be spent.

Health and Education Exclusion Trust (HEET) – a complex estate planning technique used to fund health care or education for multiple generations while avoiding generation-skipping transfer tax. A HEET must incorporate two features: the trust must make payments directly to the schools or care providers and the trust must have a charity as a co-beneficiary.

Health care agent – see *health care proxy.*

Health care power of attorney – see *health care proxy.*

Health care proxy (also known as health care power of attorney) – authorizes someone, known as a health care agent, to make medical decisions on behalf of the person signing the proxy.

Health Insurance Portability and Accountability Act – see *HIPAA*.

HIPAA (Health Insurance Portability and Accountability Act) – the federal law designed to protect medical privacy; it prohibits doctors and hospitals from sharing medical information without a patient's permission.

HIPAA release – gives doctors and hospitals permission to share medical records with specific people in addition to a person's designated health care agent.

Homestead law – a law in certain states that makes all or part of the equity in a personal residence exempt from the claims of creditors.

"I love you" will – the practice, common among spouses, of leaving everything to each other. All the assets then qualify for the unlimited marital deduction and are not taxed when the first spouse dies. But those assets become part of the survivor's estate and are subject to tax when the surviving spouse passes away. A bypass trust addresses this situation.

In terrorem clause – see *no-contest clause*.

Incapacity – a mental state in which people do not know who their family members are, what assets they have or what they want to do with them. Once someone becomes incapacitated, it is generally legally too late to make changes in estate planning documents.

Inclusion ratio – reflects what portion of assets are exempt from the generation-skipping transfer tax when exempt and non-exempt assets have been mixed in the same trust. Estate planners try to design trusts covered by the GST exemption to have what's called a zero inclusion ratio, meaning that the trust is completely GST exempt. That way, there isn't any tax on either a taxable distribution or a taxable termination.

Income in respect of a decedent – income that wasn't taxed before a person's death and would have been taxed if the individual had lived long enough to receive it. The most important example involves a traditional IRA that is inherited. Because the IRA owner did not pay income tax on the funds in the retirement account, the person or entity (such as a trust) that is a beneficiary of the IRA must pay tax as the money is withdrawn.

Installment sale to an irrevocable grantor trust – an estate planning technique in which senior family members sell assets to a trust that will benefit younger relatives and, in exchange, receive an interest-bearing promissory note. Assuming a sale at fair market value and interest at the applicable federal rate, there is no gift and therefore no gift tax.

Instrument – an estate planning document that looks like a contract and is used to create an entity such as a trust.

Inter vivos – an estate planning vehicle that takes effect during life, as opposed to one that is testamentary and takes effect when someone dies (for example, an "inter vivos trust" or an "inter vivos transfer").

Intestacy – a ranking of inheritors in order of priority for people who die without a will or living trust. Typically the spouse comes first, then children, parents and siblings.

Irrevocable – an estate planning document that cannot be changed. Examples include an irrevocable life insurance trust (ILIT), a grantor retained annuity trust (GRAT) and a qualified personal-residence trust (QPRT).

Irrevocable life insurance trust (ILIT) – a trust created to purchase and own a life insurance policy. Its main purpose is to avoid a situation in which the person insured owns a policy on his own life, because that could result in estate taxes. An ILIT can also benefit minors, who are not allowed to own the policy directly but only through a custodianship or a trust. Another trust can be the beneficiary of an ILIT (for example, a special needs trust or a generation-skipping transfer trust), and an ILIT can be the remainder beneficiary of a trust (such as a grantor retained annuity trust).

Issue – an arcane word for descendants. Still used in some wills, and occasionally by estate planners in conversation.

Joint tenancy with rights of survivorship – a popular form of ownership in which both owners have access to the assets during life, and when one of them dies, the survivor immediately becomes the sole owner of the whole property, regardless of what the will says, or whether there is a will. See *tenancy in common* and *tenancy by the entirety*.

Legacy – traditionally a gift at death of money, but now used to refer to a gift of real property or personal property, as well.

Leveraging – applying various strategies to pack as much value as possible into both the lifetime exemption and the annual exclusion. Examples include using annual exclusion gifts to fund the premium of a life insurance policy and using a grantor retained annuity trust (GRAT) or a qualified personal-residence trust (QPRT) to discount the value of the interest being transferred.

Lifetime exemption – see *gift tax exemption*.

Limited liability company – see *family limited partnership*.

Living trust (revocable trust) – safeguards assets and provides for the care of someone who can no longer handle his or her affairs, then determines who will receive the property when that person dies.

Living will – expresses preferences about certain aspects of end-of-life care, rather than leaving them up to the person named in a health care proxy.

Marital deduction – an unlimited deduction from estate and gift tax that postpones the tax on assets inherited from each other until the second spouse dies. It applies only if the inheriting spouse is a U.S. citizen. See *QDOT*.

Marital share – assets left to a spouse. They are covered by the unlimited marital deduction as long as they go to the spouse either outright, through a qualified terminable interest property trust or through a trust with a power of appointment.

Minimum required distribution – the amount that owners of traditional retirement accounts and inheritors of traditional accounts or Roth IRAs must withdraw in a given year unless they inherited the account from a spouse. The required payout is based on the account balance on Dec. 31 of the previous year divided by the individual's life expectancy, as listed in IRS tables. See *stretch-out.*

No-contest clause – a provision in a will or living trust designed to avoid legal disputes by indicating that anyone who formally challenges the document gets nothing. Some states prohibit these clauses. Also called an in terrorem clause.

Non-exempt trust – a trust that would ordinarily be subject to generation-skipping transfer tax. This tax can be avoided by allocating an individual's exemption to assets as they are put into the trust. If the exemption has already been used up, the tax would have to be paid.

Non-resident aliens – citizens of another country who do not live in the U.S.

Offshore trusts – trusts in certain foreign jurisdictions, generally set up for asset protection purposes.

One-lung trust – a single trust left to a spouse, instead of setting up both a marital trust to provide for the spouse and a separate bypass trust to provide for the spouse and other relatives. This strategy involves giving the executor the option of making the QTIP election over some of the trust funds when the first spouse dies. To make this possible, the bypass trust must be "QTIP-able," meaning that it provides (or could provide, as the result of the election), that the spouse will get all the income and that nobody else is entitled to any distributions from the QTIP portion of the trust.

Outright bequest – gives recipients immediate ownership of their inheritance. In contrast, the assets can go into a trust, which puts a person or company in charge of managing the assets and distributing them according to the wishes of the grantor, as expressed in the trust instrument.

Payable on death – a provision in a financial document, such as an application for savings bonds, certificate of deposit or bank account, providing that when the owner of the asset dies, funds should be paid out to a specific person.

Pecuniary bequest – a transfer at death of a fixed dollar amount, which can be expressed as a specific number or as a formula.

Per stirpes – when a beneficiary dies, inheritances that get passed down to a beneficiary's descendants rather than going to other members of her own generation.

Personal property – see *tangible personal property.*

Personal property memorandum – provides guidance or direction (depending on state law) to an executor about who should receive jewelry, art and other personal property not described in the will.

Personal representative – a word used in two contexts, as a synonym for executor and as a reference to someone who has the right to a person's medical information under the Health Insurance Portability and Accountability Act, HIPAA.

Pot trust – a trust with multiple beneficiaries at the same time, as opposed to just one.

Pour over – a provision in a will directing that, after certain distributions have been made, all remaining assets be paid to a trust, referred to as a pour over trust.

Power of appointment – the right of a trust beneficiary to name the next person to receive the trust property. This power may be special, meaning that she must designate someone from a certain group, or general, meaning that she can appoint anyone she chooses (or her own estate).

Power of attorney – see *durable power of attorney.*

Prearranged-sale rule – a rule that applies when a donor has a binding obligation to sell any noncash asset, including real estate, before giving it to charity. This rule forces the donor to pay tax on the gain.

Present interest – see *future interest.*

Principal – the assets used to fund a trust plus any appreciation or capital gains associated with those assets. Distinguished from trust earnings, which are considered income.

Private annuity – a sale of assets in exchange for an unsecured promise to pay an annuity for the rest of the seller's life. The payout is based on the seller's life expectancy under government actuarial tables.

Private foundation – a tax-exempt legal entity set up by an individual or a family to make grants to charities or individuals. Unlike a donor-advised fund, donors may have total control over both investment management and grant-making.

Probate – the process through which a court determines that a will is legally valid.

Protector – a neutral party, such as an attorney, accountant or family friend, who provides checks-and-balances by supervising agents under a power of attorney or trustees of a trust.

QDOT, or *qualified domestic trust* – a trust used to leave assets worth more than the estate tax exemption when they are going to a spouse who is not a U.S. citizen. Without this trust, anything above the exemption amount would be taxed immediately. Any time the QDOT distributes principal, it must withhold estate tax – at the rate that was in effect when the spouse died.

QPRT, or *qualified personal-residence trust* – an irrevocable trust that removes part of the value of a costly home from the estate and shelters future appreciation. The grantor puts her primary residence or vacation home into an irrevocable trust, retaining the right to live there rent-free for a specified number of years. During that time the trust, of which she could be trustee, owns the property. When the period ends, ownership can pass to the beneficiaries, usually children, or go into another trust, often called a drop-down trust, for the rest of her life. Meanwhile, the QPRT has removed both the property and any future appreciation from the estate. Because the trust freezes the house at its fair market value when it's transferred to the QPRT, no additional tax is due after that.

QTIP, or ***qualified terminable interest property trust*** – a trust designed to hold the marital share and qualify for the unlimited marital deduction. The trustee is required to pay all income to the surviving spouse for life and can also make distributions of principal. Distributions to anyone other than the spouse are not permitted while the spouse is alive; after that, the assets can go to whomever the trust documents specify.

QTIP election – a formality that must be observed in order to apply the marital deduction to the QTIP. The executor, who signs the federal estate tax return, Form 706, must elect to treat the trust property as if it has passed to the surviving spouse. In the process of making this election, the executor can decide how much should go to the marital share and how much to a bypass trust that preserves the estate tax exemption of the spouse who has died.

Qualified domestic trust – see *QDOT.*

Qualified personal-residence trust – see *QPRT.*

Qualified state tuition programs – see *Section 529 plans.*

Qualified terminable interest property trust – see *QTIP.*

Real property – real estate, as distinguished from tangible personal property such as art, jewelry or automobiles and intangible personal property such as stocks and bonds.

Redemption agreement – a form of buy-sell agreement used by business owners in which the shares of the owner who died will or may be sold back to the business.

Related use rule – a rule that limits the deduction for tangible personal property donated to charity. In order for a donation to qualify for a full fair market value deduction, the charity must use the asset in a manner related to its exempt purpose. A donor who gives violins to an orchestra can deduct the fair market value if the orchestra uses them, rather than sells them.

Remainder – a future interest in assets, as opposed to a current one, which typically takes effect when a predetermined event occurs. For example, remainder beneficiaries of a trust might not receive distributions until the current beneficiary dies or the trust term ends.

Required minimum distribution – see *minimum required distribution.*

Residuary estate – what is left after estate expenses, creditors and taxes have been paid and gifts of specific items or specific sums of money have been satisfied.

Revocable – an estate planning document, such as a trust, that can be amended (for example, by adding beneficiaries). The most common example is a living trust. Trusts set up to save estate taxes usually have to be irrevocable.

Revocable trust – see *living trust.*

Roth IRA – a retirement account funded with after-tax dollars, so no tax is assessed when the money is withdrawn.

Rule against perpetuities – a law in many states that prevents a trust from lasting indefinitely and sets a maximum term. Traditionally it was measured by "lives in being plus 21 years." In that case the best choice for the "measuring life" is typically someone who is young at the time the trust is created. A simpler approach, now used in many states, is to limit the term to 90 years from the time the trust is created. In states that have abolished the rule against perpetuities, it is possible to have a dynasty trust, which can last forever (assuming its assets are not depleted).

Section 529 plans – qualified state programs that can be used for higher education costs and are available in all states and the District of Columbia. These plans allow an individual to set up a separate account for each family member she wants to benefit. A private money manager chosen by each state typically manages the funds. Withdrawals from a 529 account are federal-tax exempt, provided the money is used for college or graduate school.

Section 2503(c) trust – one of a handful of trusts that meet the present interest requirement. (Another is a Crummey trust.) This irrevocable trust must have only one beneficiary, give the beneficiary the right to withdraw the assets at age 21 and must not restrict the trustee from making distributions of principal and interest before that. The trust must be includable in the beneficiary's estate if the beneficiary dies.

Section 2642(c) trust – an irrevocable trust that generally does not give rise to generation-skipping transfer tax. It can benefit only one grandchild, and the trust document must specify that if the grandchild dies before the funds have been fully distributed, the remaining funds become part of the grandchild's estate, making them potentially subject to estate tax.

Section 7520 rate – an assumed interest rate, set each month by the U.S. Treasury. The Section 7520 rate is 120 percent of the current midterm applicable rate, rounded to the nearest 0.2 percent. It is used to calculate the value of any annuity (for example, in a grantor retained annuity trust), any interest for life or a term of years (such as in a charitable remainder trust) or any remainder interest (for example, in the personal residence donated to charity).

Self-canceling installment note (SCIN) – a financing technique used in connection with the sale of assets to family members or to a trust for their benefit. With an ordinary installment note, if the seller dies while the note is outstanding, the balance is payable to the estate. With a SCIN, the debt is forgiven if the seller dies during the note term.

Self-settled spendthrift trust – see *domestic asset protection trust*.

Self-settled trust – a trust in which the person who sets it up and funds it is also a beneficiary.

Settlor – see *grantor*.

Situs – the place where an entity, such as a trust, is legally situated. This determines which state's laws apply to the trust.

Skip persons – in a family, anyone other than a spouse who is two or more generations younger than an individual; outside of the family, anyone more than 37.5 years younger than an individual. The term is used in the context of applying the generation-skipping transfer, or GST, tax.

Special needs trust – a trust to benefit an individual (whether a minor or adult) with physical, emotional or cognitive needs who may some day qualify for state or federal assistance. Having more than a certain sum of money in his or her own name disqualifies the recipient from assistance. Keeping assets in a specially designed trust avoids this restriction.

Special trustee – see *protector*.

Spendthrift clause – a provision in a trust preventing the beneficiaries from assigning their interests.

Split dollar arrangement – a financing tool in which two parties, such as a trust and a family member, share the premiums and the proceeds of a life insurance policy. Typically used to fund permanent life insurance (as opposed to a term policy).

Step-up in basis – see *basis adjustment*.

Stretch-out – the strategy, available to an IRA owner or beneficiary, of extending minimum required distributions from a traditional account or any inherited account over her life expectancy. The longer the withdrawals can be extended, the smaller each payout will be, and the less income tax will be due for the year the money is taken out.

Supplemental needs trust – see *special needs trust*.

Tangible personal property – personal possessions, such as cars, boats, clothing, jewelry and artwork, in contrast to real estate and intangible assets such as stocks, bonds and bank accounts.

Tax-deferred retirement accounts – traditional accounts, including IRAs and employer-sponsored plans such as 401(k)s and 403(b)s, with which the owner can take a tax deduction when making contributions and there is no need to pay tax as investments in the account grow. Income tax is due on funds as they are withdrawn, by the account owner or beneficiaries. See *Roth IRA*.

Tax exclusive – refers to a system of tax in which there is tax only on the sum given away, not on the money used to pay the tax. Gift tax, for example, is applied on a tax exclusive basis. In contrast, estate tax is said to be tax inclusive, meaning that the amount of tax owed is based on the entire estate, and the tax due is paid with after-tax dollars.

Taxable distribution – a payout to a skip person from a trust that benefits both skip persons and older family members.

Taxable termination – when the interests of all non-skip persons in a trust have ended and skip persons are the remaining beneficiaries. This event could generate GST tax; if so, the tax is paid by the trustee using funds in the trust.

Tenancy by the entirety – a form of joint ownership, available only to spouses, in which each spouse automatically inherits the other's share. In most states, only the couple's joint creditors have access to the asset. See *joint tenancy with rights of survivorship* and *tenancy in common*.

Tenancy in common – a form of joint ownership in which each co-owner technically owns part of the property, known as an undivided interest. When one co-owner dies, only that person's share gets included in his or her estate. See *joint tenancy with rights of survivorship* and *tenancy by the entirety*.

Testamentary – an estate planning vehicle that takes effect at death, as opposed to one that is inter vivos, which takes effect during life (for example, a "testamentary trust" or a "testamentary transfer").

Testator – the person whose property is covered in a will. Arcane term used in old wills, instead of referring to the individual by name.

Transfer tax – gift tax that applies to certain lifetime gifts, estate tax that may be an issue for assets that pass at death and generation-skipping transfer, or GST, tax that applies to some transfers made at either juncture that benefit grandchildren.

Trust – a legal wrapper for holding assets, such as cash, real estate, an insurance policy, shares in a closely held company or publicly traded securities, created by a document that looks like a contract and is called the trust instrument, declaration or agreement.

Trust adviser – see *protector*.

Trust protector – see *protector*.

Trustee – in a trust, the person or company that manages the assets and distributes them according to the terms of the trust document. A trust can have one trustee or several.

Unified credit – a term that is a vestige of an earlier estate tax system, but still sometimes used to refer to the estate tax exemption. Under the previous system, the lifetime exemption and the estate tax exemption were expressed as a total amount, and it was possible to use this "unified credit" to transfer assets at either stage or a combination of the two. Since 2004, the gift tax exemption has remained at $1 million, while the estate tax exemption has gone up.

Uniform Transfers to Minors Act (UTMA) – the law most states have adopted to regulate custodial accounts. Under this law, children are legally entitled to the money when they reach the age specified under state law (usually 21).

Unitrust – one that bases payouts to beneficiaries on the value of the trust assets, recalculated each year, rather than requiring the trustee to pay income, which can reflect only the annual earnings on stocks and bonds (not capital gains). This can be done by defining income as a unitrust amount, a fixed percentage of the trust value each year (typically 3 to 5 percent or a specific figure within that range) that is sometimes averaged over a three-year period. A more flexible approach is to give trustees broad discretion to invade principal along with distributing income, but again limited by the formula; this is called a "power to adjust."

Unrelated business taxable income (UBTI) – income to a charity financed by debt or generated by business activities unrelated to its tax-exempt purpose. This income falls outside the tax-exempt status that charities usually enjoy. It therefore defeats one purpose of donating the asset to charity, which is to avoid the tax a donor would have to pay himself.

U.S. persons – U.S. citizens and resident aliens who hold a green card.

Will – the cornerstone of many estate plans, it should transfer assets, appoint a guardian for minor children and name an executor.

Resources and Further Reading

An Internet search for information about estate planning turns up millions of sources, in print and online. Listed below are the ones I rely on most often and those that have influenced my thinking.

Finding a Lawyer

American Bar Association
A massive, national lawyers' trade association, divided into sections devoted to particular specialties. The one on Real Property, Trust and Estate Law has 30,000 members and its own area on the ABA's Web site, *www.abanet.org/rppt*, providing basic information to the public.

American College of Trust and Estate Counsel
A group of trust and estate lawyers elected to membership based on their experience and scholarship. The public area of the ACTEC Web site includes "Find an ACTEC Fellow," with a search-by-location function, and "Public Resources," with an abundance of useful links.
www.actec.org

Martindale-Hubbell Law Directory
The most complete nationwide listing of attorneys by location and area of practice.
www.martindale.com

National Academy of Elder Law Attorneys
Many estate planners work with elderly clients. Members of this group focus on some of the elderly's particular concerns, including Medicaid planning, maintaining independence and geriatric care. Includes a tool for finding an elder law attorney nearby.
www.naela.com

Special Needs Alliance
A national network of attorneys dedicated to assisting families with special needs planning. Many became involved in the field because members of their own families were affected.
www.specialneedsalliance.org

Books

The Harvard Manual on the Tax Aspects of Charitable Giving
Carolyn M. Osteen With Martin Hall
8th edition (1999, Harvard University)
Published by Harvard's Planned Giving Office, this has become an essential desk reference for people concerned about philanthropy. Its highly readable style makes it as helpful to consumers as it is to the professionals who were its intended audience.

Life and Death Planning for Retirement Benefits
Natalie B. Choate
6th edition (2006, Ataxplan Publications)
Without dispute, this is the Bible on the subject for lawyers and financial advisers. Consumers with an appetite for detail may also find it a valuable resource; among other things, it includes sample letters to use when communicating with financial institutions.
www.ataxplan.com

Making the Most of Your Money
Jane Bryant Quinn
(1991, Simon & Schuster)
The eminent magazine and newspaper columnist who once took on the insurance industry offers a comprehensive guide to all aspects of personal finance. Although it has not been updated since its initial publication, much of the book's savvy advice remains useful.

Mrs. Astor Regrets: The Hidden Betrayals of a Family Beyond Reproach
Meryl Gordon
(2008, Houghton Mifflin Harcourt)
A saucy tale of events leading up to the criminal trial of the New York philanthropist's son and lawyer, who were convicted in October 2009 of conspiring to take advantage of Brooke Astor's diminished capacity. Though the author doesn't say so, there are lessons here for us all: Anticipate your possible mental decline and go outside the family for help if you can't trust your kin.

The QPRT Manual: The Estate Planner's Guide
To Qualified Personal-Residence Trusts
Natalie B. Choate
(2004, Ataxplan Publications)
Surprising as it may seem to devote an entire book to the qualified personal-residence trust, or QPRT, there's no unnecessary material in this, and it has become a go-to source for advisers. Before setting up a QPRT, a complex but potentially useful estate-planning tool, clients might also want to read up.
www.ataxplan.com

The Retirement Savings Time Bomb...and How to Defuse It
Ed Slott
(2003, Viking)
Written by a CPA with a knack for plain English and comical metaphors, this guide to IRA distribution rules and associated financial strategies is an invaluable resource for consumers.
www.irahelp.com

Silver Spoon Kids: How Successful Parents Raise Responsible Children
Eileen Gallo and Jon J. Gallo
(2002, Contemporary Books)
A psychotherapist and her husband, who is a trust and estate lawyer, team up to offer a highly creative approach to teaching children about money.

Smarter Insurance Solutions
Janet Bamford
(1996, Bloomberg Press)
One of the few books devoted entirely to insurance that offers an independent perspective. Out of print but available through libraries and through the used book market by searching for the book's title on these Web sites: *www.amazon.com, www.barnesandnoble.com* and *www.alibris.com.*

Wealth in Families
Charles W. Collier
(2001, Harvard University)
A look at motivations and methods for charitable giving, written by Harvard's senior philanthropic adviser and intended for the university's fundraising. This slender volume became a classic for advisers and families interested in fostering a spirit of giving.

Newsletters and Magazines

Chronicle of Philanthropy
With its nonprofit news and grant announcements, this biweekly newspaper is required reading for fundraisers, and the heart-warming success stories will inspire donors.
www.philanthropy.com

Ed Slott's IRA Advisor
Addresses both consumers and advisers with monthly updates and recommended strategies from Ed Slott and other leaders in the field.
www.irahelp.com

Steve Leimberg's Estate Planning Email Newsletter
In the rapidly changing world of estate planning, staying current is essential. With frequent updates on breaking news and analysis by leading experts, this newsletter, delivered electronically, fills a pressing need.
www.leimbergservices.com

Tax Wise Giving
Conrad Teitell, a writer, speaker and authority on the law of charitable giving, leavens his advice with plenty of puns and homespun humor. His artful turns of phrase make this monthly newsletter interesting to both fundraisers and donors.
www.taxwisegiving.com

Trusts & Estates
A monthly magazine with timely articles, mostly written by lawyers for lawyers and other advisers.
www.trustsandestates.com

Software

Brentmark Software Inc. (www.brentmark.com)
Offers a variety of products to help professionals and consumers evaluate retirement strategies (based on various scenarios), such as the precise benefits of maximizing the stretch-out in an IRA and whether it makes sense to convert a traditional IRA to a Roth IRA.

Tiger Tables Actuarial Software (www.tigertables.com)
Created by Lawrence P. Katzenstein, a trust and estate lawyer in St. Louis, this software computes the value of the interests transferred and those retained through a variety of tools for estate planning or charitable giving, including: grantor retained annuity trusts, interests for a life or for a term of years, charitable remainder trusts and qualified personal-residence trusts. The program incorporates the mortality tables used by the Internal Revenue Service for various purposes and automatically updates the Section 7520 rate – an assumed interest rate, set each month by the IRS, that is essential to the calculation. A free demo is available on the site.

Web Sites

www.estateplanningsmarts.com
The home of this book, where material will be updated to reflect legal developments that might affect your estate plan. As sections of the book are revised, they will be made available on the site. You can register here to receive e-mail notifications about these changes.

www.fairmark.com
Hosted by Kaye A. Thomas, a tax lawyer and author, this site provides consumers with a wealth of information about personal finance.

www.savingforcollege.com
State-by-state information on Section 529 accounts.

IRS Publications

Tax forms referred to in this book, as well as helpful Internal Revenue Service publications, can be downloaded from www.irs.gov. IRS publications are a lot simpler to read than the tax code, though they are not binding, as only the law can be. Here are some that may be useful:

513 *Tax Information for Visitors to the United States*
519 *U.S. Tax Guide for Aliens*
555 *Community Property*
590 *Individual Retirement Arrangements (IRAs)*
Includes all three Life Expectancy Tables used to calculate the minimum required distribution from an IRA. The two that most people will need are in the Appendix of this book. The one that is not is the Joint Life and Last Survivor Expectancy table, which consumes 13 pages in the IRS publication and applies only when the spouse is the only beneficiary and is more than 10 years younger than the IRA owner.
970 *Tax Benefits for Education*

Single Life Expectancy

*For use by beneficiaries**

Age	Life Expectancy	Age	Life Expectancy
0	82.4	28	55.3
1	81.6	29	54.3
2	80.6	30	53.3
3	79.7	31	52.4
4	78.7	32	51.4
5	77.7	33	50.4
6	76.7	34	49.4
7	75.8	35	48.5
8	74.8	36	47.5
9	73.8	37	46.5
10	72.8	38	45.6
11	71.8	39	44.6
12	70.8	40	43.6
13	69.9	41	42.7
14	68.9	42	41.7
15	67.9	43	40.7
16	66.9	44	39.8
17	66.0	45	38.8
18	65.0	46	37.9
19	64.0	47	37.0
20	63.0	48	36.0
21	62.1	49	35.1
22	61.1	50	34.2
23	60.1	51	33.3
24	59.1	52	32.3
25	58.2	53	31.4
26	57.2	54	30.5
27	56.2	55	29.6

*Spouses who are the only beneficiary and more than 10 years younger than the IRA owner need to consult the Joint Life and Last Survivor Expectancy table, included in IRS Publication 590, available at www.irs.gov.

Source: Internal Revenue Service

Single Life Expectancy

For use by beneficiaries*

Age	Life Expectancy	Age	Life Expectancy
56	28.7	84	8.1
57	27.9	85	7.6
58	27.0	86	7.1
59	26.1	87	6.7
60	25.2	88	6.3
61	24.4	89	5.9
62	23.5	90	5.5
63	22.7	91	5.2
64	21.8	92	4.9
65	21.0	93	4.6
66	20.2	94	4.3
67	19.4	95	4.1
68	18.6	96	3.8
69	17.8	97	3.6
70	17.0	98	3.4
71	16.3	99	3.1
72	15.5	100	2.9
73	14.8	101	2.7
74	14.1	102	2.5
75	13.4	103	2.3
76	12.7	104	2.1
77	12.1	105	1.9
78	11.4	106	1.7
79	10.8	107	1.5
80	10.2	108	1.4
81	9.7	109	1.2
82	9.1	110	1.1
83	8.6	111 and over	1.0

*Spouses who are the only beneficiary and more than 10 years younger than the IRA owner need to consult the Joint Life and Last Survivor Expectancy table, included in IRS Publication 590, available at www.irs.gov.

Source: Internal Revenue Service

Uniform Lifetime

For use by:

- *Unmarried owners*
- *Married owners whose spouses are not more than 10 years younger*
- *Married owners whose spouses are not the sole beneficiaries of their IRAs*

Age	Distribution Period	Age	Distribution Period
70	27.4	93	9.6
71	26.5	94	9.1
72	25.6	95	8.6
73	24.7	96	8.1
74	23.8	97	7.6
75	22.9	98	7.1
76	22.0	99	6.7
77	21.2	100	6.3
78	20.3	101	5.9
79	19.5	102	5.5
80	18.7	103	5.2
81	17.9	104	4.9
82	17.1	105	4.5
83	16.3	106	4.2
84	15.5	107	3.9
85	14.8	108	3.7
86	14.1	109	3.4
87	13.4	110	3.1
88	12.7	111	2.9
89	12.0	112	2.6
90	11.4	113	2.4
91	10.8	114	2.1
92	10.2	115 and over	1.9

Source: Internal Revenue Service

Index

Adjusted gross income (AGI)
 charitable deductions and, 147,
  240-241, 242, 243
 Coverdell Education Savings Accounts
  and, 130
 deducting unreimbursed medical
  expenses of a dependent, 185
adoption
 adopting an adult, 46
 married couple and non-biological
  children, 65, 68
 partner in unmarried couple adopts
  biological child of partner, 70
 previous marriages, children from,
  69-70
 single person, 68
 unmarried couple and non-biological
  children, 70
advance directive. *See* living will
advisers. *See* lawyers and advisers
AFR. *See* applicable federal rate
Alaska
 domestic asset-protection trusts in, 259
 dynasty trusts in, 199
aliens. *See* domiciliaries; non-citizen
 spouse; non-citizens; non-resident
 aliens; resident aliens
alternate beneficiary. *See* contingent
 beneficiary
alternate valuation date, 277
American College of Trust and Estate
 Counsel, 271, 299
American Council on Gift Annuities, 234
American Jobs Creation Act (2004), 178
annual exclusion. *See also* gifts
 amount 41, 125, 139, 163, 174, 183, 187,
  213, 222, 266

 appreciating assets and, 210-211
 best time to make gifts, 43
 capitalizing on, 209-211
 cash gifts using, 183, 187, 195,
  210, 219
 Crummey notices, use of, 83, 119, 188
 deadline for making gifts with, 211
 death (imminent) and use of, 266
 defined, 41, 125, 183, 277
 determining what gifts qualify for,
  200-201
 expatriate rules, 166
 foreigners and, 159
 funding life insurance premiums with,
  119, 198, 210
 funding trusts with, 83, 89-90, 116,
  130, 133, 174, 178, 188, 193-194,
  198, 200-201, 210, 214, 219
 generation-skipping transfer tax and
  cash gifts, 195
 grantor trusts and, 214
 leveraging gifts with life insurance,
  115, 198
 partial interests, giving away,
  139-140
 present interest requirement, 83, 130,
  132, 186, 188, 197, 210, 219, 284
 relationship to lifetime exemption,
  42, 50, 125, 211
 right to withdraw portion of gift to
  trust, 83, 119, 188, 219
 Section 529 plans and, 127, 184, 196, 210
 transferring business interests to
  family members and, 174
 when to report gifts using, 186, 219
applicable exclusion. *See* estate tax,
 federal exemption amount

Photo Credits

Cover: Gold locket ©Paula Connelly/istockphoto.com; pocket watch ©Andrew Parfenov/istockphoto.com; antique keys ©Donald Erickson/istockphoto.com; young girl, first row by Laura Zavetz; grandfather and granddaughter, first row, courtesy of the Stern family; family, second row, courtesy of the Jacobs family; wedding couple, second row, courtesy of Dianne and Richard Oh; mother and child, third row left, by Howard Bushman; young girl, third row center, ©Tammy Bryngelson/istockphoto.com; couple, third row right, ©Catherine Yeulet/istockphoto.com; boy in hat, fourth row left, by Ken Stern; mother and daughter, fourth row center, courtesy of Yamnarm family; man, fourth row right, courtesy of the Zavetz family; girl with ax, fifth row left, courtesy of the Van de Walle family; father with daughters, fifth row right, courtesy of the Eisenstein family; couple, bottom right, courtesy of the Stern family; boys on beach by Ken Stern; boy with pots by Ken Stern

Page 1: Gold frame ©Jakub Krechowicz/istockphoto.com; Renoir photo, Réunion des Musées Nationaux/Art Resource

Page 11: Clockwise: Teacup ©Achim Prill/istockphoto.com; girl by Laura Zavetz; children on swing by Ken Stern; children in tree by Jerry C. Jacobs; woman with dogs by Jerry C. Jacobs; boy and baby by Stacey Horan

Page 31: Chinese dragon ©Jamil Nasir/istockphoto.com

Page 45: Couple, top left, ©Andrew Lever/istockphoto.com; couple, top center, ©Linda Rosenthal; couple, top right, courtesy of the Stern family; couple, bottom left, courtesy of the Kosonocky family; couple, bottom center, ©Catherine Yeulet/istockphoto.com; wedding rings ©Elnur Amikishiyev/istockphoto.com; couple, bottom right, courtesy of the Hordyke family

Page 63: Rocking horse ©Susan Stewart/istockphoto.com

Page 79: Three generations, top left, courtesy of the Van de Walle family; man with child, top center, courtesy of the Sinclair family; mother and child, top right, by Laura Zavetz; woman, bottom left, courtesy of the Fenster famly; child, bottom center, courtesy of the Stern family; pocket watch ©Andrew Parfenov/istockphoto.com

Page 93: Couple, top left, ©Anna Bryukhanova/istockphoto.com; couple, top center, ©digitalskillet/istockphoto.com; woman, top right, courtesy of the Jacobs family; woman, bottom left, ©Loretta Hostettler/istockphoto.com

Page 111: Umbrella ©Carlos Alvarez/istockphoto.com

Page 121: Eyeglasses ©Pali Rao/istockphoto.com; student, top center, ©Joshua Hodge/istockphoto.com; student, top right, ©Island Photography, Inc.; pregnant woman, bottom left, ©digitalskillet/istockphoto.com; man with cane, bottom center, ©Selin Ogeturk/istockphoto.com; child, bottom right, courtesy of the Kosonocky family

Page 137: Vacation home exterior, top left and interior, bottom right ©Ann D. Gleason, AIA; man with children, top center courtesy of the Jacobs family; road sign, top right, by Ken Stern; young girl, bottom left, by Carolyn Hordyke; condominiums, bottom center, ©Tony Tremblay/istockphoto.com; antique keys ©Donald Erickson/istockphoto.com

Page 155: Antique globe ©Jessica Morelli/istockphoto.com

❧
About the Author

© Marianne Barcellona

Deborah L. Jacobs is a lawyer and award-winning journalist specializing in legal topics. In her new book, ***Estate Planning Smarts,*** she draws on more than a decade of writing about the stressful issues that surround estate planning. Her articles for *The New York Times, Bloomberg Wealth Manager, BusinessWeek* and many other publications have been widely cited and circulated by both advisers and consumers. Readers appreciate her clear, concise explanations of complex subjects and her ability to combine real-life stories with reassuring, practical advice.

Jacobs has been a syndicated newspaper columnist, newsletter editor and entrepreneur – she has had her own company, producing a variety of written products on legal and financial matters, for most of her career. She is the author of *Small Business Legal Smarts* (Bloomberg Press).

A native of New York and a graduate of Barnard College, Jacobs received her J.D. degree from Columbia Law School and her M.S. from the Columbia University Graduate School of Journalism. She lives in New York City with her husband and son.

Keeping Current

The material in this book will be continually updated to reflect legal developments that might affect your estate plan. As changes occur, the pertinent sections of this book will be revised and available at *www.estateplanningsmarts.com*. You can register at the site to receive e-mail notifications of these changes.